In Your

Build Your Team For Success

Sky Andrew

ISBN 978-0-9955521-0-4 (pb)
ISBN 978-0-9955521-3-5 (hb)
Ebook ISBN 978-0-9955521-1-1

Thank You Mum
Your Strength and Love is Always With Me

Contents

Introduction

The beginning of your life does not have to determine where you end up. For as long as I can remember, I have had an interest in how people think and the psychology behind why certain people succeed and fail. We are all born into a world of so-called *opportunity*. Each one of us has the opportunity to achieve almost whatever we want – if we want it badly enough. This book will show that the people *In Your World* and the team you build can determine whether you can fulfil your full potential. This is, in fact, important for all of us, as do we know what's going on around us? Are we aware of both good and bad influences? Do our families, friends, colleagues and even spouses want the best for us?

Eugene Luther Gore Vidal was an American writer who died in July 2012 at the age of eighty-six. A man of brutal honesty, he once said the following:

'*Whenever a friend succeeds, a little something in me dies.*'

So is that the truth? Do friends suffer when someone succeeds? The saying: You can choose your friends, but not your family, is true but we can still choose who we have around us and who we listen to. But working hard, alone, isn't enough.

For you, you have to work-smart, have the right people around you, listen to the right advice and hopefully get a little luck. Knowledge is such a powerful thing, but who is going to give you the knowledge? If you surround yourself with the right people, you will receive knowledge and information that will help you in your future life. So many people talk about dreams and aspirations, but never actually start on the journey. So many people have dreams that they don't want to talk about, aspirations they don't share with anyone and ambitions that some would feel are unrealistic.

If you lack the courage to start, you have already finished. Being scared of failure is often a reason not to try and an uncertain future can make people feel uncomfortable – but one thing is for sure:

If you don't try, you will know the outcome.

If you try, you are uncertain of the outcome. An unrealistic starting position is sometimes an obstacle; why do some people feel that they shouldn't have to start at the bottom? There is no better journey than the one that starts on a winding road and reaches a fabulous motorway. Everyone has dreams and aspirations and the moment we start, our odds go up dramatically. Of course, having the right people around us, and getting good advice makes the chance of success greater. For some inexplicable reason, there are people who just know they are destined to do something great and are meant to be successful or famous. Those who know they have the potential are haunted by it and it often keeps them up at night. Knowing that you should be doing something, but you don't know what or how, can eat away at you. Like a plant in a greenhouse; if you're in the right environment you will grow. With the right people around you and good advice anything is possible. Politicians are deemed to be the most powerful people in the world; they are also supposed to have a high-level of intelligence, and in fact, most are educated to a very high level. If they hire advisors to make decisions, then why do so many people refuse advice? The point I'm going to make here is that politicians place an extremely high importance on advisors. They take advice from experts and they listen to advice. They have to make important decisions and want to make sure they get things right. In fact, it's fair to say that no matter how good a politician is, they are only as good as their advisors and ultimately, decisions. So if politicians are smart enough to have advisors, take advice and have the right people around them, why do so many people feel that they either don't need advice, or do not place any importance on who is around them in their world?

We all have to make decisions and crucial ones determine how our lives pan out. And to that end, if you make the right decision, at the right time, in the right frame of mind, then you have a great chance of making huge steps forward. Decisions in theory should be made to achieve positive results, but people sometimes try and save face or place their ego and emotions ahead of making the right decision – that of course can be very dangerous. People who have made lots of good decisions historically can start believing that they are infallible and don't need to listen to anyone. The ego then becomes more important than making the right decision. Similarly, people can make bad decisions when in an emotional state and don't care about whether the decision is right; they just want to prove a point because it makes them feel better. One of the hardest things in the world to do is to stop and say: '*I am not in the right mind-set to make that decision.*' Also, being able to ask for advice from people who normally see you as the leader and indestructible. If you don't have smart, strong and long-term thinking people around you, decisions will be made based on ego and emotional point scoring. Being too proud is another dangerous area; even if you know what the right course of action is, being too proud stops you and harms your future. That's why it is so important to have people around you who will be strong and be willing to fallout with you in order not to cut off your nose to spite your face as the saying goes. You are only as good as your environment, who's around you and who you listen to. Everybody has some form of talent, ability and possibility, but how can someone fulfil their potential? I also thought about how much an individual could achieve if his/her environment was conducive to getting the most out of their life and career. Who you listen to and the people *In Your World* has a profound effect on how successful you become. We rely on input from others more than we realise, so how much can we achieve by receiving the right advice and having someone give us a motivational talk just before a performance, job interview or challenge?

People seeing something in us is of great importance.

We are not best placed to judge what our talents are or where our journey should go. Smart, experienced people in different fields can help us on to the right-path, because they recognise the talents that we don't often see in ourselves. But if we don't surround ourselves with the right people, we have no chance of that happening; the moment we do, our odds of achieving our dreams goes up dramatically. Smart people, with bad experiences to tell, can help us too, because they can articulate why certain things are bad (from experience) and stop us from going down that same dark road. How beneficial would it be not to have a catalogue of wasted years on our CVs because we had people around us who were not wasters or riddled with resentment? If we could identify what and who needs to be in our worlds in order to get the most out of life, surely we would all do it? Whilst playing table-tennis for England, I travelled the world and met so many interesting people. The mental side of the sport could be applied to so many situations in life. It prepared me for my next life as an agent/manager. I hope to give you some anecdotes and philosophies that will get you thinking. Most importantly, we all have to think about our worlds and what input we have and why we create and have created certain worlds. Your world is the people around you; the family you listen to and spend time with and your thought process. The one thing I have found is that your mind-set and who you listen to has so much to do with how your life develops. There are people who create a world where they basically just go round in circles, discussing the same things and continually blaming everyone else and making excuses. They will say that they want to do certain things, but deep down they are scared and insecure. So they create a world where they can't move on. Those who have the power of their convictions, create a world of opportunity and, in it, they have people who show them how to move on and tell them things they don't already know.

Fear and risk are parts of life that can be deemed negative. And stepping in to the unknown is something that, at times, is impossible to do on your own. But without risk, fear and the unknown, what do we have? To succeed you have to embrace those things and appreciate the positivity they bring in order to be successful. Having the right people around you with the right mentality can help us achieve unimaginable success. Somebody has to be the next Richard Branson, David Beckham, Beyoncé, Barrack Obama, Usain Bolt, Oprah Winfrey and Bill Gates; so why not you? Someone will discover the next Apple, Microsoft, Google, Twitter or Facebook and your world is the setting where this can happen. Bob Geldof and Emma Parry were innovative in the way they raised money for charity; they could never have done it on their own, and they will go down in history for their philanthropy. The bottom line is that we all have to assess our world and decide if and when to make change.

Who Am I?

If you want to build a successful world and have the right environment to grow, there are two critical things you have to address; who am I? And who is around me? This section focuses on the: '*Who am I?*' dilemma. So, the *who am I*? Is the question is the first part of your most important journey. This should be easy. It's just you. But when you stop and actually think what it is that makes the person that you are, things can get rather complicated. This Ontological thought was what Scottish philosopher David Hume referred to as '*Bundle Theory*'. It concerns the collection of parts that make an object what it is in order to create your world and make it conducive to your growth; you have to figure out who you are and what pieces are needed to complete your jigsaw puzzle. You have to also take into account that certain elements of you will change. When you are younger you have the future, as you get older history becomes more important and how you have developed as a person and the relationships you have. Early twentieth century anthroposophist, Rudolph Steiner considered the '*Seven Year Cycle Theory*' and stated that: '*Your body regenerates its cells every seven years.*' This brings us to the question of whether you are the same person you were seven years ago? And if so, what part of you is the same? Sometimes memory itself is unreliable. As an older person, you may not know anything about the eighteen year-old you once were, but you know a lot about yourself now. An analogy to your journey is like having an old car, you may have repaired it many times over the years, replacing the bumper, exhaust, bonnet, doors and maybe even reconditioning the engine. Then one day, you realise that not one piece of material from the original car is still part of it. So is that still your car? If you named your car Austin the day you bought it, would you change the name now? It would still be Austin, right? Lots of people have false impressions of themselves. Some truly believe they are somebody they are clearly not.

This false impression can go on for years if someone doesn't front them up and detail what is real. This can be someone who has a negative or positive opinion of how they are. But, all the way along your journey, the aim should be to grow and improve. That will happen if you are always aware of who you are and who is around you. Something important to remember is, that maybe it's not about similarity, but about continuity. If similarity was enough to define you, then the *college you* and the *businessperson* you, would be the same person. The thing to acknowledge here is, that you can share experiences with people who are personal to you and no one else on Earth. As you develop and build your world, you will be connected with people and environments that will form an unbroken string of continuous existence. Things like your moral and ethical compass are a mainstay in who you are and what you stand for. It's a long chain of overlapping memories, personality traits and physical characteristics. For different reasons, fair-weather friends and colleagues will allow individuals to live a life of false-hood. In sport and entertainment, the so-called '*hangers-on*' perpetuate the myth and are passengers for as long as the ride lasts.

A crucial element to understanding yourself is to have complete honesty when you look in the mirror.

That statement sounds ridiculous, because surely everyone is honest with themselves? Right? At different stages of your journey you will grow in some aspects and understand more about yourself in others. There will be times when you are strong and times when you are weak and in need of some form of help and/or assistance. Often, it is easier to only learn the hard way so difficult lessons are hard to take; but are a reminder of who you are and how you react to situations. A manager of a team may not know about his/her assistant until a really difficult situation happens. The manager may be wondering if the assistant will break under the pressure, give support in the right way or use it as an opportunity to get their job.

The assistant on the other hand will look to see how his/her boss reacts and if the boss will try and blame them. A protection mechanism for some many is to hide behind a mask; but surely when you are alone, and you look in the mirror, the mask has to come off? Not for some. The removal of the mask can help people deal with unresolved issues. Some people will have those conversations with friends and family, where they are told something about themselves and the denial is deafening. People may respond by telling themselves, that they are not like that or that people just don't know them well enough, but it is sometimes the case that the individual is still wearing a mask and failing to know themselves. Not knowing or understanding yourself is a huge problem when trying to build your world. Sometimes the impact we want to make in our world is not what is really going on. If you really want to know what the people *In Your World* think of you and the impact you are having on them, get someone neutral to speak to ten people who know you and listen to the results; it may not be what you think. Ultimately, all of us have to rely on our internal structure. We have to work on ourselves and make sure that no matter what happens in our World, we can deal with the consequences.

If you hang your identity on external structures, when they disappear you can lose yourself.

In business for instance, if you know that you're good at dealing with people but bad with money you have a good chance of finding the right people to complement the operation. On the flip side, someone who doesn't know who they are and believe they are great with money, when they are not, could get into serious problems. Even though it can be really difficult to hear, the people who know you best are your closest friends and family. When they are telling you who you are, listen. The biggest reward for working out who you are and what you need is the relationship that will be formed with your spouse. People who understand themselves can communicate who they are and what they want.

The assistant on the other hand will look to see how his/her boss reacts and if world. In the USA today, seeing a psychiatrist has become all the more common; suggesting we live in a world where we want to understand ourselves. However, in Britain, a tradition or culture of pride has created an opposing view; one where seeking professional help, is seen as weak or even taboo.

People We Meet On Our Journey

As the great seventeenth century philosopher - John Locke suggested, we are all born with a blank slate, with the possibility of anything happening. Along our journey we all meet many people, some good and some bad, but we can learn something from all of them. It's amazing how certain quotes, pieces of advice and life-pointers can have a dramatic effect on how we think. Ironically, we can also learn a lot from people who are not friends or don't have our best interests at heart. What we learn from them is what to look out for in people and what to avoid. We can actually learn very little from people in our lives who over-protect us, or have blind-faith, so to speak. There is no short-cut to experience and no short-cut to learning; but taking on-board certain bits of advice can help us become successful faster. It's interesting how much we remember as the years go by. There are always little quotes and sound bites that stay with us forever. For instance, someone once told me a way in which to remember how to wire a plug. They told me to take the second letter in blue, so 'l' and the second letter in brown, so 'r'. So, now, I can always remember that the blue wire is on the left side of the plug and brown is on the right. Everything can be simplified in a way that we can understand and remember. Computers are arguably the most complicated machines, yet they work using binary code applying so just the digits zero and one.

Situations that seem complicated can be simplified and then made understandable and executable.

Arsène Wenger was someone whose quotes had a positive influence on me. During the period when Sol Campbell first joined Arsenal, I would have conversations with Arsène about life and football. For me, one great quote stood out like a beaming ray of light and is still relevant today. It goes right to the heart of why certain people are more successful than others.

He said: '*There are two types of people in life, smart people and stupid people. Smart people know what their priorities should be in life.*' That's why he has no time for people who don't have the right priorities. When he spoke about Aaron Ramsey, Wenger said: '*He is obsessed with improving.*' A young player needs to be able to see the benefit of doing everything within their power to improve. Self-improvement is key to becoming successful. Some people did not understand why Wenger kept playing him even through difficult periods; the answer is that Ramsey's priority in life is and always has been his football. He works like crazy and he's a really good footballer, so Wenger rewarded and continues to reward him with loyalty. If you want to be a professional footballer, football must be your passion and your life's work. Whilst we are on the subject of legends in football, David Dein is an extraordinary person. During his career, he was not only a great operator in football, but also someone who took care and attention to each relationship he had and consequently built a family that had hundreds of thousands of people in it. He of course was, and still is a great family man, and so had a way of making everyone connected with the club feel like they were in a family – that is not an easy thing to do. He knew who was on *the team* and who wasn't; if you were on *the team*, then you were part of the family and he would be generous in his spirit and time. '*Spirit*' in a team and a group can do great things, and it is that spirit that often comes from the top. Alan Sugar on the other hand had a different way of dealing with people during his career in football and quite enjoyed a bit of a '*street fight*'. He was basically a '*street fighter*', who had grafted his way to success and would fight his corner vehemently. His demeanour meant many people found him quite scary and not very friendly; he didn't have much time for small talk, as he just wanted to get things done. Our relationship was strained to say the least, but I understood where he was coming from. It's ironic that he is on a hit reality show now, because when he was the chairman at Spurs, that was the last thing I could ever see him doing.

He didn't seem to care that much for his own PR, and didn't feel that he needed to explain how he did things. In those days the last thing on his mind was to go on TV and have a chat about what was going on. Because he didn't do lots of PR and TV, there was a huge misunderstanding over certain issues; one of them was over the fans thinking he wasn't spending any money. He spent a hell of a lot of money but didn't get value for it and that just didn't make business sense to him. When the fans gave him stick he was bemused. He didn't like some of the people in football, especially agents and *smoozers*. Back then, the interesting aspect of his character was how loyal he was to the people he trusted and those he considered to be on his team. There were people who worked for and with him for many years, and in my experience, people don't do that unless they feel appreciated. He would speak to people in a certain way, which made them feel that he didn't like them; but he knew which people were '*straight*' and who were '*double-dealing*'. Agents who didn't have their clients' best interests at heart might still have got deals done, but they would not have had his respect.

I've been in football for a long time; over twenty years in fact. Alan Sugar was and is one of those people you would rather have on your side than against you. Having said that, he definitely wasn't on my side in the various meetings and discussions we had and some of them were very difficult. But, I couldn't help but have huge respect for him because of his work ethic and determination to do things correctly. He came from nothing and created an empire in his vision.

I know the Spurs fans gave him hell but he was trustworthy. Even though he didn't particularly like '*smoozers*', he too knew what people were about. I was always amazed at how astute he was about people in football and how he dealt with some of them through gritted teeth. He would often have me in stitches about his views on certain individuals. Not many people understood his sense of humour because it was so brutal, but I did. Something he said that resonated with me was:

'Business is all about systems; set up a good system, then find the right people to fit in.' It is so true for both companies and football clubs. If you have a successful structure, then you just need to find individuals to fill it. And strong structures will last, even if the individuals leave. Although he gave the impression of not being that sensitive to the character and makeup of people, he was in fact very aware of who he needed around him and in his companies. I even picked up on something as simple as the way he had his desk situated; it had a table joined to it, so that it made a 'T' shape. There was something about the way it was set up that gave me a good feeling about it. He could have meetings with people sat at the table whilst he was at his desk. But, the thing I learnt most from him is that you are only as strong as your lawyers and boy, his lawyers were aggressive. If anybody tried to take liberties with him, he would take it all the way legally. He was – and most probably still is – a fierce character. For example, if anybody tried to use one of Amstrad's patents, or did something underhand – then God help them. A few people had to write out some big cheques to Alan, of which, he donated to Great Ormond Street Hospital. I learned from Sugar that you just cannot allow people to get away with illegal practice or anyone trying to take liberties with you or your company.

Taking Responsibility

Everybody wants some form of success, whether it's with family, business or relationships. In order to have a better chance of success, you have to take responsibility for who you have around us and who you listen to. A common mistake is to overvalue, or underestimate yourself. This can be dangerous and lead to a catalogue of mistakes. It is important to remember that success is like a jigsaw puzzle; you're one of the pieces and you need to take responsibility and have a say in how the other pieces fit. However, not everyone wants to do everything possible to have the best chance of success; some people want to blame other people when things go wrong.

If someone gets the right people around them then there are no excuses – they can't blame anyone else.

Tennis players are the guys who take absolute responsibility for who is around them, because who is in their world and who is part of their team can lead to sporting success. They want to be pushed to the absolute limit, because if they don't, others will get the right team and will get the most out of themselves.

There is an irony about taking responsibility for who is around us. Some people are scared of using that responsibility because it doesn't give them anything to moan about. Even in personal relationships, you will know friends who are with the wrong person; the type of person who definitely does not get the best out of them but they persevere and feel comfortable complaining and blaming others. '*If I wasn't with him/her I'd be taking on the world.*' In business, the successful people are often the ones who know their strengths and crucially weaknesses. Everyone is happy to display their strengths, but few are happy to acknowledge their weaknesses. In business you often need *front of house* and *back of house* people and they complement each other.

Front of house people are the sociable types, customer-friendly, and can win more business. *Back of house* people are generally those with good organisational skills; an understanding of structure and a love of numbers.

There's a *school of thought* that you need to be a genius to be successful. This is not the case. Someone with average intelligence but with great teambuilding skills will always be more successful than someone who is super-intelligent, but is not aware of how to have the right people around them. Creative people are often not business people and vice-versa. There are so many people in the world with great ideas, but need some form of structure. There are the *one-offs* like Charles Dyson, who had an idea and developed it with smart business people around him, but most people don't have the full skillset. In order to go forward, and develop as people in life, we have to take responsibility for who's around us. Destructive individuals will hold back development in all areas. Positive, forward-thinking and thought-provoking people will help create an environment where there is continual development. Networking is crucial to self-development; if you don't network, then you never get the chance to meet others who might fit into your positive puzzle. We all get invited to various events, but how many times do we just not feel like going or that we can't be bothered? If unsure, we should go, because we never know who we will meet.

Relationships

Close your eyes and let's look into the future; you are eighty years old and sitting around a table having dinner with your family. You look around the table. Who's there? Close your eyes and imagine you are part of an amazing team. Who is in that team? Close your eyes; you are ninety years old and in a rocking chair and someone is holding your hand and asking if you are okay. Who is that person?

The relationships you have *In Your World* are key to your success as an individual. An honest relationship with the right people can help you immeasurably. Being honest with dishonest people will be your Achilles' heel. The wonderful poet, David Whyte, wrote this in his poem: *Sweet Darkness.*

'Give up all the other worlds except the one to which you belong. Sometimes it takes darkness and the sweet confinement of your aloneness to learn anything or anyone that does not bring you alive is too small for you.'

So, the most important world is the one we create and take responsibility for. We should not have people around us who do not magnify us or *bring us alive.*

Sometimes we need to be alone and be able to think clearly in the peacefulness of darkness to be able to understand what is going on in our world.

The most important advice I can give is to ask for the things money can't buy; love, support, respect and honesty. If we allow people in our world to treat us badly or with a lack of respect then that is what will happen. We all need to take responsibility for the messages sent out to people in our world. Whether in business or personal life, people will take liberties if we don't demand a certain level of respect. Even if we are nice and good people, that can be taken for weakness or being soft. We've all heard the saying: Taking kindness for weakness.

So, as soon as someone disrespects us or does something that is unacceptable, our reaction is key to how our relationship develops in the future. We should think carefully about how we respond and try not to have a *knee-jerk* reaction. In a loving relationship, saying one thing, because of an immediate reaction, and then doing something different is a recipe for disaster. If we tell friends, family and colleagues what our non-negotiables and deal-breakers are, then they really have to be what we say they are. We have to set the rules in our own world. By not having any, it can be a major risk. If we can identify what we give and want to receive in relationships, our world can be an amazing place. From family and friends we normally want love, support and communication. In work-life, those of us who want to succeed need creative and hard-working people around us. In order to understand where people are coming from and whether to have them in our life, we have to decipher what they say and what they mean. People will often say something or make a big issue about situations, but the root answer is a simple one. It's like having a pain in our belly and going to the doctor, but it just keeps getting misdiagnosed. After trying many different avenues, it ends up being a simple digestion problem. Well, a lot of time can be wasted by trying to help friends, family and colleagues solve problems that are, in fact, a cover for something else. These situations are often a complete waste of time because there is seldom a satisfactory outcome or conclusion. There are many people who can be creative, loyal, inspirational and ambitious *In Your World.* What you have to accept and be aware of, is that there may be something going on with someone that will be a blockage to them being productive to you. When you spend a lot of time with someone, their world has an influence on yours. The key to having positive relationships is not getting dragged into situations that are time consuming, non-productive and have no possibility of resolution. Sometimes it's just simply that someone wants something from you. It could be love, money or attention, but once they get what they want, all the negative behaviour stops.

Even more difficult is if someone close to you is secretly suffering with something serious like depression or a form of mental illness. They do not mean to be disruptive or difficult, but when someone is fighting against an illness that affects your whole being in that way, no amount of advice or support can help unless they admit to what is really going on. With the backdrop of such an overwhelming issue, there can be no successful conclusion without dealing with the root problem. Relationships can become strained and the quicker root problems can be identified, the sooner you can move forward in a positive vein. If you ever watch, *The Jeremy Kyle Show,* you will see families and friends arguing with passion and venom about a perceived reason. During the altercations someone will say something that almost seems irrelevant, even petty. But, the seemingly insignificant statement can be the root of the problem for the person who said it. I remember watching a show about couples, it was a kind of fly on the wall show that filmed couples at home and tried to help their doomed relationships. In one of the episodes, a couple in their fifties acted *like strangers in the night*; in short, the house lacked love and togetherness. They had been married for over twenty-five years and couldn't put a finger on why their relationship wasn't working. After numerous on-camera conversations and counselling, the lady of the house made a telling comment. She said: '*When he makes a cup of tea he never asks me if I want one and it's really upsetting.*' So for years she had harboured that resentment, but she had never said anything and he didn't feel it was a big deal.

The little things in life can help when building a relationship.

Doing little things for your friends and family plays a big part in building trust, respect and loyalty. There is so much to gain from giving support to the right people in your network and helping them through difficult periods. Letting people close to you know that they can tell you anything and the support will be there, is something that gives relationships amazing strength.

In sport, athletes carry secrets, insecurities and apprehensions; in many cases an athlete can limit their success by not being honest about their fears and insecurities. It's still surprising why more sports people do not use psychologists and life-coaches because it is so beneficial. There are still a lot of people hiding parts of their emotional makeup. I admit myself that if I had used a sports psychologist and been completely upfront about my fears and apprehensions, then my sports career would have been even more successful. Everybody feels better after getting something off their chest and a tremendous weight can be lifted off an individual's shoulder if they can communicate their inner thoughts and fears. Frank Bruno famously discussed fighting his inner demons prior to the fight with Mike Tyson. Most relationships reach a critical point at some stage and who we seek advice from and what action we take is so important to the dynamics of our worlds.

Who we listen to and what action we take is a major factor in the paths we take.

Anyone who underestimates the importance of their partner, friends and family in their lives, as sports people or business entrepreneurs is making a huge mistake. We have all heard the saying: Behind every successful man is a strong woman; well behind every successful person is a mentor, strong friend, partner or family. When a relationship reaches a critical point we seek advice from people around us and sometimes complete strangers. Ironically, sometimes strangers can give the most rational and impartial advice. In order to make an informed decision you have to understand any agenda of the person you are seeking advice from and take that into consideration. Dr Brad Blanton has written about '*Radical Honesty*', which is about the importance of being honest to the right people. He says that the person who learns to tell the truth is the most free, most alive kind of adult human being you'll ever see, but is more insecure than normal. The insecurity comes from having fewer beliefs to rely on for security.

Blanton says that although it is important to be truthful to our loved ones, it is also important to recognise that truth changes. He says we can become lost in our own minds and fail to recognise when truth changes. His theory is that, whilst holding on to the idea of what used to be true, we become liars. He uses the example that if at 8:00pm you are mad at your partner; you tell them about it and get quite worked up and your partner gets mad back and you talk about it, if then, you stay committed to the conversation, there is a possibility of getting over the anger; there is a good chance that by 8:45pm you will laugh and have a drink and not be angry anymore. It was true that you hated your partner's guts at 8:00pm. But it was no longer true somewhere between 8:20pm and 8:45pm. In contrast, people who are stubborn and live according to principles, stick to the presumed fact that: '*I hated you then, and for good reason, so I still hate you now.*' Those people can never get over things.

Blanton goes on to say, in colourful language, that life goes on and yesterday's truth is today's bullshit. Even yesterday's liberating insight, is today's jail of stale explanation. The ability to acknowledge that what you considered was true has actually changed is intriguing. Sports managers and coaches are sometimes guilty of the above. Football coaches find it extremely difficult to change their opinion on a player they had an experience with. To be fair, a lot of the time people just don't change, but the ones who do push themselves to the absolute limit in order to fulfil their potential. So if anyone closes their mind to the possibility that people can change, they miss out on the experience of working with someone who has learned a tough lesson. In 2008 a talented young footballer, Jay Bothroyd, called me and said he wanted to talk; he explained that he was fed up of wasting his talent and wanted to change. Now here was a guy who was at Arsenal as a kid and very highly rated. He was tall and had lots of ability, great feet and blistering pace. He was sold to Coventry City FC after throwing his shirt at the much-respected coach – Don Howe after being substituted in a youth game.

Blanton says that although it is important to be truthful to our loved ones, it is and Mick McCarthy, who was manager at the time, wanted him out. He saw Jay as someone who wasn't professional enough and lacked desire. In fact, Bothroyd had been at so many clubs that most managers just believed he flattered to deceive and didn't have an interest in working with him. So, I drove to the midlands and had a three hour meeting with him, in which, I basically tore him to pieces explaining how bad his attitude was and what he had to do to fulfil his potential. We talked about everything; how he conducted his life, what people thought of him and what he could achieve. He was also honest as well, but the most impressive thing about him, at that time, was his willingness to change, something nobody in football would have believed. To many managers and coaches, the truth about Bothroyd was that he was flash, big-time and not willing to work hard. That was their truth and as I spoke about earlier some people are just not willing to change that truth. During the conversation with him, I realised that this was someone who really wanted to change – I could see it in his eyes.

I said to him:

'Let's get back to basics, go into training early tomorrow, wear normal boots and get rid of the Bentley. Nobody respects someone that lives the life of a superstar and doesn't put in the work at the training ground.'

I told him that he would be one of those fifty-year-old guys in the pub telling people how he could have done this or that. Amazingly, he literally changed his character overnight and for the next three years he was the consummate professional; he played for Cardiff City FC in the Championship and eventually won an England Cap against France. Bothroyd wanted the trappings of success and something tapped into his psyche that told him he could have everything he ever wanted if he worked hard and performed.

Blanton says that although it is important to be truthful to our loved ones, it is Cardiff City FC manager, Dave Jones, should get a lot of credit for helping Bothroyd fulfil his potential; he was his manager for three years. He understood Bothroyds' personality and knew how to deal with him. Jones also had the ability to see that what someone was before, doesn't have to be what they are now. What Jay did in football is unprecedented; never a World Cup or Champions League winner, but a successful professional who turned his life around. And Jay should be proud of this triumph. There are many *Bothroyds* scattered around and they just need to find the right environment to grow; the same way in which flowers need a greenhouse. Breaking a negative cycle not only takes guts, but it means dealing with an uncomfortable reality.

It's a lot easier to blame everyone else and not look at yourself.

In football the guys who are on the subs bench may think going to another club will all of a sudden change everything and they will play every week. Well, you can go to as many clubs as you like, the club will change but not the player. It's not rocket science that the players you see in the team at one club, go to another and are in the team every week there as well. You guys reading this book may get the opinion that I'm biased towards tennis players but I have a huge respect for many of them because they are brave and mainly take responsibility for all aspects of their life. Look at Johanna Konta, the UK's top female tennis player in 2015. She hired coaches and trainers then told them to train her as hard as was necessary and not to take any notice of how upset she became. Konta admits that she does get upset and sheds the odd tear, but she wants to be the absolute best she can possibly be. Therein lies the relationship people have with themselves. Konta, Murray and the like have an honest relationship with themselves; they look in the mirror and say: '*I want to be the best; what do I need?*' Honesty with yourself, can simply be:

'Do I want to do this? Do I want to be as good as I can possibly be or am I too scared to try? Am I scared of the possibility that after trying absolutely everything what happens if I fall short?'

How many people do that? How many of us have people in our world pushing us to the absolute maximum even when it hurts? Many people grasp onto principles that are hard for them to get over, or get beyond or let change themselves for the better.

People choke the life out of themselves by tying themselves to a chosen thought process.

Johanna Konta, like Andy Murray, is obsessed with not leaving a stone unturned. She will no doubt reach her potential and for her bravery, she deserves to. Dr Blanton says that we must be willing to tell the truth. Telling the truth frees us from entrapment in the mind. The alternative to freedom is to live out a program imposed by prefabricated internalised moral resolves. Living this way is a gradual suffocation, which makes us simultaneously more desperate. People that try to keep up a pretence, or try to live a life for what others want, end up using their mind in a negative way which leads to life as a victim rather than an artist. The relationship that Bothroyd and I formed was one of absolute truth. Dr Blanton would call it '*Radical Truth*'. We both benefitted from the experience. Because of that he was able to release himself from the façade; the burden of living a life that wasn't justified.

It takes a lot of energy to 'put on a front' or lie about who you are and how you feel, it is a source of human stress.

If you can engage honestly, the energy that is wasted maintaining a persona becomes available for real creativity. If you can admit your pretences to people who genuinely want to help you (coaches, managers, mentors), you can create a powerful relationship for the future.

Radical Honesty is direct communication that leads to relationships that become stronger and more powerful. There are people in great romantic relationships, who have a wobble, then either partner will seek advice from a close friend. If that friend is single and unhappy, they will encourage you to break up with the partner. Sometimes, this isn't done maliciously, it's just because they want their friend back and that would ease the pain of having to be constantly reminded of a great relationship. Ironically, it is those we hold closest to us that can do the most damage to our career. Many young footballers find themselves in relationships which result in them being given advice by inexperienced people. It's not surprising because we were all twenty-one at some stage and we all thought we knew it all. Sometimes a calculating partner, friend or family member can cause irreparable damage to a career by encouraging the impatient, naïve, *you are amazing* and *you are so successful*, mentality. Once anybody believes that they have made it, or are infallible, then it's downhill from there. Having said the above, many footballers have a positive input from people close to them. The media tends to exaggerate how good or how bad someone is at any time. There are lots of really good parents, partners, family and friends out there who keep a footballer's feet on the ground by not getting carried away with the hype or the difficult spells. It's quite simple; older people who can articulate experiences are the best mentors and people who should be listened to. Young talent, who have the possibility of success, have the difficult task of making sure that everyone in their world knows the boundaries. Conversations along those lines are very difficult and it takes a very mature, young person to build their world so that lines do not get blurred. Great sports people listen to their coaches and professional advisers, when it comes to their craft. The Chinese dominate the sport of table-tennis and they often win by the smallest of margins. If you have never seen a table-tennis match, watch one and look at the absolute respect the players have for their coaches.

In sport, everyone looks for marginal gain; the edg
difference between winning and losing. By believ
return, having your coach believe in you, will g
point of having a coach or adviser if you're not going
energy to have a coach who you are not listening to or giving th
that you are listening but you're not really. When you go into battle, in sp
life, you have the total belief in the people around you. They will often seek support and advice from close friends and family but then it takes maturity and genuine care for those to support and not try to advise in areas they know nothing about – that is a complete disaster. When there are critical decisions to make, the best advice I can give anyone is to take a step back and try to look at the whole picture and why certain people are saying certain things. People *In Your World* who have bad intentions, will not want you to take a step back because they don't want you to see what's going on. There is something that I have battled with over the years and that is the need for someone else to see something in me. We, as individuals, are not best placed to identify our talent, our position on a football field or our placement in a company. The amazing people in our world will see a talent, a specific thing that we, as individuals, don't see. For instance, a good football coach or manager may say to a player: '*I know you're playing as a striker, but you're a centre-half*' or advise a player to change the position he/she is playing in. That kind of advice can be a big difference to how a footballer develops because when we are developing our true talents, improvement and development is more natural and faster. It's interesting that someone else *seeing something in us*, is totally out of our control unless we have forward thinking/creative people *In our World*. How many different crafts could an individual excel at? There's a school of thought that everyone has a book in them. I'm testament to that, as I sit here tapping away thinking: '*Why didn't I do this years ago?*' There are so many people frustrated in the workplace because they know that what they are doing is not what they should be doing.

' is that they are often not sure what profession they should pursue. . I was at school, a lovely man called Len Hoffman used to come round .e a week on his bike and hold table-tennis classes at our school. In those ıays (eleven-fourteen years old), I was playing cricket, football and athletics to a high standard, but Len came in one day, watched me playing around on the table-tennis table and told me I had a talent for table-tennis. He saw something in me; he encouraged me to play more and instilled lots of confidence in me. In those days, as a kid, I was playing football and cricket for my district; I was a pretty good sprinter and high-jumper as well. But Len Hoffman inspired me in a sport that wasn't as fashionable as football or cricket. If it hadn't been for Len, I would never have competed in the Olympics, never mind the fourteen National titles and three Commonwealth gold medals. He sent me to Fairbairn Boys' Club and I fell in love with the game. Then I struck gold again with Arthur Thomas, who recognized my talent and helped me develop. I would turn up to the boys' club in my green football kit from school and my old table-tennis bat and absolutely loved every moment of every game I played. Most nights I would catch the bus from around the corner with different people. On some occasions, I would walk to the bus stop with a guy called Adrian Elliot, who would buy pie and chips from the shop next to the bus stop. He never gave me any and I would always think: *'One day I want to be able to afford to buy pie and chips every night.'* When I turned up to table-tennis at Fairbairn, I can remember being the only kid without all the proper clothing; the others would make fun of me and it was not funny at the time. Having things tough like that instils character and when I look back, I wouldn't have had it any other way. The advice I got from Len and Arthur was that it didn't matter who had the best shorts, shirts and bats, it was who wanted it the most. They were also the fairest and most honest people I knew; everything they said was like little gems or pearls of wisdom. Everybody knew that they were coaches because of their genuine love of the game and a desire to help young players.

Having Len and Arthur as mentors was a stroke of luck for me, as my parents didn't seek them, they just happened to be there. But these days, parents need to seek the right teachers, mentors and advisers. Good parents want mentors to be an extension of their moral views and characters. It's so difficult for parents, in that they bring their children into the *world*, nurture them, then have to pass their kids on to someone else for further education, whether academic, sporting or entertainment. Talented kid, at some stage, often stop responding to their parents; then the parents have to find the right mentors and that becomes the most crucial time for all parties. A talented youngster's world should have input from family, advisers and qualified coaches. The parents have to take the lead as to how the structure should work. The wrong adviser for the wrong reason is a disaster. The right advisor for the right reason is fantastic. No advice at all is better than bad advice and there is still a chance that talented people can come through. Table-Tennis was obviously the right sport for me to pursue; I might not have played to a as high a senior standard as the other sports, but I won three Commonwealth gold medals, fourteen National Titles and competed at the 1988 Olympics. My mum was just amazing; we both knew that table-tennis was never going to give the family financial security, but she worked long hours in that Fray Bentos pie factory, in order to give me that ten pounds needed for me to travel around the country playing the game I loved. The relationship I had and still have with my mum is one of love and support. I always felt so strong and able to take on the world no matter what I did, because I had that feeling that I was doing what I was meant to do. I never, ever lost my focus; it was like I was in a trance. So we agree that relationships are important and that we all need to identify who is good and bad for our world? Identifying people who are toxic and negative is absolutely paramount. When you are building a business, a team or relationship the key to success is having people around you who want to solve problems and find solutions. One of the defining factors of successful relationships is when team members come together to solve problems and figure out a way forward.

Having Len and Arthur as mentors was a stroke of luck for me, as my parents will blame everybody else. The wrong team members will treat everything as an attack on them personally. So, when there is a problem or issue and you need to resolve it with your team, they create an atmosphere where you start walking on eggshells and the team becomes worried about addressing certain issues. So, in a team situation where the manager is speaking to them as a whole about mistakes being made and how to move forward, the toxic person believes that everything being said is directed at them. Because the toxic individual is only interested in themselves and feeding off negativity, they seize every opportunity to accuse people of picking on them. Inevitably an argument pursues and the situation becomes unproductive. Instead of the situation being about improving and adding to the team, everything becomes about not upsetting the toxic person. Toxic people are very good manipulators; they place the blame on others and make everyone believe that it's not them who have a problem but somebody else. They look for someone in the team or group they can influence and manipulate. If they find such a person then their ambition is to bring that person to their knees. Philosopher – John Whyte, once said:

'We are like chameleons; we take our hue and the colour of our moral character, from those who are around us.'

Toxic people will most definitely affect your '*hue and colour of your moral character.*' He said that quote in the seventeenth century, yet hundreds of years later it still rings true.

Loyalty

Loyalty is a subject that sparks debate on various platforms. Loyalty and commitment are two of the most important attributes to have as a person. People *In Your World* with those same attributes can make you feel strong and protected. Being loyal to people around you is something that, when reciprocated, can be of the highest importance. But beware, unscrupulous people will use your loyalty as a reason to make you feel guilty and to make you do what they want. My mum is the most loyal person I've ever known; even after everything that happened in the marriage to my father, she stuck in there over fifty years later. It is fair to say that whilst my siblings and I were growing up, my father did things he must regret now. He wasn't around for us and got caught up in the vices lots of people enjoy– although, drugs was never one of them. My mum suffered. There was one occasion when she had absolutely no money and gave me hot water to drink to try and stop me from crying.

Some will say that my mum should have left the marriage; everything that went on is certainly another book that may never be written. But, what this shows is that there are people like my mum who just stick to a relationship regardless of what goes on. If we can identify bad traits in people and situations early, then we should have the power of our convictions and leave the situation. In order to identify people and situations that will abuse your loyalty you need outside help and assistance. Often, the second impression you get of someone is truer and more informed; and as summed up from the thoughts of Dr Brad Blanton, we must have the ability to change what we see as true. Plenty of good people form an initial impression of someone and then refuse to change their opinion or view. Part of this is not being able to admit: '*I was wrong*' or not being able to break the routine. Whether it's a personal relationship, working for a company or playing for a football club, some of us would rather stay in a routine rather than break it; even if breaking it is the right thing to do.

Having said that, patience is key to getting the full picture of a situation. By having patience and the power of conviction (at the right time) you can win. Patience gives you the ability to see, learn and character build. Power of conviction gives you the courage to walk away or stay (for the right reasons). Sometimes if you can overcome testing times, your relationships may get stronger as a result. People stay in relationships for years and years even after knowing that it's not working out. How many times have you heard: '*I knew it was over years ago?*' We need to use time productively, so when we feel that something isn't working out, every moment from that point has to be used positively. Something has to come out of staying in a situation we are not sure about. The first port of call is to communicate with whoever is in the relationship with you. We all need that for closure or to cement the situation. Even when someone may not seem interested, keep trying to communicate until you feel you have truly had enough. When a decision is made to stay or leave, you should know the following:

1) You gave it every opportunity to work out.
2) It's made you a stronger person
3) The experience has taught you something

Once you have all the information you need, your decision won't be made with regret or doubt. In football there are players who have been loyal to the wrong people and still to this day do not realise the disservice that has been done to them. One of the ways agents in football, for instance, get away with doing a disservice to their client is by letting the client think that it was all their idea. Football is an emotional sport and players will say things from time to time, but it is the responsibility of the representatives to be honest and advise clients not to do things that will hurt them publicly and in their careers. Effectively, you are what the public sees and if you don't care about your image then you can't expect the public to be loyal to you after football.

Outside the tribal following of particular clubs, the rest of the public are looking at other aspects of a footballer's character. Once you have the loyalty of the public anything is possible. David Beckham could open a chip shop and the public would queue up around the block to buy his chips. The power of the public's loyalty is undeniable, but they are not stupid. The public see through any pretence and under-hand dealings; however, they give loyalty to people who communicate with them and who lay all cards on the table. Football is very public – not only in the UK, but worldwide. What has to be remembered is that lots of people don't watch or have an interest in football but they will become aware of issues that make the news. Any situation where a player is breaking a contract and looking bad in doing so is never a good thing. The general public get snippets of information and will only be loyal to those they can identify with. Loyalty is sometimes conditional. In the world of football, loyalty can only be defined during the term of a contract. There's often talk about footballers being *one club players* and much more talk about them being disloyal. Footballers seem to be in a position where they can't win. If they want to leave during a contract they are castigated and if they are doing well with their contract running out then they are accused of being disloyal for not signing a new contract – regardless what any proposed offer may or may not be. Why are footballers continually accused of being disloyal? In any other walk of life, a person who is offered a better job is fully expected to accept it as they are trying to better their lives and the lives of their family. What seems to be the situation some are happy with, is that a footballer should never make a decision to move forward but wait until they are all washed-up and of no use to anyone, then they can be released and nobody will criticise them. Football managers get it even worse; most get sacked and if any dare be ambitious and get offered a job elsewhere, then all hell breaks loose. So, like footballers, they will never be called disloyal if they wait to get sacked. Footballers or managers who honour their contracts are not applauded or even acknowledged.

Outside the tribal following of particular clubs, the rest of the public are looking contract with a club they should also be negotiating their divorce. That may sound negative but it's a fact that managers are more often than not, eventually sacked, so they have to negotiate what happens when they do. It's like a kind of prenuptial agreement that details what happens when the relationship goes sour. When it comes to marriages, the Americans have been signing prenuptial agreements for years. It's just seen as practical as people change when a relationship goes wrong; some will get nasty and go to any lengths if they feel wronged, cheated or underappreciated. By going into an arrangement knowing the terms of the breakup, there can be no grey area when and if the breakup happens. The press may know deep down the ethics and morals of certain managers and footballers, but never make a big deal about them, because it's not a big story. Big stories are when the above are doing well and leave for another team.

Ultimately, people are loyal to people, not companies, football clubs or institutions.

A footballer will invariably follow a manager who always looks after him; a great example of that was when Kevin Nolan left Premier League Newcastle United to follow Sam Allardyce to West Ham United who had been relegated to the Championship. The loyalty to each other was clear to see but was glued together by a trade-off, Allardyce giving Nolan a similar salary, the captaincy and regular football. Nolan gave Allardyce a top Premier League player who would help get the team back to the Premier League. But still, the element of loyalty to each other was the one variable that made the whole situation happen. Loyalty is often conditional, as both parties have to be happy with an arrangement in order for it to work. In football, loyalty is conditional on either party (club or footballer) living up to each other's expectations. If a player loses form or has problems for a considerable period of time, then a club will not or cannot afford to keep the player in the squad.

Sometimes clubs just cannot be loyal to a player for financial or business reasons and have to find a way to let them go. Players often just want to know where they stand in terms of the team and sometimes no one can tell them. There's so much going on and things change so quickly that there is often a lack of information given to players. A very simple way of letting players know where they stand is by letting them know if they are in the '*Red*', '*Amber*' or '*Green*' Zone. So in terms of football, '*Red*' would be you're not doing enough to be in the team and you might have to look for another club. '*Amber*', you're in and out of the team; likely to be on bench or substituted if playing. '*Green*', you're in my starting eleven. The above situation can change from week to week but at least footballers get a sense of where they stand, because not knowing is a major frustration to most. But importantly, it will be up to the footballer how they react to knowing where they stand. Normally, someone who is asking to know where they stand is either not in the team or on the periphery. For the coaches, if they do not get the right response, then they also know where they stand in terms of the player's character. One of the situations that I find totally unacceptable is when a club decides a player is surplus to requirements, but the player wants to stay and certain tactics are put in place to force the player out. Making a player train with the reserves and not select them for the first team squad are common tactics. Surely that is not being loyal to someone who has signed a contract in good faith? Likewise, a player who decides he wants to leave and decides to go on strike or train badly is also not the way to go about your business. In personal relationships many of us fixate on past experiences and get stuck in that mind-set. Past experiences can be mistaken for current experiences, which itself can confuse loyalty. A woman may ask her husband if he loves her and his response could be: '*Of course I love you, we've been together for ten years.*' Evidence from the past doesn't prove anything about current situations and experiences. Many people just drift along, not addressing how their relationship is going, this can be with other individuals, teams or companies.

Then one day, someone turns around and tells you, for example, that they are leaving, that you are sacked or that they are selling you. The response by the party who has been dumped is total shock and normally a reference is made to how long the relationship has been going. It is deemed that the longer the relationship has been intact, the more of a betrayal it is. Sol Campbell was deemed disloyal by Spurs fans when he left the club in 2001 after his contract expired, after spending two years at football's School of Excellence, he went back to Spurs at sixteen and stayed until he was twenty-six. As I spoke about earlier, loyalty is a two way street and more importantly, history is significant but current experience is reality. When people have the power of conviction and options then loyalty over a period of time should be treasured more. Throughout his early to mid-twenties, Sol was courted by other clubs but never left. He honoured his contract and only left when it ended, but he did not and has not received the respect he should have done. Some fans today still sat that they weren't happy with what he did or that he shouldn't have left. One fan said to me once: '*Come on, deep down he would have been happier at Spurs; he might not have won stuff but he would have been happier.*' These words were not just lip service, as he truly believed what he said, because like a lot of fans the loyalty to their team is undeniable and they will not have any empathy with a situation that reflects negatively on their team. However, in my opinion, football fans are mainly the most loyal people you will find (along with footballers) and the most important people in football. Although fans are incredibly loyal, sometimes they feel cheated, let down, tricked and even taken for granted but they keep supporting their team. Fans walking out of a stadium will say things like: '*Never again,*' and '*that's it; I've had enough.*' Or '*I'm ripping up my season ticket.*' But they just keep going back. Although fans are ultimately loyal to their club, they don't always have the same sentiments towards players. Sometimes it's because of the information they get from the press or sometimes it's purely because they don't think the player is pulling his weight on the pitch.

Then one day, someone turns around and tells you, for example, that they are are passionate about their club. I think they understand players will come and go, but that still doesn't soften the blow when players leave (only the ones they wanted to stay). Football can be extremely political behind the scenes and the fans seldom get to see or hear what is going on. Footballers (that are in demand) are on the whole made to look bad when they leave a club, even if it is for a big transfer fee. Those who haven't performed or are not wanted can tiptoe out of a club without anyone noticing. The fans react to what they hear and read, so all of a sudden a player who was loved can overnight become *'greedy'* and a *'traitor'*. It's impossible for most fans to stay loyal to a star-footballer, unless he is a great communicator with the club and media. Conversely, in the one off case of Sol Campbell, it wouldn't have mattered what he did, as his move to Arsenal was deemed so controversial. Beckham, Henry, Ferdinand, Gerrard and even Frank Lampard are heroes at the clubs they played for in the Premier League. I say: '*Even Frank Lampard,*' because there were minor rumblings when he played for Manchester City after leaving Chelsea. But even though Jose Mourinho was not happy with the fact that Lampard had joined a rival club, the fans stayed loyal to him. The fans acknowledged that Lampard had given the club his best years and could not deny him the opportunity to join Manchester City for the short spell. Both Beckham and Henry carefully planned their careers and protected their hero status at Manchester United and Arsenal respectively. Their careers were similar from success in the premier league; big-money transfers to Spain (La Liga) and later moving to the US (MLS). The two left no possibility of the fans being disloyal towards them by not playing for another club in the Premier League. Legend is a word used often, but Thierry Henry is a legend and great communicator. His communication with Wenger, the fans and media was with such class, it helped him be even more revered. Like Sol Campbell, Frank Lampard played for a rival. These were very different transfers however, as Frank's stint was a short spell at the end of his Premier League career, whilst Sol's was at his peak years.

There was no way the Spurs fans were going to show any loyalty towards a great player going to a rival. Although there was a small minority who displayed their anger in unacceptable ways, I felt for the genuine fans who saw it for what it was; their captain leaving to try and win trophies. But Sol Campbell joining Arsenal sparked a huge loyalty debate and it will be discussed for many more years to come. Just like any top achiever, in any walk of life, he moved jobs to try and be successful and he was. Moving away from football, we all believe our interpretations of reality intensely, and we want other people to join us in our beliefs to make us feel secure. There are people who will say: '*I don't trust anybody*' and that puts them in '*mind-handcuffs*'. Normally it's because of a bad experience where someone was disloyal. It stops the possibility of building relationships and developing loyalty. There are lots of people out there who will be loyal and h*ave your back*, but you have to play your part. Identifying those with the right characteristics becomes easier once you start identifying the common denominators in people. There are billions of people in the world, but not billions of completely different people. People have long-standing relationships, but that doesn't mean that they are loyal. There are people who will stay in a relationship but are not loyal or faithful. An example of this is someone being continually unfaithful in a relationship whilst portraying the image of a family person. There's nothing worse than not being sure if your partner, colleague or employee is courting others. A few of us occasionally escape the *mind-handcuffs*; however, most of us die with them on. Some of us simply do not want to address the situation or just want an easy life. All of us have the amazing possibility of getting beyond the handcuffs of our own minds. We have to be brave in questioning our own thought process and be prepared to be let down by people. But the positive outcome is to learn from the information received and build relationships with the right people. Very few relationships will give 100% loyalty, but the amount of pain we may suffer finding them is worth it. Most importantly, we have to know that although we will give 100% to the people in our *world*, current experience will always rule over history.

When Loyalty becomes *Enabling*

Being a loyal person is an amazing trait to have and loyalty on the whole is positive. But, there is an aspect to loyalty that we have to be acutely aware of and that's when it enables someone to continue harming themselves and others whilst knowing they don't need to change because the loyal folk are around to bail them out. If your partner cheats on you, hits you or has destructible traits and you don't leave, you start to become an enabler. Threats don't mean anything to *Mr* or *Mrs Destructible*, because they know the loved and loyal ones are only saying it to try and get change. Of course, the discussions and explaining of how you feel have to take place but people who are on a self-destructive mission mainly do not change. There are a few cases where an individual will find the strength and character to change, but normally that has to come from within and if the loyal folk around don't address the situation, in the strongest terms, then nothing changes. There's only one thing worse than telling someone to leave your world because they are not growing, and that's keeping them *In Your World* with them not growing. Sometimes the only way people can grow is to not have the constant safety net that enables them to continually mess up. I will talk here, a little about Jermaine Pennant. I doubt there are many relationships in sport closer than that between my *'adopted'* son (so to speak) and me. After becoming his advisor and father figure when he was fifteen, I had to accept that whilst helping him achieve his so-called dreams, I also enabled him. I feel strongly that once you make a pledge to represent someone then you should do that through thick and thin and rich and poor – just like a marriage. Many footballers have told me horror stories of what happened when they stopped making money for their agents. In the sports and entertainment world, the agent/client relationship is often one that is conditional.

Loyalty depends on what each party is getting out of the relationship.

Jermaine and I have been through more than most agent/client relationships. We had a constant battle where I was trying to push him forward and help him reach his potential; yet he was determined to self-destruct. I'm known for being intensely confidential, but at this time, Jermaine wants to put his past career into the public domain and is writing his own book. So, with his blessing, I am speaking a little about our relationship and hoping that the next generation, who have the intention to self-destruct will take heed. We both believe he over-achieved, though many think that he could have done a lot more. But, for someone who went to prison, was convicted three times for drink-driving and was doing things behind the scenes which, at any time, could have ended his career; he over-achieved. All will of course be revealed in his book. Regardless of what he did or the trouble he was in, his expectation was always to get what he wanted. The financial deal he got with Birmingham City after prison was more than generous and the move to his boyhood club, Liverpool FC, happened when most of the clubs in the Premier League were seriously concerned about his character. It's difficult to tell someone that they need to do everything a certain way to become successful, when they have served time in prison and then received a dream move to Liverpool. He played good football at Birmingham City, but behind the scenes, I was drumming into him that he had to be professional and conduct his life in the right way to get what he wanted. So, when he got what he wanted, I became an enabler. The great thing about our relationship, on my side, is that I've always been able to be brutally honest with him and that is as a massive plus. Now I realise, that he did continue to mess up because of his belief that I would always pull a rabbit out of the bag. He admitted to this in the speech at his wedding. I have first-hand experience of that horrible situation of wanting to help someone close, but knowing you are also enabling them. Loyal folk can help people they care about by not rewarding things that will cause long-term harm. Only people close to Mr and Mrs Destructible know what's really going on and they can enable or make a stand. There's a saying:

You never really know what's going on with people behind closed doors, and that is so true. At the height of his career he could have been disloyal to me, but he wasn't. For all the things that have been written about him, loyalty is a characteristic Jermaine holds. Everybody, not just sports stars, need a constant in their lives; someone who is always there, someone who knows their flaws and insecurities. There is a lot of papering over the cracks in relationships and then one day the proverbial pack of cards comes crashing down. Loyalty isn't just about hanging around as it's also about the honesty that might cause a problem in the short-term but is for long-term reasons. I can sleep at night knowing that I did everything I could for him and he is still alive, playing football and can pass on valuable information to the next generation about what not to do. Not many footballers achieve *Man of the Match* in a Champions League final; this is something both Jermaine and I are hugely proud of. When people sign contracts they should honour them, in reality, an individual's loyalty can only be judged during the terms of a contract. You should only ask for a divorce under irretrievable circumstances. If standards aren't that high then it's very difficult to fulfil your potential. During a period in any situation, you have to be able to see things out to its conclusion. That doesn't necessary mean that you will do that, but you need to know within yourself that you can go all the way. When Sol Campbell was at Spurs he was asked the question after a match: '*Are you staying?*' He replied: '*I'm going nowhere.*' During that time there were on-going discussions about his future. He could only be held to that statement under the terms of a contract; if he had asked to leave and broken his contract then people would have had the right to question the statement. If you asked someone during a marriage: '*Are you staying?*' When they had no intention of leaving, they would say: '*Yes.*' A contract is normally between two parties; each having to play their part because if one becomes unhappy then there is a problem. That doesn't mean that the unhappy party has to ask to opt out.

Perseverance can lead to successful relationships. Many people go into a contract or relationship without doing due diligence and without taking enough time to negotiate the situation properly. Even in a relationship you need to discuss, even negotiate, important issues properly before getting married. If you want kids and you know your partner doesn't, then surely that's a deal-breaker. Likewise (but nowhere near the importance of having children), if a player signs a five-year contract with the ambition of winning the Premier League but realistically knows there is no chance of it happening, why sign a five-year contract?

There is a 'sign now and worry later' mentality especially in football.

The way someone feels when signing an agreement, can play a major part in how they feel during the period. People can sometimes feel pressured into signing or they feel they cannot research or prepare properly; these situations can cause resentment and in turn cause one or both parties to want to terminate. How many times do we see someone sign a contract then very soon afterwards declare their unhappiness with it and request of a new one? If a club is underachieving or not competing at the highest level, then a player, who is at the top of his game, may still want to fulfil his ambitions. This often brings up the question of loyalty and this is where the lines get blurred. If a player is underachieving and let go or sold, then nothing is said, not even a murmur. But if a player leaves one club to play for another that is on an upward cycle then all hell is let loose. In my opinion, footballers would fight more to honour their contracts if a clear message was out there: '*Honour your contract and you'll receive no criticism.*' But, footballers get criticised no matter what they do, except for one golden sequence of events. The footballer, who always performs and stays at the top of their game throughout the period at their club, regardless of how the club performs is deemed loyal; and in return will receive hero status when they retire.

The ultimate super-heroes are the likes of Steven Gerrard and Alan Shearer. These two stand, almost alone, as individuals who were faithful to their clubs and cities – true loyalty. Gerrard and Shearer deserve hero status because their loyalties had no conditions. Neither has won the Premier league and both had the opportunity, at different times, to join teams that would have almost guaranteed titles. Some people may say they lacked ambition, but these guys had that deep sense of loyalty that you can't just learn or be convinced of. They genuinely loved their club and city. They also had a desire for success and wanted it with the club they loved. A question could legitimately be asked: *'Would the clubs have been loyal to the players if they didn't perform or had a loss of form over a long period of time?'* But, the clubs did reward the players for their loyalty, with great contracts and hero status. Also, the two parties (club and footballer) always agreed contracts that satisfied both parties; there is no doubt that the clubs had to be competitive with the contracts; they paid to these two heroes. It was inconceivable to not give these guys fantastic contracts. Gerrard and Shearer played for massive clubs, where loyalty played a huge part in the relationship. Players who played for the likes of Man' United, Chelsea and Arsenal, during the last couple of decades, have had periods of success so their loyalty included the fact that they fulfilled their ambitions. There is no better feeling than doing a sport you love, win and get paid your market value. Most of the best players gravitated towards those clubs because they won the titles over that period, but the guys playing for the clubs outside the top four, often had a decision to make. The realistic situation was that they would have to move in order to win the Premier league. Sol Campbell is someone that most people following football in North London would talk about and discuss in reference to the loyalty angle. Even though Sol honoured his contract, there were still lots of people who had a major problem with the situation. Everyone could understand fans being upset that he went to a rival team, but when folk had an issue with him leaving when his contract had expired, then this was and is a problem.

Some have said that he left and the club didn't get any money; well that would be a legitimate argument if thousands of players were not being released and found themselves out of work. When a contract is approaching its end, there are different situations going on everywhere. Some players are desperate to get a new contract for different reasons; sometimes it's just to do with their family being settled and/or their kids being happy at the school they attend. It is the worst thing in the world when a player is not offered a new contract. It can be like a death in the family. Then you have the very rare situation where a player is of value to a club and his contract is running out, then, it seems to become a major issue for everyone. Everyone gets involved and the player is often vilified. It's amazing that there are probably 500 players released, to every one player who has value and honours his contract; yet no one says anything about the guy being released. Clubs have to decide who they want to keep and who they want to let go. When they decide who they want to keep, it is important to communicate with the player and secure his services at the right time. Secondly, a player should just concentrate on playing football, conducting himself in the right way and not breaking their contract. Sol was accused of saying he was staying at the club and some tried to imply that it meant he was staying beyond his current contract. An extension of a contractual relationship has to be negotiated and every person has the right to have a say in their future; yet some thought that Sol was just going to say he was staying, regardless of any negotiation or aspirations of the club. Although Sol wanted to stay, he was a strong character and wanted things to be right. It is strange how individuals are sometimes not applauded for standing up for themselves and what they believe in. People like Sol just want things to be right and there's absolutely nothing wrong with that. Many people in life don't have a say in their own career or life in football.

Negotiation – The Mind Game

My mother always taught me to do the right thing at any cost - that sounds ironic doesn't it? Why should it be at all costs? The reason is, that if you want to do things in the right and most ethical way, it doesn't mean that your adversary will give you any credit; in fact, there are people out there who will publicly criticise you, if they don't get their own way.

In a negotiation a lot of people focus on the headline guaranteed financial figure.

A football club, for instance, would have a figure that they will not go over and a player would also focus on a figure that they want. The above facts make an agent's job easy, because they don't have to worry about negotiating clauses as well. A situation that has happened in the past, was that a player would want a certain figure, so the club could have easily asked the agent for an option of an extra year or two. That basically meant that there would be a guaranteed length of contract (maybe four years) with a further two years; that was an option for the club only. The Professional Footballers Association will tell you that this is not a good situation. You can imagine that a player can sometimes see no light at the end of the tunnel and decide to do something irrational. I have always taken great care and attention to the clauses in contracts, because if an agreement has good incentives and triggers that reflect a player's performances and successes, they are less likely to want to break a contract. A week is a long time in football, never mind four years. Is it realistic for there to be a four-six year contract, with no clauses or triggers and everyone is happy? The agent may be content because they get a longer period of commission. So there is a slight conflict; a contract with no triggers or clauses equals a bad negotiation, but more money for the agents and less chance of loyalty during the terms of a contract.

People, who have succeeded, hire professionals and experts to assist them. Then, the right incentives need to be in place to encourage the professionals and experts to do the very best job they can. If a footballer says to his/her representative: *'I want x pounds a week and I don't care how I get it.'* Then that is selling himself down the river, and encouraging both the representative and the club to weaken his position in other areas by length of contract, option years or less bonus payments. In some cases, it may be better to have a little less money and more structure, so greater opportunity to be rewarded with success. So, some agents believe that there is no point in fighting their client's corner. Clients come and go, but institutions are there forever. In order to negotiate the best contract for a client, the agent and client have to have a strong partnership. They must also see the benefits of being open with each other about the objectives. The obvious objectives for some, is to just get the most money and to disregard incentives, clauses and the general structure of the contract. But, a contract can be much more valuable, by having the right clauses and structure. A client can earn more money and success by not focusing on the guaranteed salary. In football, clubs are happy to do that because the headline figures stay within their budgets. Clubs can end up paying players much more than they expected to, because the agent and client had a secret – the client was always going to be successful. So, if you are going to be a success then you are going to reach your potential and financial aspirations. Everything should be geared up for success because if you are not going to deliver then what are you doing in your chosen profession? A successful negotiation has so much to do with timing; even a bad negotiator can have success if a deal is concluded at the right time. But when is the right time? One thing is for sure - if you don't have patience you will make it infinitely harder to find the right time, as a deal will be done because of that very reason. If your focus is purely on money then you will do a deal purely because there is more money.

The ironic thing here is, that you will probably get more money by focusing on important things, like, whether it is the right time, and what you need to perform at your optimal. Money is relative, just because someone offers you more money doesn't mean you should sell yourself short or forget your standards. We've all been in situations where we think we know what we want financially, but what is the objective? To get what you want or to get what you deserve after performing? Do you want to earn £1,000,000 a year guaranteed and capped or the possibility to earn £1,500,000 with a lower guaranteed sum? If you're not in the game to perform then, what are you doing in the game? Is the possibility to earn more going to give you an incentive to perform? Money used in the wrong way can demotivate an individual and be a negative influence on a career. People who over-emphasise what they want, are undoubtedly not helping themselves. Employers have to think about the *bottom line* because of the financial structures in place. But, they should be happy to reward success and that's where clever negotiation can come into play. The famous opening gambit for someone is: '*I want this*' (starting high); the other party then says: '*We'll give you this*' (starting low) and then you meet somewhere in the middle. American lawyer and politician Henry Clay once suggested, that a good compromise leaves both parties dissatisfied. When you ask for something, two reactions will most likely happen. Initially, you have put all your cards on the table and will definitely not get what you asked for. Secondly, you now have to wait for a response. That is of course in relation to finance. If you listen to most people talking about how they negotiated this or that, they always make it sound like they have just reinvented the wheel by starting high or low and then agreeing at the adjusted level.

If you ask for something you're not getting more and risk the possibility of the opposite side losing respect for your position.

By going in too low, the inevitable feeling of being insulted is felt by the other side. So, research is key in a negotiation, not just lazy figure throwing. You must have an idea of what is available, so who you are negotiating with and other test cases, then you are already head of the game. Your focus must be on more important issues, such as improving your career. Financial remuneration can be used in a positive or negative way; the most positive way, is as an incentive to perform; not that talent should need extra incentives to perform, but if it adds something then it's good. The negativity comes from someone just earning money and not linking it to anything. In other words, that's how much you're getting come rain or shine. So as an agent you are sometimes faced with the protecting of your client and the fighting for your client that could upset the person you are negotiating with, at say, a football club. Or compromise yourself so the chief executive or chairman is happy and they then give you recommendations. You may think: '*Is it possible to keep everyone happy?*' Well a very well-known chairman once said to me that: '*A good agent makes sure both sides are happy.*' The most important thing is that people respect you for the right reasons. There is a constant battle in football that a footballer has to try and win, and this also concerns how to deal with money; it can have a destructive effect on an individual and those around them. It is so important for a client to have people around them that do not make money their '*God.*' But, when you are young and impressionable, people professing to offer someone a deal that's too good to be true, is often just that. So representatives, who are not in the business to genuinely look after clients properly, have to find a way to get their attention and hold some form of control, without doing the hard graft they should be doing. There are agents, who tell potential clients, that if they let them do the deal, the agent will give the client 50% of the commission. The whole premise of this book is to take responsibility for who is *In Your World.* By accepting the above offer, it gives confidence to all the scammers and makes genuine agents/managers feel there is no point in building long-term careers.

By going in too low, the inevitable feeling of being insulted is felt by the other make sure the client gets less than he should do and more on the agent's commission. So not only does the client have someone around them, who is not going to give them a complete management service, that person has taken 50% of the money that should have gone into the client's pot (wages).

In Your World is all about the people and influences around you. Why would anyone have people in their lives with a '*smash and grab mentality*'? It's because some people use whatever skill, ability or ingenuity they have to fool people. If you allow people into your life, who will turn your head in five minutes then let you pick up the pieces for the rest of your life, then good luck. All of us have to identify which people have our long-term interests at heart and who will do us harm. People in a hurry to get us to do something quickly are often the ones who are bad news. Look at it this way; a good financial advisor will give you prudent advice for your long-term financial security. How many of us want to listen?

Table-Tennis

I loved table-tennis; I loved training, competing and the many conversations I had with some of my teammates and players from across the world. Table-tennis has many similarities to tennis; one major difference is that in table-tennis, you have to be selected for major international tournaments, whereas in tennis you can just enter yourself into qualifying competitions and then it's up to you. I met so many good people and formed lots of good friendships, but table-tennis was and probably still is a very insular and often claustrophobic sport. You would play in tournaments, often in sport-centres, seeing the same people over and over again. Unlike tennis, where you can surround yourself with people to protect you, in table-tennis the lack of space and the intensity of the sport, meant it was easy for opponents to try and get in each-other's heads. You spent so much time with the same people that certain individuals would constantly try and get an edge psychologically. Most players didn't bother with mind games and there were those who didn't understand what was going on, but felt inferior to those one or two who took every opportunity to exert their perceived importance. Unfortunately for me, I noticed a lot and was acutely aware of what was and wasn't going on. One of my best friends in table-tennis was someone I would sometimes speak to about stuff and he would look at me as if I was from another planet, because everything went straight over his head. That worked for him and he always slept like a baby, but there was a profound effect on him. Mentally he never believed he would be the best, nor did his mentality develop to a level to perform at the highest level, even though he was a major talent. Table-tennis taught me lots of important things: One is that you have to be aware of the influence some people have around you, even if you don't understand or cannot articulate it, you know how you feel. Really smart people who want to manipulate you, will do it without you knowing; they'll keep chipping away with negative comments and will never give you credit for achievements.

It will stifle your thought process. We've all been on a plane, train or bus where someone is sitting next to us and we start thinking: *'Oh no, I'm stuck with this person for X number of hours!'* The reason why I mention that is because that image is the ultimate frustration as you don't want to spend time sitting with someone who is negative, downbeat or purposely wants to get in your head. Unless you're sitting next to someone on a plane and can't move, you are in control of who spends time with you. In a team situation there are always good people who have a positive and healthy outlook – attach yourself to those and develop ambitions together. Because there wasn't so much money then, the focus for some people was to assert some sort of political power within the sport. Until I was nineteen I hadn't trained particularly hard, then one day I decided that I was going to change this and train so hard that people would have a different opinion of me. It made a difference to me, but unfortunately not how people viewed me. They still viewed me as the joker, which I only was when I wasn't training. No matter how hard I trained, my personality went before me. I couldn't understand why some people would never admit that I trained hard. It was because a guy, who trained hard, couldn't be the guy who enjoyed life and laughed a lot. It didn't fit into a box. The guys whose personality you could put in a matchbox and still get fifty-two matches in, were taken much more seriously. You shouldn't have to be miserable to be taken seriously. So it got me thinking that a guy who is serious all the time and trains fairly hard will always get credit. Those who have a little bit of a personality have to train twice as hard to be taken seriously. At eighteen I realised that I just had to find a way to win. The way I played was unconventional, as it was a combination of watching different people play and my own natural game. It wasn't pretty to watch lethal serves, loaded with spin followed by a quick topspin; the points were often quick. Most of my success was due to being so awkward to play against because I hadn't had any real coaching, so I played an unusual style that nobody could understand.

It will stifle your thought process. We've all been on a plane, train or bus where someone is sitting next to us and we start thinking: *'Oh no, I'm stuck with this person for X number of hours!'* The reason why I mention that is because that ways of winning a point; you could win it or your opponent could lose it by making a mistake or unforced error. You had to be mentally strong in both cases. Some players could allow a player to *play* and return so many balls that their opponent would make mistakes because of the increasing pressure. Then on the big points their opponents would often make mistakes because of the pressure on them to hit the ball hard or do something special. As a risk taker, I would always try and win the point. One occasion springs to mind when I had match point in the National Championships against, arguably our greatest ever player, Des Douglas. Des had never been beaten by an English player and it was the semi-finals. I played the game of my life and held match point, 20-19 in the fifth game. He was serving. I'd never seen him look so nervous. All I had to do was put the ball back across the net and history was mine. He was going to make me *play*, and keep the ball on the table hoping I'd make a mistake. I was obviously going to attack the serve and try and win the point quickly. Des, with sweat on his brow, performed the softest serve with no spin; crouched over the table, I attacked the serve. It was like slow motion, as the ball missed the end of the table by millimetres. I then went on to lose the match. Afterwards I sat there thinking, for just once, couldn't I have made him '*play*' under that highly pressured situation. But how could I? No one had empowered me with belief or the mental capability that I could win such a point – even though I knew what to do. I saw the signs. In sport and in life, sometimes it's really difficult to allow things to take their course and have the belief that you can cope with what happens. No one can have control all of the time. The problem for lots of sportspeople is that they are told that they need to be in control all of the time in order to win, and that in itself, can create a negative and disabling view.

In any sport, a period of competition is a mixture of situations; sometimes things are going well and you have control and sometimes things aren't so good and your opponent(s) have confidence. If you can draw a positive from all situations then you always have a chance of finding your top game and overcoming difficult periods. If you watch someone like Djokovic, his opponents always have periods in the game where they are blasting shots and winning games; but Djokovic normally comes through, because he is always focused on the big picture; but that is easier said than done. He is only human and will be affected a little by periods when he's not winning points, but it's about the belief in knowing that the percentages are in his favour. Ultimately, everything boils down to percentages and knowing that gives you mental strength. For instance, imagine that you have four bad days in a row. If you believe that the chance of having another bad day is low then you will be optimistic. The alternative is to sink into a dark and gloomy place. Djokovic knows that the percentages are with him; his overall game will come through, if he stays focused and competes. Whilst we're on the tennis theme, let's talk about two completely contrasting legends of the game: John McEnroe and Jimmy Connors. God help anyone if they went against McEnroe because he was a confidence-player. By his own admission he played on a red, amber or green light. If he won the early games, his play would go amber, then green and shots would flow like the Suez Canal. If he were under pressure, then he would play on red light, and play the percentages heavily. Jimmy Connors invariably started slowly, but would grind his opponents down and would fight until the bitter end. The funny thing about playing Jimmy Connors was, that unlike McEnroe, he played better when he was losing. How many times was that guy two sets to love or two sets to one down? This guy played the percentages heavily; he knew that in a best of five he would win three sets and he almost enjoyed breaking people mentally. Often, the Achilles' heel for someone is when things are going well, because they stop putting their flaws under the microscope.

In any sport, a period of competition is a mixture of situations; sometimes teams are performing badly then that's when there is a focus on what needs to be put right. That's when extra training happens. Many people just cruise when things are going right. Often, results just '*paper over the cracks*' and don't always represent how much hard work and improvement is going on behind the scenes. Thinking you've made it or that you're doing great is the absolute worst thing that can happen because you've never made it and you always have to improve. The wrong environment can set the wrong standards. I fell victim to thinking that because I'd reached the quarter or semi-finals of tournaments that I had done well and there was this underlying acceptance that we were only going to reach those levels. Some of my teammates did better and they won more tournaments, but I am convinced that some of these guys I grew up with could have been greater champions with the right mental messages. Winners and go-getters can be nurtured from an early age with the right messages.

Does Privilege Guarantee Success?

Our backgrounds, where we come from and the family we're born into, has a profound effect on how our lives pan out. Just because someone has come from a privileged background, it doesn't guarantee success and it certainly doesn't give people attributes like desire, determination or the right attitude. People from difficult backgrounds are always given more credit for success than people from so-called '*privileged*' backgrounds. In fact, a person's background does not guarantee that they will be successful or have the capability of listening to the right people. Laziness, lack of ambition and bad attitudes are common place in the privileged and under-privileged. Whatever your background, it is important to focus on a goal and respond positively to whatever people say about you. Most do not have sympathy for those from so-called privilege backgrounds, but in a world where we all want recognition, the privileged have to work very hard in order to receive the acknowledgement they deserve. Those from difficult backgrounds, who succeed, develop a '*no choice*' policy. When you have nothing to lose, you only look forward and fight to move forward. When you have perceived privilege, those with ambition have everything to lose because they are expected to succeed and know they probably won't receive any credit even when they do. It's not the fault of an individual that their father or mother is or was successful; all that situation does is make options available, and it's up to them whether they want to be successful in their own right. In the mid-nineties I first met Rio Ferdinand and Frank Lampard on an evening out in Essex. At the time I remember thinking that they were both good guys, who were focused on their football, but very different. I'd see them from time to time and although they came from completely different backgrounds they were similar in so many ways. Rio's background was not as stable as Frank's, but he had a calm, assured way about him; he was one of those people who had *star* on his forehead. Frank wasn't seen as a star by the fans and had received the privilege of going to a very good school.

What these two friends showed is that, no matter what your background is, you can still make it. You just need to take the opportunity. They were both developed at West Ham United FC and whilst Rio, the guy from the '*ghetto,*' was always deemed the big talent, ironically Frank Lampard was the one who had to prove himself, because of the so-called privilege he had. Rio was just so talented, a lot came easy to him, but he developed a work ethic that took him all the way to the top. When you are deemed talented at a young age, it is really difficult to deliver the necessary work ethic because you are ahead of your peers. History will show that most super-talented kids never develop the desire, determination and attitude needed to reach the top and that is why Rio is such a fantastic role model to young players with talent. But while Rio was receiving acclaim from the fans, Frank Lampard, was having to deal with uncalled for abuse from the same fans because his father was the coach and his uncle the manager of West Ham United – the team he played for. Many footballers have family in football, but most do not reach the heights of Frank Lampard. Yes, he had a fairly privileged background and went to private school, but what Frank has achieved, even with the negative inferences of his family connection in football, is quite outstanding. He has earned credit; he deserves recognition and is a fantastic role model. Some people do not want to give credit to certain people because they cannot accept that it is possible to do certain things or that credit shouldn't be given to those from so-called privileged backgrounds. So, no matter what Frank Lampard did, there were those who would not give him credit. But, let's be *Frank* here – excuse the pun – Lampard did not become one the best midfielders in the world because his family were in football. He achieved success because of the unbelievable work ethic and professionalism he showed over many years. It's not by chance that he scored great free kicks and penalties. He spent extra hours practising his craft and technique. The Chelsea legend played 164 consecutive games during a great spell at the club, which in itself showed his professionalism and the way he conducted his life.

If you speak to anyone who has worked with him, Lampard always did extra training and was and is the consummate professional. At this point you're thinking: *'Am I supposed to sympathise with those who are from a privileged background?'* The point being made here is, no matter what your background is, you can make a case why you shouldn't try; why you shouldn't bother because you will never get the credit you deserve. Frank Lampard carried that burden of people thinking that all he had to do was turn up and he'd get selected. He also knew that no matter how hard he worked, some people were always going to throw the *privilege card* at him. Talented people from tough backgrounds can make a strong case for why they shouldn't try; why they will never get a fair chance and why privileged others have a better chance of success. It's normal to expect a difficult upbringing to have a negative effect on individuals; that's why we applaud the ones who come through and make something of themselves. But, having the right voice in your ear no matter your background, is key. To add to this point, the voices you hear have to be coming from the right place and if it's an experienced voice, then in my opinion, you have a greater chance of success. Frank Lampard had his father, who was a successful footballer, and businessman; this man had the experience, know-how and respect from his son and regardless of what people said, Frank Lampard, maintained a focus and determination that was encouraged by his father. When the difficult decision came to move across to Chelsea, Lampard saw this as an opportunity to have a fresh start and go on to prove he was going to be a top footballer, which he did. The rest is history. Being successful is difficult for everyone; realistically, the odds of becoming a Premier League footballer, film producer or prime minister are so great, that most people can only dream about achieving such things. *You can use 'where you come from' as a reason not to try or as an incentive to succeed.* Rio and Frank have shown that you can make a success of your life no matter what your background is.

Mentality

When seeking why they are not getting a promotion or being selected for a certain team, an individual will say things like: *'I'm working just as hard as they are, so what are they doing that I'm not doing?'* So then the response would be from someone giving good advice: *'Why don't you work harder? You just have to be better than everyone else.'* The person receiving the advice will question why, in fact, they have to work harder than everyone else when actually that's not fair on them. But, life is often unfair. And people are sometimes content with settling for mediocrity and doing the same as everyone else. Surely you should want to be better? Want to work harder and aspire to be the very best? It shouldn't be a negative thing to be better than everyone else. So, the way in which someone interprets a situation says a lot about whether they will be a success in life. Most of us will interpret some situations in a negative way. It's often a safeguard against what is happening to us at any given time. On many occasions, when I was a teenager playing table-tennis, I didn't get the benefit of the doubt on certain selections. A major turning point for me in my career was when I should have been selected for the European Championships in 1984. I was shocked when I wasn't selected, even though my ranking justified it. For weeks I remember thinking about how unfair it was, and how easy it was for people to take something away from me or someone else – if given the opportunity. From that point, I trained like a man possessed and fought in matches like my life depended on it. On the one hand I look back and think I reacted in the right way to a negative situation; on the other hand why did I need that to happen to train harder and fight harder in matches? Why do people need something to happen, in order for them to realise what they want and how much they want it? Why do we have to lose something before we realise what we have? If we have people in our world who are totally honest when we are not pulling our weight, then we understand more a lot quicker.

Having continual conversations with a wise mentor helps us to understand situations in a more constructive way. Motivation is something that we all lack at certain times; when we're less motivated, less gets done. My mentor, Raymond, would call me in the morning and remind me about the big picture. If I ever sounded a little demotivated, he would be straight with me and use a few expletives. If he thought I wasn't listening he would say: '*Hello, hello, hello! Do you want to be one of those guys sitting in a pub saying I could have done this and I could have done that?*' That was a scary thought, because you can't get back all the years you waste. When you have opportunities whilst younger and in good health, you have to take them. When you're older you can look back and say: '*I tried and gave it a real go.*' Anyway, I made nearly every major tournament after that, until 1994 - World, European and Commonwealth championships, and even the Olympic Games in 1988. There were still occasions when I didn't get the benefit of the doubt, in terms of selection. But I was so focused that those moments didn't faze me. I truly believe that there are defining moments for all of us and the way we respond says whether we want to reach our full potential or not. Someone patting you on the back and telling you well done is one thing, but someone telling you, that you can't do it or you'll never be anyone, can fuel some of us to achieve. We can all give a reason why doors aren't opening for us; because of colour, sex, religion, height, looks, and the list goes on. But surely we've all got to say: '*This is my lot and I'm going to do the best I can.*' And then use what we have positively. People often talk about me being the first black licensed football agent. I can honestly say that I never thought about that, until someone mentioned it. Yes, sometimes there is a challenge to be taken; especially in examples like a male-dominated industry, where a woman achieves success or in an industry where few ethnic minorities are prevalent and then someone breaks down the barriers and succeeds. For me, my heroes are those with physical and/or learning difficulties who succeed and achieve in an able-bodied environment, because that is still a major problem in society, which we all have to acknowledge.

So we all have to do the best with what we have. The happiest people are not the ones with the best of everything but the people that do the best with what they have.

Talent, looks and God-given gifts are not as effective as attitude, work ethic and determination. All of the above are in very few people; the amazing Beyoncé springs to mind, and this girl works like a Trojan. When you have that much talent and stunning looks, it is easy to rely on that, but her supreme success comes from incredible hard work and some creative people around her. Not everyone can be Beyoncé, but you can go a long way by having determination and a little luck. Take Katie Price for instance; she's not everyone's cup of tea and her chosen career might not feature in the national curriculum, but she has achieved incredible success with the alleged '*little she has*'. Her work ethic and desire to succeed is at such a level that she has now become one of the most famous women in the UK. Most people can't remember why she was famous in the first place, but trust me, she received unprecedented criticism for the topless career that kick-started her success. She quickly kicked that to the curb, when she realised and understood the power of being in the public eye constantly, whether in the press or on TV. Her reality show put her on another level in terms of public awareness. It takes a certain type of human being to allow a TV camera to take over their life, and trust me, most of us wouldn't cope with it. Whether you like her or not, whether you respect her or not, Katie Price is the epitome of anything is possible. All the people giggling in the corner saying: '*She's got no talent.*' Should take note that success is not about just about talent but other attributes like determination, attitude and work ethic.

Fame, Celebrity and Money

The desire of *fame and celebrity'* is possibly one of the biggest curses to our society and to legitimate character. Those who pursue a career for gratification of their craft, are much more likely to have longevity even if they dislike being in the public eye. Fame is a highly sought-after commodity, this is mainly because of self-esteem and some people want to feel that they are better than others. The irony with the pursuit of this fickle existence is that people seldom enjoy the experience over a prolonged period. Being too well known is in direct contradiction of our basic human rights. If you cannot be anonymous and feel free to go for a walk in the park, then what do you have? One of my well-known friends would always sit in the corner of a restaurant with her back to other customers. Another compared it to being an animal in a zoo, with people constantly pointing and staring. Being famous can also be very stressful, because there are no longer any boundaries. Many famous people are uncomfortable with that part of it. It elevates the level of stress and depersonalisation. People who are in that position find it difficult and need some professional help to still retain their self-worth and self-respect. A lot is said about people who are famous for no reason. Those individuals will sometimes find that they are surrounded by like-minded folk and do not seek substance or encourage the pursuit of a craft or a credible existence. Too much importance is placed on fame rather than actual achievement. People don't often stop someone on the street and tell them what a good person or parent they are and compliment them on their charity work. But a, so called or branded, *'bad'* person or *'terrible'* parent, who happens to be on reality TV has the paparazzi chasing them down the street for a photo. Those who have excelled at their craft, and have had to deal with fame, still have their craft and that is what will keep them sane – a love for it. But we are living in worrying times; where it's more important to be on TV than at university; where it's more important to be famous than educated.

Being famous is like living in a cage. As a famous friend of mine once told me that life is about having freedom, anonymity and going for a walk in the park without being followed or bothered. So why do so many people want, crave or become desperate for fame? Most who get it actually don't like it; although it might be fun for a while, it becomes a tedious and boring routine of running, hiding and being paranoid. Being famous is a very lonely place; once you cannot communicate with people freely then what do you have? Meeting new people without them pointing or having a heart attack goes to the core of life. After all, we live on a planet with humans, so why not get to know them? People who have a strong network of family and friends around them can deal with the spotlight a lot better. Being down to earth and dealing with fame is not rocket science. One of my friends, Angela Griffin, has been famous since she was a teenager, but when you meet her you wouldn't even believe that she has ever been on television. She's a strong character with even stronger morals and ethics. Although Angela has a strong family network, what helped her considerably was meeting Lisa Faulkner and Nicola Stephenson on the set of *Holby City* many years ago. The three of them became friends for life and all the way through their careers they have supported each other and shared the journey. When you meet them, you see a family; a group of girls who don't focus on fame, but on relationships. It really is an amazing thing. Now, they all have children and families, but nothing's changed. It doesn't matter how famous any of them are, they have the most important thing – genuine friendship. In a world of fame and celebrity, people who underestimate the importance of honest relationships and friendships are just waiting to get the shock of their lives, when they wake up and there is no one around them. All the conditional relationships (dependent on being famous) have disappeared and not only are they alone but they've forgotten how to communicate with people on a normal level. Fame and celebrity steals the desire to have meaningful conversations and relationships.

A proper conversation is one when someone is genuinely interested in what someone else has to say and they do not believe they're better than that person. However, it is difficult trying to leave the fame at home or put it in a box, because, they are constantly being reminded by others that they are famous and important. Genuine friendships are based on a reciprocal selflessness; friendship is the sole and end goal. Fame can make someone feel that they're just so important – it can make them talk nonsense and not listen to what anyone's saying. The irony that comes with a lot of celebrities, is that there isn't as much money as people think. Just because someone is famous, doesn't mean that they're earning money. So that creates the problem for the so-called '*celebrity*' and that they must be seen to be doing certain things, because the public think they're rich. It's a vicious cycle, but unfortunately, some who seek fame drop their friends as they climb the fame ladder; this is because they are constantly looking for new fair-weather friends to keep their celebrity status alive. '*Celebrity*' is a word that often rubs certain people up the wrong way. People who have a craft, that happened to make them famous, hate the word '*celebrity*' as they feel it's demeaning to what they do. Parts of the media obsessively portray the good life as people with fame and money. So we've come to the conclusion that fame and celebrity can be a disastrous mix, so as well as this, let's add lots and lots of money to make things just absolutely ridiculous. Some footballers get a lot of stick about the way in which they earn lots of money and buy expensive things. Well, could anyone deal with fame and money in their early twenties? I know people don't have sympathy for footballers, but having so much money at such an early age and no experience is a seriously difficult situation. Then on top of that, their friends are supposed to accept the situation as normal, and this is not usually the case. Many young people, not in just football, find themselves having to deal with fame and money Singers, actors and TV personalities also find themselves in the same boat.

The truth is this, nobody is ever as good and never as bad as the press say they are; that's why in the exaggerated world of celebrity, it is just so important for those around talent not to get carried away and not to join in the hype. For this type of situation, the parent who doesn't get carried away and reminds their child that they are only as good as their next performance are the best parents. Money can do so much good when used selflessly and be so destructive when used for selfish means. Everybody with excess money should be advised to do some philanthropy and to help others in need. It is a great leveller to do so; it gives great karma and develops a strong relationship and keeps someone connected with the outside world – so to speak. Money creates a world, which is not normal and can take some people out of touch with reality. It is always so reassuring when you meet someone who has fame and money, but they are down to earth. In the late '80s, I sat in a restaurant next to a couple in their late thirties. We soon struck up a conversation. After a short while they asked me what I did and I explained that playing professional table-tennis was my job – they were genuinely interested. I then asked what they did; the man said that he was in the music industry. I thought that was great, so asked what he did within the industry and he told me he was in a band. Then, I asked what kind of band? And he said: '*Queen.*' It was unbelievable. It was John Deacon, who had purposely decided that he wasn't going to seek fame and wanted a normal life. He told me about how he lived in a fairly normal house, caught the bus and tube with no one recognising him. A short time later, my friend and I were his guests at Wembley Stadium and were watching him on stage in front of over 50,000 people. Afterwards we went backstage and amongst all the craziness of one of the biggest bands in the world, there was John Deacon, just acting normally. Here is someone who knew the importance of a life; a normal life – the one thing money can't buy.

Coaches and Managers

The name of this book is *In Your World.* It's all about the people *In Your World* who influence you, guide you and/or mentor you. The best coaches and mentors are not necessarily people who have competed at the highest level or who reached the highest echelons of business. In fact, people who think they are qualified to get things as a manager, coach or agent just because they competed in a certain sport will be overtaken by people who have the hunger and who have the interest in understanding what is needed for success. Here's something else to note, the best coaches and managers don't have to be experts in rocket science, they just have to be respected. After a while, talent will hear the same recycled bits of advice and almost know what their advisors are going to say, but respect has longevity. If you don't respect the person in your corner, it doesn't matter what they say; it won't inspire you. If the manager of a team does not have the respect of his/her team, then the *'edge'* needed to win may not be there. Whilst talent should always have the intense appetite to learn and improve, coaches should always be ahead of the game and have the ability to change and improve their methods. At the very least, coaches should constantly be looking to improve their EQ (Emotional Intelligence). At the highest level of sport, the mental side becomes more and more important. Coaches need to be able to tap into the psyche of their team. People often attach intelligence to how high someone's IQ (Intelligence Quotient) is, but this is not important in the world of a coach, mentor or manager. The level of EQ a coach has is much more important. If a coach can understand the emotional status of talent and then communicate in a way that helps them express themselves, then that is a lot more important than having a high IQ. Coaches with a high EQ, understand themselves and have the ability to understand, empathise and tap into the psyche of others. A coach can have their theory on coaching or implement what they have learned from courses and manuals, but if they cannot get under the skin of talent and really understand them on an emotional level, then there is a limit to the impact they will have.

Sometimes, individuals don't perform because of their emotional state of mind and not because they don't have the talent, ability and desire. A coach with a high EQ will always have the advantage over one who just has experience in any given craft. Coaches, mentors and managers with high EQs can also become leaders, because they understand the importance of relationships, collaboration and teamwork. There are of course the exceptions; the guys who have a way of doing things and rely on their ability to put a fantastic system in place and ask everyone to follow. Sir David Brailsford, revolutionised cycling in this country and helped produce Olympic Champions and Tour de France winners. The word *'revolutionised'* makes it sound like Brailsford invented some new, magical way of competing on a bike. What he did was to focus on something much simpler: *Marginal Gain.* People want huge improvement in return for hard work. The truth is that steady improvement especially against your competitors will bring success. Dave Brailsford said:

'The whole principle came from the idea that if you broke down everything you could think of that goes into riding a bike, and then improved it by 1%, you will get a significant increase when you put them all together'.

Brailsford also talked about how his cyclists washed their hands really well, slept on the same pillow every night and had every aspect of their lives improved, as well as their bikes. That philosophy must carry weight; just look at the success British cycling has had. So, a good coach, mentor or adviser, will identify areas where improvements are needed and no matter how marginal they are, when all added up together, the difference can be substantial. There are many people who have succeeded in football, who didn't compete at the highest level or even played for that matter. Mourinho, Wenger and Ferguson are example of people who didn't set the world alight with their footballing skills. In fact, Mourinho was a translator, who whilst translating for the likes of Bobby Robson at Barcelona, was obviously watching, learning and thinking: *'I can do this.'*

When Mourinho was translating in Spain, imagine if he decided to tell people that he wanted to be one of the world's greatest coaches. He would have been *laughed out of court* – especially by the *'you've never played the game'* gang. There are different ways of being a successful manager. It is easy to become obsessed with what level someone played at and their coaching qualifications, but it's possible to be a great manager by having the right people around you and having the ability to identify the best coaches and scouts. Arsène Wenger is an amazing mentor and coach; he hasn't needed to develop his team skills as much as other managers. He has ultimate belief in himself and doesn't really need to have protection around him. So everything in Wenger's world is designed by him; people around him are there but not because they make him look good. If you asked a fan on the street who the coaches are who work with Wenger, most fans could name just one person. At Manchester United, under the incredible reign of Ferguson over almost three decades, the coaching-staff were very visible and the fans knew who they were. Ferguson was obviously a good enough coach, but his unbelievable skill was managing the coaching team and the players. Also, his ability to identify what was needed for his team was quite extraordinary. He also had an almost physic ability to know when to get rid of people. He rarely got that wrong. Ferguson is inspirational to all of us, in that he showed that being a smart, strong person, and knowing how to construct a team, can bring you success. Ferguson is probably the greatest coach of our time but nobody could have predicted that this kid from Glasgow would have gone on to achieve what he did. Coaches/mentors are some of the most influential people *In Your World*, because their specific job should be to give you the right and appropriate advice. Incentive, direction and seeing a *light at the end of the tunnel* often comes from the top. Even chairmen and directors can send out the wrong message to teams, groups and individuals. Young footballers seeing that none of their peers are getting a chance can cause long-term damage.

When Mourinho was translating in Spain, imagine if he decided to tell people that he wanted to be one of the world's greatest coaches. He would have been *laughed out of court* – especially by the *'you've never played the game'* gang. table-tennis team, myself and others battled away to try and break into the top few. Places were limited and we all desperately wanted a place in the team for big competitions like World, European and Commonwealth championships. Team spirit and legacy can be damaged by a coach or manager bringing someone in at the wrong time and by that I mean when you have people who are almost '*there*' and people who have worked really hard to get to a point where they are waiting for the proverbial nod. In 1990, the ETTA (English Table-Tennis Association) decided to bring in a Chinese player called Chen Xinhua. He had gained UK citizenship and was indeed a great character. At that time there were a few players just below myself in the England rankings (5-10) who were playing full-time and sacrificing a lot to table-tennis. Even though Xinhua was a fantastic player and personality, many players saw his introduction and believed they may not get the chance. Of course, to have a winning mind-set, would be to believe you are good enough no matter who comes in. My view is that additions to the group (in sports and business) have to be a much higher level than already in place and the manager has to communicate why the addition has taken place. Most importantly, a manager has to be prepared to replace the addition with one of the mainstays if it is justified. Managers will often bring someone in and then refuse to replace them, no matter how badly they perform – that is a very dangerous precedent to set. No individual is bigger than a team. Group ethic is of key importance. In football, Arsenal FC and Manchester United FC have nurtured players from their academy who have gone on to be first team regulars. That gives a major boost to their whole set-up. People often talk about talent and the point may be aimed at Arsenal and Manchester United as they have had the best youngsters and that's why they produce them.

My view is that talent is an overrated attribute; the most talented sportspeople don't necessarily come through, and instead, we see the ones with other attributes like attitude, character, determination and raw desire. But they still have to be mentored and nurtured. The famous group of Giggs, Scholes, Butt, G. Neville, P. Neville and Beckham all came through together at Man' United. The standard was set for these boys and they rose to it in spectacular fashion. In their *world* they could prosper and satisfy their ambitions. We all remember Alan Hansen's comment: '*You win nothing with kids,*' after a Man' United loss featuring the above players. He would have been right if those players were at any other team in the world at that time. In their world, Butt, Scholes, Beckham, Giggs and the Nevilles were nurtured by a manager and the coaching staff; all the right values were set and what anyone else thought was ignored. In sport, once a youngster has been coached to a certain standard, the mental side becomes more and more important. '*Over-coaching*' is a term I've heard used from time to time. The truth is this: the best coaches are the ones who nurture individual talent and accept that sometimes they can't add that much to natural talent. If a coach has a big ego and wants to impress on someone how things should be done, then that can cause a narrow way of thinking. Some coaches just want individuals to stick to what they say so that they can take the credit. The best coaches are the ones who can judge characters and situations.

When I played table-tennis, I was told things like: '*Don't play to his backhand, play to his forehand,*' and '*play wide to his forehand then down his backhand.*'

What does that mean? That I should play that way every point? If I won a point another way, then the coach would be disappointed? I used this uncreative coaching approach to my benefit. You see, I was one of those players with a great forehand and a less than average backhand. So, I taught myself to serve and lean on my backhand side to get my forehand in and how to impart really heavy topspin from wide on my forehand, in order to allow me to get back into position to play another forehand.

My view is that talent is an overrated attribute; the most talented sportspeople your opponent's strengths or have a positive response when your opponent is having a good period and playing to his/her strengths. Because if you are coached in a way that means you are scared or worried about your opponent's strengths, then it is difficult to compete under that pressure. Stellan Bengtsson, a former World Champion, said in his book, that when he is leading a match by six or seven points, he then plays directly to his opponent's strengths and fights hard to win those points because if he does his opponent is broken. Mental strength comes from knowing you can deal with all situations. Level of performance has a lot to do with your state of mind and confidence. Timing is so important in sport; knowing when to do certain things is a talent in itself, which coaches and mentors can empower you to develop. The way you strike a ball has everything to do with timing. When I wanted to hit the ball, I would hold my bat so tight that I could only hit a few balls in a row. But applying yourself mentally to know that you can hit the ball just as hard by focusing on timing, would allow you to hit the ball hard time and time again because you would not be gripping your bat so hard. Look at Federer, watch the way he hits the ball and glides across the court. Does he ever look like there is tension in his arm? The link between wanting to hit the ball hard and the way you approach it mentally, is something you have to be taught at a young age, otherwise you can never separate the mental aggression from the physical aggression. In football you see footballers, who have lots of pace, but hardly ever pass anybody; that has everything to do with mentality, bravery, knowing when to *go* and when to *give and go.* For non-football people, my apologies for that terminology, it just means when to run and when to pass it then run. So the question is, why can't a player run past another one who is far slower than him? It's because he mentally does not have the *know-how* and confidence. A coach may say to him: '*Just run past him,*' but it's about empowering the player to leave his opponent uncertain about what he's going to do, thus making it easier when he does take him on.

Tactics are something that coaches are always given a lot of praise for, but asking a talented person or group to regimentally stick to certain tactics can have negative repercussions. Everybody wants to see talent flourish. A team's mentality often comes from the top, the manager, coach or other people in charge. The smallest thing can send the wrong message to the group and affect team spirit and in turn affect performance. In a situation where a manager or coach continues to select someone, even when they are not performing, that group cannot achieve great success. Even worse is, if the group sense that any decisions are political, the group is damaged. Certain members will take their '*eye off the ball*' and start to place some importance on political actions. Managers, coaches and people in authoritarian positions should not be there if they are going to set the wrong standard, because it will filter down into the psyche of up-and-coming players. Then you have a real problem of talent not coming through with the winning mentality. There were times, when other team members and I felt, that no matter what we did it wasn't going to make a difference to our ranking or selection. Of course, it would be fantastic to go from 50th in the world, to becoming World Champion but it was impossible to make a jump like that without day-to-day nurturing. Managers have to set the right standard and respect; a thriving environment that encourages everyone to improve and sends the right messages to the youngsters. All situations should have positive repercussions. If you lose, work harder and learn from your mistakes. If you win, work harder and build on your success. If you're losing the race, you have nothing to lose, but if you're winning the race, build on your success and win it. So much time is wasted by not spending time improving yourself, learning and seeking. Imagine a giant egg timer in your bedroom, filled to the top, and it represents your career or life. Every morning you wake up, you see a little bit more in the bottom - it's not a great image. People often complain about there not being enough personalities in sport.

For someone with character to come through, he has to have people around him who don't take a negative view on his character and that happens a lot. There are so many people from minority sports, who have continual debates about why they don't get more column inches or TV airtime. I heard it said many times, that if we had a World or European Champion then things would change and we would all of a sudden have lots of TV, Press and Sponsorships. The truth is, that there are some people in those sports who are desperate for their sport to be big but there are others who are scared of losing control of their sport. In their world they are happy to talk about why their sport isn't on TV, but won't make the changes needed. In order to be high profile you have to accept that there will be all sorts of press. You have to also accept that you may have to get people to the venues for other reasons than the sport. It doesn't matter why they go, but once they're there they will fall in love with the sport.

When you're fighting for airtime and column-inches, you have to be creative. Those who standout need to have the support of the sport and need to be branded. It is always a problem in minority sports, because the mentality is, often, that only certain people can get media attention and they can often be the least interesting to the public. To return to table-tennis, I will discuss a little about what I learnt from different mentalities. I was a fairly good player and reached twenty-nine in Europe and mid-fifties world ranking. The reason why I didn't go any higher was because my winning mentality wasn't good enough and I wasn't prepared to change my game against certain people. Having the confidence to employ tactics you're not comfortable with is not an easy thing to do. There were certain players I knew I would beat by playing my normal game, but there were other players who I found really difficult to play against, so I went into those matches with a negative frame of mind. Those players were the ones who could deal with my major strength – heavy spun serves with an even heavier follow up forehand.

My nightmare opponents were people like the late Andrej Grubba and former World Champion – Jorgen Persson. Most opponents were either scared or a little wary of my game. My variation in serves and strong forehand topspin was quite awkward to play against, but those two guys in particular let me hit my big shots and kept getting balls back, especially on the big points. Their mentality was that, although, I might hit some balls passed them, they would win the percentage game. Most importantly, they were preparing themselves for the big points, which is what champions do. Everybody in life whether it's sport, business or entertainment, can win a situation. That is the key difference between champions and also-rans. One of the most unbelievable turnarounds I have ever seen, was when the greatest table-tennis player of all time, Jan-Ove Waldner, played in the 1992 World Championships. In the team competition, Waldner lost 21-9 to Vladimir Samsonov. It was embarrassing because Waldner was the world's best and Samsonov was an up-and-coming talent. Waldner then had to play Samsonov again in the singles; it was unbelievable, and Waldner ripped him to pieces – a real lesson. The thing with Waldner was, that he always performed when it mattered. Yes, the team competition was important, but for his world ranking and standing, it was all about the singles and whilst Samsonov was wiping the floor with him in the team event, Waldner was making notes for the real event. Nobody can be great all the time, but if you're great at the right times, you can leave a legacy and make history. There were certain players who were regularly two games down in a best of five and they would come back to win. There were guys who would always win the close games, as they would perform on the big points. This fascinated me, because winning and losing was such a small margin. There were a hundred guys who could get to nineteen points against anyone, but only a few who could regularly get to twenty-one. I spoke with some of the guys and learnt a lot. So much of the emphasis in our sport is on getting a good start, but this can have very negative repercussions on certain people, because it actually makes you think that if you don't get a good start you can't win.

It can also make you incapable of dealing with difficult moments in your match or competitive events.

Winners get to the finish line whether they have a good start or not.

It's not a coincidence that Man' United come from behind so many times. It's not a coincidence that Jimmy Connors won so many matches from two sets to love, down. When I played, some coaches would continually say that getting in with the first topspin was imperative so in your mind a picture starts to build, that if you don't make the first topspin, then you will probably lose the point. But, the great players knew that even if opponents played the first topspin, they could still control the point and countering quickly would not give the opponent time to react. What you are told by coaches (especially when young) moulds your thought process. If you watch old Jan-Ove Waldner footage, he sometimes allowed opponents to topspin attack; this lulled his opponents into a false sense of security. Because, opponents are never sure when they will get the opportunity to attack, and when they do it is often a weak-shot, which Waldner counter-attacks quickly. Just because someone is attacking, leading or shouting the odds, it doesn't mean that they are in control. Waldner was in control even when he wasn't attacking; situations like that are demoralising to opponents because most people's mentality, is that you should win the point or situation when you are attacking. If you allow someone to attack, you basically lull them into a false sense of security, because you can react quickly with a counter-attack. When Waldner served, his opponents never knew where the ball was going so they couldn't prepare and would seldom get in a strong attack. Even when opponents got in a strong topspin, Waldner would just step back and do what's called, '*fishing*' in table-tennis terms. This would sometimes break opponents mentally because if they can't win the point when attacking aggressively, then how are they going to win? People would watch Waldner and not understand what he was doing, but enjoyed the beautiful way he played.

His game was based on capitalising from the indecision of his opponents (me being one of them). There would be a mixture of giving his opponents the run around, then at certain stages he would be away from the table – '*fishing*' and just putting the ball back on the table. At this point, his opponents would start hitting the ball harder and harder, thinking: '*I have to win this point.*' He, of course, was at the back of the court with the proverbial cigar, sending the ball back with high looping shots. Winning those rallies broke the morale of his opponents. It was like winning two points in one. It's about winning the race and there are always different stages. If you try and sprint the marathon, you obviously will not finish. Just like Murray and Djokovic, they know that the psyche of opponents are that they must win the point when attacking, so they defend with vigour and focus; knowing that winning those points are huge mental gains. In some respects, obvious coaching methods are very easy to compete against. Someone telling you to just be aggressive without explaining the different ways of winning the mental game can actually be negative. You're not going to beat the Waldner, Persson, Djokovic and Murrays, by having a plan of just aggression. In fact, these guys need to be allowed to be the aggressors for certain parts of the match, so that they feel uncomfortable when not winning points. Key messages have to be given to kids when they are learning their sport. That it's about finding your '*A*' game and finding a way to win no matter what happens. People perform better with a positive mind-set and you can draw a positive mode from any situation. When I asked a former World Champion how he managed to come back from two games down to win, he said: '*No matter what is going on, all I am trying to do is find my game because when I do I will win eventually.*' I then asked him whether he gets worried when he's losing, he said: '*When I'm losing, my opponent is looking backwards and I can only look forwards; he gets nervous and I get stronger*'.

The Achilles' heel in sport can be when someone or a team is on the brink of winning, then something happens and they are paralysed for the rest of the match or competitive session.

That is why another sporting legend told me that when he was a match point down or close to defeat, he would always think about what it will do to his opponent mentally if he could get the next two points. How many times have you seen a tennis match where someone is two sets to one up and has match points, then doesn't convert any of them and is destroyed for the rest of the match? That is why turning points are so important in competitive situations. Instead of performing at a lower level because you're not winning, you up your performance in search of the turning point. These are all positive messages to enhance a positive, mental performance in competition. When sportspeople compete at an intense level and under pressure, they go into autopilot and they will win or lose in that mode. That is why positive messages in their subconscious are so important. In fact, our subconscious mind is 30,000 times more powerful than our conscious mind. Our subconscious mind controls everything we do; so by having positive messages embedded deep in our psyche, we will perform under pressure and on big moments. Taking in what's actually happening in the sporting arena whilst under pressure is a real difficult ask, but great sportspeople just know what to do in certain situations. A lot of our mentality is getting a good start then everything will be fine. But when it comes to the so-called *'big points,'* why aren't we winning them? Empowering our youngsters to focus on the big points is important because you are judged by just a few points in each tennis match because it's the difference between winning and losing. There is very little difference between the top 100 player – if tennis was played up to four or five games – but there is a massive difference between the top few and the rest when it comes to winning those last games and points. To refer back to Jan-Ove Waldner, he was a genius; a talent that transcended all sports. He would win matches from impossible situations and would invariably win the big points. I asked once why he won so many big points, and he didn't know; he couldn't explain. But when you watched him, he always knew what to do in pressure situations and that comes from knowing.

It's about the end and not the beginning and middle. At tournaments there would be sixteen tables then, as the tournament reached the latter stages, there would be less and less tables, until there would be just one left for the final of the men's and women's singles. It always interested me why certain people played so well when the hall was full with lots of tables, but fell to pieces when the spotlight was on them. One guy, who never fell to pieces, was Mikael Applegren; he came into his element when all eyes were on him. I would think what a shame for those who had played so well all weekend, only to crumble in the spotlight. Some people can only go so far and deep down they know this; what a shame that is. Mikael Applegren once said to me: '*It's not easy playing in front of all those people; if you make a mistake everybody sees it, but it's my stage.*' So his mentality was that when there was one table, it was his stage to perform, so he could go all the way; he could win tournaments and there was no glass ceiling. That is a mentality he gained from an early stage and the people around him nurtured it. Anyone who cannot perform on the big stage can never be a champion, a hero or a legend. History will tell you that it is all about the big stage. The one thing Maradona holds over Lionel Messi, is that Messi has not weaved his magic at a World Cup with Argentina. When he does, he will be considered the greatest or one of the Greatest. Belief is so important and being empowered by knowing what your opponent is feeling will give you success. One of our greatest ever middle-distance runners is Sebastian Coe. We all remember that moment in Moscow, when he won the 1500 metres after losing the 800. He hit the front and with 200 metres to go sprinted for home. The amazing thing about that, was the amount of pressure Coe put himself under to win. He had lost the 800, which was his best event, and had spent every minute of every day after the 800 thinking about how he would win the 1500. Ovett, on the other hand had won a gold medal and he probably didn't spend every minute of every day thinking about the 1500. Probably because he had forty-five straight wins at the distance.

It's not often in sport you see that level of desire, determination, relief and joy, but all that was a repercussion for losing the 800m. So it's ironic that in order for some champions to reach a level of supreme performance, it has to come after some form of adversity. A hard working person with little talent will always do better than a talented person who doesn't work hard. But why can't we get the best out of the highly talented individuals? If we did, then we could have people able to reach the top of their craft. I have a theory, most coaches like to impart information to young people in a structured way: From a coaching manual and if the youngster follows the manual, then he or she is more likely to be fast-tracked. Unfortunately, some coaches take a negative view on a talented person who doesn't follow the instructions given. So, many talented people are misunderstood and, in turn, hate training and performing in a way that is not natural to them. How many times have we heard talented people say things like: '*He wants me to be a robot,*' or '*she keeps telling me off for doing something different?*' So, how do we nurture talented people and not lose them because of coaching structures? My view is that everything is a system or has an element of system in it; so even highly talented individuals who seem to be doing different things have an element of structure and things they do regularly. When I stopped competing, I coached for a while. I would do summer camps and take classes at weekends. When I coached, I was conscious of allowing the youngsters to express themselves and not necessarily dictate to them and tell them it had to be a certain way. Whilst coaching I developed a technique called '*PLAY AND ADJUST*'. There are probably many of my ex-students reading this and putting their head in their hands saying: '*What the hell was he going on about?*' But seriously, it was a system that gave each player a purpose/strategy in the way they approached games; it also gave them a way to play when they were not in control of a point. So for instance, they would look to play a backhand, but if it went to the forehand then they would adjust and play a forehand with limited movement (because of the limited time to play the shot).

You see, not every person is structured; there are some sportspeople who are, and they have their routine with not many changes. Highly gifted people often seem to play '*off the cuff*', and the '*Play and Adjust*' system helps them because it always looks like they know what they're doing, especially when the adjust shots get better and better. Footballers with sight of goal on either flank of the pitch are told: '*Always shoot across the goalkeeper because if he saves it, the ball might go to one of your teammates.*' That is a textbook coaching quote. But what if the player sees the goalkeeper move and leave a gap at the near-post? Is that in the manual? So shouldn't the player look to shoot across the goalkeeper, then adjust his shot if he sees an opening at the near post? The *Play and Adjust* theory can be applied to anything in life. It's better than waiting for something to happen, or having an obvious uncreative plan that can't be changed. How many times do we hear: '*They Have No Plan B?*' Are you surprised when people are being taught to stick to a structure?

No 'Plan B' is a result of people not being taught how to adjust.

Olympics 88

The excitement about the 100 metres final was unbearable and to add to that, my mate, Linford Christie was running in it against Ben Johnson and Carl Lewis. In Linford's world he had his coach, Ron Roddan, and didn't really listen to anyone else. He made himself untouchable by not fraternising. Nobody knew what he was thinking – he was so strong mentally – that he made his world unbreakable. The night before the race I made the mistake of asking him if he really thought he could win the race; he looked at me as if I had stolen all his money and said: '*Why not? Why does it have to be Carl?*' That statement has resonated with me ever since. His belief was so great and quite rightly so. Why couldn't he win? That was as close as anyone was going to get to his psyche; that's why he won silver in Seoul, then went on to win gold at the age of thirty-two. *In Your World,* you have to protect yourself from people who will burst your balloon, mock your ambitions and generally not support you. There are many successful people like Linford, who make a decision to fly solo and find inner strength to get to where they want to go and sometimes that's what they need to do. The Athletes' Village is a classic example of how certain environments can influence you in a positive way and make you believe that anything is possible. I was there to play doubles with table-tennis' all-time great – Des Douglas. He was an absolute legend and I was just happy to be there. We had qualified at a competition earlier in the season in Austria, where we had some crazy results including beating one of the world's best duos – Lupelescu and Primorac. In table-tennis doubles, the best combination is a right-hander with a left-hander. This is because service and returns happen on the right hand of the table and you don't get in each other's way. The next best combination is two right-handers for the same reason. Last and least is two left-handers; this is because you just get in each other's way. Yes, Des and I are both left-handed.

Table-tennis bosses were not going to enter a second doubles pairing, probably because it was deemed a waste of time due to the combinations available.

I realised that my opportunity of going to the Olympics was to play doubles with Des Douglas, but no second pairing had been entered. The call I made to Des to convince him to ask for me and him to play doubles in Seoul, South Korea is one of the most important I've ever made. He was happy. I asked the question and the rest is history. We seemed to not have a chance of qualifying for the Olympics, but qualifying was exactly what we did. It was one of the happiest days of my life. Des Douglas was and is such a great man, a guy who reached the pinnacle of his sport but maintained a *down to earth* quality and had time for everyone. Others would get a couple of good results and think they're world-beaters. Des respected everybody, treated every opponent with respect and never '*counted his chickens*'. To be honest, we had no chance at the Olympics but a combination of being around the great man and mixing with like-minded athletes gave me great confidence. We beat the Swedish combination of Applegren and Waldner – two of the greatest players to ever play the game. Furthermore, one is left-handed and the other right-handed; Des and I are both left-handed and got in each other's way, but found a way to beat one of the tournament's favourites. Many other victories ensued, but we missed out on qualifying for the knockout and medal stages by a couple of points. I learnt so much from Des; he never thought he had achieved greatness as he always focused on the next match and was never overawed by others. At the games, GB athletics had some really big names, including Daley Thompson. There was a poignant moment when Des and I were walking through the Athletes' Village and Daley Thompson was sitting talking to someone. He then saw Des walk past and he said to his companion: '*That's Des Douglas.*' Des didn't notice and just carried on walking. I later told Des that Daley had recognised him and he looked back at me nonchalantly and replied: '*Why would he do that?*'

Displaying his modesty and level headed character. I loved the Olympics: The competition; the mentality of all the athletes and the togetherness for a common goal. The most important thing I got from the experience, was the focus on *personal bests*. Everybody wanted to improve themselves and everybody wanted to improve their performance by whatever margins. Whilst there was a focus on medals, the vast majority of athletes talked about getting a PB (personal best). Isn't that what we all should be doing, constantly trying to get PBs in life? The Olympics made me realise (if I hadn't already) to keep improving myself and to always try and do better. We are all in control of our own self-improvement.

Agents and Double Agents

The profession of being an agent/manager has changed so much over the past years. I have always felt that there shouldn't be a need to have a written contract with a client. That's because a piece of paper with signatures on shouldn't mean anything if the representative and client do not have a good relationship and perform as agreed verbally. Also, as an agent, I've always felt that if you do everything right, and work hard for a client, they won't let you down. In the USA, everything is about the contract; lawyers are king and emphasis is on clauses and airtight scenarios. Any business needs three types of *capital*, which are: *Finance capital*, *creative capital* and *relationship capital*. It's fair to say that *relationship capital* is very important in the *management of talent* business. Gary Lineker has had the same agent for almost forty years – John Holmes and they have never had a written contract. When a client and agent have that type of relationship both parties can take a long-term view on strategy and development. Agents, once a pledge is made to look after a client, should give time, effort and creativity to the client's career, regardless of successes or failures. On the other-hand, clients will have success and difficult periods with their representatives and in my opinion, should not change representation unless absolutely, bona fide necessary. Sometimes, clients will make a complete change because it may seem like the right thing to do at a certain time, which is often a low or difficult point, in their career. Being strong during difficult periods and adding to the team can make talent even stronger in the business. It can be a mistake to lose the network, support and work ethic of people behind you. The key is adding to your team to become stronger and not losing people to become weaker. However, I do wonder about whether the twenty-first century agent is helping change the mind-set of talent. What has happened to the '*old-school*' agent, who cared about their client as they were friends and had time for anyone who called the office or wrote a letter?

I have spent my whole life as an agent/manager telling clients to honour their contracts. The philosophy was to not approach anybody to represent them, as I always believed that talent should choose their representatives and not the other way round. But, the problem with that is talent are being approached all the time; companies are pitching to them and the business has become ruthless. In some quarters, no one cares if your client honours their contract. It's not about conducting yourself in the right way and doing things in the right manner, but whether you do the popular thing. Henry Brook Adams once said: '*Morality is a private and costly luxury.*' That is so true, because you can try and do everything right, but in the end, it's a very private thing that almost certainly costs you in different ways. But no matter what people say or how much money you could have earned doing things another way, the most rewarding thing is that private feeling of good karma. For the most part the profession has become smoke and mirrors. Agents doing deals with film studios instead of clients, football clubs instead of players and buying into the masses instead of the individual. Agents aim to have a power-base and do this in different ways; the most popular one is to have strong relationships with third parties. For instance, a football agent would have more interest in having a relationship with a club so they will always be used by the club. Players would then become reliant on the agent for their trade. Most agents take the view that longevity is in the partnerships with third parties. Although it may look like an agent is representing footballers, the truth is that few agents would put their neck on the line for a player because of the possibility of falling out with any club. In show business, Hollywood, for instance, the top agents have partnerships with the big film studios and so an actor becomes a pawn in a very big game of chess. The USA agent way of doing things is to cover every possible angle. In the film industry, the big agencies represent everybody who can be involved in the production of a movie; writers, producers, directors and actors.

An individual with any sort of ambition in the film industry, has to have an agent; it's just not possible to succeed without one. That environment of huge insecurity for the talent has been created by the agents and further strands of insecurity have been created in previous years. In the US, a sport's, TV or film star has to have: A manager, an agent and a publicist. The question is why? Was that system designed to offer talent a better service or a crude way of giving more to different representatives? In the good old days, an old school agent did everything and did it well. Shouldn't an agent be qualified to manage, negotiate and brand their clients? Some agents rely on a combination of the personal relationship that they have with their clients and the work they deliver. I'm a believer in personal relationships and understanding your client on a one-to-one basis. I also believe that no matter how much you may like the client, there must be a clear focus and vision on the client's career. Sometimes it is possible to lose the professional vision and feel secure within the personal relationship, but that can do a disservice to the client, although some clients do place more of an importance on the trust in a relationship. The ideal scenario for a client is to have a really smart, creative agent who thrives on creativity; because they will always look ahead; they will always look to move a client's career on because it's what they live for and it's their passion. So few agents are like that. This is because the art of being an agent, has become the art of holding the power with the institutions and not by doing the craft of representing a client to the best of their ability. A client should always have the balance of power, but unfortunately a footballer can often find themselves as a pawn in an elaborate chess game. If anyone looks around their life and can't find a pawn, chances are it's because they are, in fact, the pawn. Once an agent holds power with an institution – a football club, film studio or powerbrokers – they do not see the value in developing the real relationship or work situation with a client. The reason why so few football agents bother to develop their craft or skill in the areas of brand, PR and negotiation solely for footballers, is because they don't see the value and don't have to.

The most important thing an agent can do is to see the qualities in a client and help them develop their talent. Ironically, the agents who are genuine and focus on delivering the best service for their clients, whilst enjoying excellent personal relationships, are not in as strong a position as the agents who have the relationship with third parties who talent rely on. And that, in a nutshell, is why so few agents focus on working one-on-one with a small group of talented people, because the feeling is that there is no value in putting in all that effort. All most clients want, is quality personal management. Something else agents can do is to *condition* clients to think in a certain way. The worst *conditioning* is when clients are taught to think it's all about the money and then sign contracts without any research or preparation; because they can throw in a transfer request, go on strike or behave in such a bad way that they have to be sold. In that situation, the agent is in the background counting the cash and the client looks terrible and has an almost irreversible image. The most important thing an agent can do, doesn't often involve money. For instance, a client's image, brand and negotiating position can all be made stronger with some hard work behind the scenes. Every client has the right to have an element of control over his or her career. No one should have to sign a contract when it just isn't the right time to do so. Pressure can often be exerted on someone to sign something when the timing suits someone else rather than them.

Timing is everything when negotiating and signing a contract.

A strong agent who solely represents his client, will have done their research and know the market; they will also judge when the right time is to negotiate and finalise a contract. The agent may come under pressure from third parties to agree a contract at a time that isn't good for the client, but a strong agent will resist. This is often difficult because agents have families too and the longer they leave the finalising of a contract, the more chance there is of being let down by the client because the client becomes an interesting proposition to more and more people.

Some agents will make a client totally unattractive to other agents, by negotiating an extremely long contract. This means lots of money for the agent involved and no opportunity the footballer to ever be in a position of strength. A footballer would never be able to have a say in their career unless they forced through a move by acting in a bad way. Even then, they would have to wait until the club decided to sell, no matter how desperate they were to move. The argument for signing a long contract would be *'security,'* but there is no security in a sport like football. Furthermore, a week is a long time in football and the landscape changes regularly. Every footballer should be in the game to be successful and they have to set themselves up to be so. My view is, that if they are not setting their plan to be successful, then why be in the game? Every player should want to be as good as they can and not just sit on a long contract thinking about security. I understand that there has to be an element of security, especially when they have a family, but they should put themselves under pressure to succeed. Short contracts leave them a little on edge to perform and deliver; it also gives them the opportunity to have some input into their own career. Some of the best players, ever produced in this country, have made big decisions with a year or year and half left on their contract. Why? Because in an industry where players are normally pawns, they had an opportunity to have an input in their own careers. Beckham. Gerrard, Owen, Ferdinand, Rooney, Lampard and the list goes on; it's not rocket science. But you have to be strong and your representative has to be strong, just to have a say in your own career. In my opinion, management should create a world for clients, which is conducive to them becoming the best they can possibly be.

But, some agents condition clients to think in a way that suits them rather than the client. A common theme is for an agent to tell a client that their commission is on top of the client's fee and that they are not taking any of their fee. This of course is music to a client's ears because they think: '*This is not costing me anything.*' It also justifies the agent's fee.

I was once negotiating a deal for a new non-footballing client and told him that I would make sure all the groundwork was done properly and then would get him the best deal possible and the agent's commission would be 20%. He then said to me that I should put the commission on top of whatever I got for him. I tried explaining that the '*pot of money* 'was the '*pot of money*' and that agents say their commission is on top to make the client feel that no money is coming out of their deal. I was fighting a losing battle. He had already been conditioned to accept anything an agent put to him, as long as the agent's fee was on top. In other words, agents can do a client a disservice by negotiating an average fee and then anything they want on top, because it's not coming out of the client's deal. Clients have to empower their representatives to do the best deal they can and know the commission they get. Agents have to encourage a team ethic with clients and always get the best deals possible; knowing that everyone is happy with the arrangement between client and agent. There is a dark world in which clients have no idea what their representatives are getting because of the *commission on top* mentality. In football there are some decent advisers who have looked after their client's whole career. By having the same adviser you build trust and a team ethic. After a chat with Sol, we agreed that I would represent him. I felt comfortable with the whole thing because I had represented myself all the way through my own career. During the last years of playing sport I had a brief fling with a company, that although professed a desire to represent me, they also had hundreds of clients; I honestly felt like a very small needle in a very big haystack. So, when I started as an agent, I made the decision to always represent a small group of people and always give them the attention required to manage them properly. More importantly, I decided that all my clients would always honour their contracts and that I would always be brutally honest with them, no matter how difficult the conversation would be. I also felt that sportspeople needed to have some '*stickability*', win their battles and obtain strong characters that would hold them in good stead for their careers and lives after.

That was the world I felt was right for my clients and business associates to work within. I was in for a shock, not necessarily from my clients but from some people I would deal with whilst managing my clients' careers. My first ever discussion with a manager was with Ossie Ardiles at Spurs. I remember walking up the stairs thinking, *'am I really going to be good at this?'* I passed Alan Sugar's office and he gave me a look I'll never forget. But anyway, Ossie was great; he loved Sol and didn't have a massive ego. He also didn't try to put me in a position of: *'If I didn't do as I was told then I would have problems.'* He loved his table-tennis and told me a story about playing for Argentina juniors. I happened to say to him that I'd give him nineteen points start in a game; considering that games were up to twenty-one, he wasn't happy. *'I'll give you 100 grand if you beat me'*, was his response. Dealing with Ossie and Steve Perryman lulled me into a false sense of security, because they were great, honest guys who didn't try to influence any negotiations. The players loved those two guys and wanted to play for them; for Sol it was a great time to start his professional career. After that nice start to my career as an agent, things got remarkably harder. What was particularly daunting was not the difficult conversations or dealing with the rollercoaster that is a player's career, it was actually making sure I did not compromise myself or my client. Because the industry dictates that if you side with your client completely, then you will have problems. Clubs often pay the fees and the agents don't want to fall out with the clubs. So, a lot of agents profess to represent footballers, but in fact they are representing themselves by this simple fact: *Players come and go but the clubs are always there.* It takes a very strong agent to put his neck on the line for his client, so the question is: Do clients get the right advice? There is this weird atmosphere in the relationship of players and agents. Some agents begrudge how much money their clients earn and vice-versa. So you end up with agents not wanting players to know how much they get and players not wanting to know how much the agent is earning. That creates an opportunity for some agents to do deals and get more than they should be getting.

That was the world I felt was right for my clients and business associates to governing body (Football Association). You see, you're supposed to send a copy of any representation contract to the governing body and in that contract it will say how much commission an agent should get and how. The problem with that, for the participants, is everyone knows what the agents are receiving or should be receiving. Agents then have to abide by the rules and regulations set out by the governing body. Unlicensed individuals are a major problem because these guys don't come under the governing body's rules and operate behind someone who has a license. In a footballer's world, if he has these types of people around him, it's difficult to build a legitimate team. To the public this seems ridiculous; why should there be any grey area? You can't disagree with that and to be quite frank, if a client wants to help create a world where his or her agent cannot be compromised and is encouraged to fight the corner and give the absolute true advice, then everything needs to be open. Everyone has responsibility here. The client has to make sure that their agent has the right incentives and fair commission. The agent has to be totally transparent and be committed to getting the client the best deals possible and advising in the best possible way. The agent has to also be happy with the financial remuneration and to do all the other necessary work free of charge; for example, associating the client with the right charities and initiatives. The absolute worst scenario is when the agent doesn't care for, nor understand, the importance of a client's image and brand. Some agents will give that part of the job no time whatsoever because it doesn't pay. If a client is advised not to do something because it doesn't pay, the consequence of this could have a negative impact on their brand. The way to build a brand and image, is to do things which don't pay, so you have control of what's going out and you can do lots of it. Then once your brand is out there, you can charge what you want. The reason why so few people have amazing brands, like David Beckham, is because it is generally really hard work and takes up energy. But if you like it then it's not so difficult. One of the important things agents, advisers and mentors can do is to *see something in you.*

This basically means, seeing something (talent or character), which they can then help a client to develop. Just one piece of forward-thinking advice from someone with experience and wisdom, can help guide you on your particular journey. Even the opportunity to weigh-up what might happen in the future, and discuss the possibilities with your advisors are very important. This is because a client may not know what road to take or what their skill-set is. Someone directing you on the right road, whilst utilising your skill-set is such a big thing that it's difficult to explain the enormity of it. Football coaches are well placed to guide young players to making the right decisions on where they should play on the pitch. So obviously, lots of coaches see agents as just a pain in the backside. Imagine this: Coaches can nurture a footballer and give them all the information needed to have the best chance of fulfilling their potential. Then along comes an agent and says: '*Forget all that crap; it's all about the money.*' This voice has an agenda that is all about getting as much money in the quickest way possible. Footballers cannot possibly get the right advice for their careers from those types of agents. It also contradicts everything footballers have been taught by coaches and the like. When a kid plays football at school and at their local clubs, the emphasis from coaches is to learn the craft, enjoy the game and everything will follow. The industry allows, and is in some way, encouraging to agents who keep moving players around. The press love the speculation and give big profile to transfer stories. The appetite to fans for new transfers and speculation about new players is insatiable. The whirlwind of a transfer and the euphoric short-term feeling players get when moving clubs can also become very attractive. So agents feel under pressure to continually give players information about the possibility of a move and interested clubs, and of course, it's always to bigger clubs with more money. Excuse my sarcasm. The truth is that most professional players will not move to one club from a bigger club or higher league interested in them. Every footballer believes in himself/herself so it's natural that there will always be the thought: '*I can play for a bigger club.*'

Double Agents

Most talent have agents and representatives and most people buy and sell their houses via agents. The most infamous of agents are indeed football and estate agents, but whatever the public opinion is of the dreaded middleman, they're here to stay because there is a legitimate role to play in business transactions. In an ideal world, an agent would give talent the right advice. Their intentions should be to use their knowledge and expertise to give you the best advice. Unfortunately in life, this is not always the case, because most agents learn how to represent the side with the bigger powerbase and financial muscle and that is often not the individual. So, individuals/talent need to create a world where their representative has incentives to advise them properly. Clients and agents (especially in football) find it awkward and uncomfortable discussing money. There's this strange standoff, where agents try to get paid without the clients knowing how much they get and the clients either don't want to know or don't want to pay for the service. If a *client fronts up* a conversation about what they want out of their career long-term, and has input into the remuneration and bonuses the agent should get, then odds of them getting the right advice goes up dramatically. The odds of getting the right advice shortens even more if the client gives clear direction that the more success they get, the more the remuneration the agent will get without a glass ceiling. The '*agent's fees*' phenomenon is a major issue in both football and in the property business. Estate agents are much maligned; mainly because they are often seen as a problem in the middle of a transaction. The first thing to accept is that they will always represent the person who is paying them and that is the vendor. So even when you go in an estate agents and you try to buy a house, the information you are getting is in favour of the vendor:

Often you will hear that the seller won't budge on the price or there are lots of other people interested in the property. God help you if you give off that: *'I've just got to have that house'* demeanour, because then you really are in trouble. In that business there are two fundamental problems:

1) Estate agents in this country get 1-3%. In America they get 5-10%. If fees are not realistic, then people will play a numbers game. Albeit, some greedy people will play a numbers game regardless.

2) A business has developed within the business where some estate agents will sometimes get paid by both sides and then whoever is paying the most will get the right advice.

I always wondered why it was so difficult to have confidentiality. Too many people knowing your business, weakens your position. You can be as strong as a team, if your opponents or non-team members don't know your training methods, tactics and/or weaknesses. Historically, governments all over the world employed spies; there has always been this intensity to know other people's secrets. That is why unscrupulous people are willing to pay a '*King's Ransom*' to people who will '*double-deal* 'or give-up information about their own team, company or government. When Sol Campbell came out from behind the boards to be unveiled as Arsenal's new signing, it was a total shock to everybody because nobody knew it was going to be him. It was a natural thing to not discuss a client's business with anyone; I also have always believed that a strong confidential team can achieve great things. In football, the footballers are and should be the stars of the industry. Also, they quite rightly, get paid very well. Footballers have short careers and they quite rightly deserve to maximise their opportunity to win trophies and achieve financial security. A key point is that footballers should have the opportunity to have some control over their own careers and not be traded around like pieces of meat.

So, here is the unsettling fact, more agents are '*double-Agents*' than '*single-agents*' (representing their client without compromise). Double-dealing in football and business is rife because some people will go to any lengths to have control and information. Information gives people power and if you know what someone's next move is going to be, then you can plan accordingly. *In Your World* it is important to identify who the double-Agents and double-dealers are, because if you don't then your position is weak and you have people who are poking your Achilles heel. The good thing is that when you identify who they are, you can actually use them in a positive way by giving them the wrong information to pass on. That actually makes your position stronger. Footballers and other talent don't know what advice they have been given until their career is over. That is why it is so important to have an input into the mechanics of how the client/agent relationship should work. The client can create great incentives for the agent to ensure there is no double-dealing. Don't get me wrong, the best situation is to have a team where you have that common bond and confidentiality, because you can take on the world. Advisers can take the view that '*clients come and go but clubs are always there*' so then their job becomes not to represent a client, but to play the double-game and the better you play it the more money you make. Anyone who represents a client and does not double-deal, but instead, helps them to utilise their career by giving advice solely for them, can find themselves in a position where the view can be to discredit them or not encourage footballers to join them because the footballers hold a certain amount of control over their careers. The fact is this: Most of the richest agents are not the ones who represent clients without compromising themselves or putting their necks on the line for them. As I've mentioned, in every team, workplace and group, there are people who feel hard-done-by, bitter and feel they deserved more. These people are often misguided or not willing to put in the hard work needed to succeed – it's much easier to blame everyone else.

The most dangerous individuals are the ones who thrive on that negativity; the ones who live for gossip and bad blood. Their resentment becomes all-consuming. These types of individuals live for those situations much more than their work or craft. Jealousy can sprout its roots from the above situations and then the problem can become cancerous. *In Your World,* individuals with such negative aspirations have to be identified, sooner rather than later. So how do you identify people who are *In Your World* but don't want the best for you or your team? Well, jealousy comes from a very insecure place. It comes from a lack of confidence and the belief that they want something that someone else has. Leaders have to make sure that they set the right standards and goals for their teams; once that has been done, members who do not respond in the right way need to be looked at closer. Also, people who have hidden agendas cannot hide their true feelings indefinitely; they will talk and try to get others on their side. There's a saying: Big Business, Small World, and every environment is a small world, because people talk. I have always been someone who loves to have good people around me. Like-minded people with the right intentions and a good work ethic are key to success and happiness. I have always admired people who have achieved and felt inspired by the achievements of friends and colleagues. Sometimes you can't put your finger on it, but something just doesn't feel right about someone *In Your World* and it's often because they don't share in your success, seldom give positive comments or encouragement to you, friends or colleagues. Then, you have no choice but to confront the situation because you have nothing to lose. Sometimes you fear the worst with people close to you and don't want to create a situation. One of the worst is the feeling that your partner is cheating on you and even worse – with one of your friends. Sometimes friends do that deadly sin – the ultimate betrayal some may say.

Weak friends, colleagues and teammates are prime targets for double-agent roles.

The most dangerous individuals are the ones who thrive on that negativity; the taking for people within your world is a recipe for disaster and those who partake in such vices often keep it secret. A compulsive gambler can never have or earn enough money and at some point they will sell you down the river. The drug-taker can never be relied upon completely and eventually they will let you down. Many families have faced people intent on destruction, they often cannot be helped and you can feel helpless. Sometimes you need to go through the process of trying to help, especially if it's someone close to you. But you'll find that being *cruel to be kind* is the best way forward. Being an '*enabler*' is the quickest way to make your world anti-productive. Time is the most valuable commodity and it's important not to use good time on bad situations. We all have a limited amount of time, so it's important not to let people and situations steal it. Like, *time Stealers*, who say:

'*Can you come round to my place as I'm going to tell you all my problems and not allow you to help me? Furthermore I'm not interested in what's going on with you and if you do start talking about dreams and aspirations, I will be negative.*'

Yes, that person just pick-pocketed a couple of your hours. But in business, you can't keep people who are continuously a liability. Time has to be used in a positive manner; it is for building and not destroying.

Talent

Coming from a *purist* point of view, the representatives of talent should not compromise themselves, but give 100% undivided commitment. The sports and entertainment industry has been an interesting education for me. It's immeasurable how important the people in the world of talent are. Whoever is in their world will guide them to oblivion or fulfilment of potential. In an ideal world, talent would be able to work out who they should have around them, but unfortunately a lot of talent have people around them who are often short-sighted and not particularly qualified. In my opinion, aspiring talent or entrepreneurs need the following: Some history, some future and some here and now. If the above is mixed badly it can be a recipe for disaster. So what do you need? You need someone around you who knows you and who can be completely honest; you also need someone who is creative and forward thinking. Finally, you need someone who can coach and mentor you through the immediate challenges. When you're young you have the future but the older you get, the more important history becomes. If you lose people around you who are there for the right reasons, then you lose the foundation of who you are. Regardless of where you go or what you do, you always need to confide in someone you trust. The wrong people, like unscrupulous agents, can take you down a fast running stream. At some stage you will have the chance to get off, as it's impossible to swim against the current, if you don't get off, you will get washed down the river and end up at the bottom of it. Scary but true. Agents can say all the right things, in order to get the attention of valuable talent and unfortunately some will fall for it. Some agents prey on vulnerable families, who are often working class and acceptable to offers of cash in return for signing off their talented son.

When I think about that it makes my stomach turn, but some parents just believe that's the norm and some basically sell their kids down the river. Having said that, the vast majority of parents do not entertain that kind of approach to their talented kids, and quite rightly so. What kind of start in a player's career is it when someone is offering a loan with a huge APR of finance and morality? Smart parents realise that they need to get the right advice during the formative years of their child's sporting life and that has to come from people with the right intentions. Smart-talent will always keep their core people around them, but also have someone who can add a little extra. It's disastrous for them to get their heads turned and then drop everyone around them, because someone has sweet-talked them at their weakest point in order to make money. The lesson here is, if someone approaches you and gives you a whole load of promises, it's not because they're family or want to help you become a philanthropist; they are doing it to invariably make money for themselves. Talent should choose agents and not the other way round. There are two ways of looking at everything and if you take the wrong option, then it could cost you long term. For instance, an agent approaching a young footballer and saying to his parents: '*Our company is massive, we represent 500 players, and we've got some big names.*' You can either go: 'Wow, that's impressive' or 'how can you look after all those players?' Young footballers and parents need advice over a period of time and speaking of '*time*' that is exactly what people need who are not familiar with the business. David Beckham is someone I admire greatly; he took control of his career because he hired a personal manager and then chose his PR, branding and assistants. David and Victoria have taken the whole marketing and branding skill to another level. Their world is conducive to their success. They are taking advice from the best possible people and reaping the benefits. Anyone who ignores the importance of an individual's or their own brand really doesn't understand the effect it can have in so many ways. Some people have questioned why certain teams signed Beckham and even suggested that it was because of shirt sales.

Even if that were true, it helped prolong his career at the highest level. I personally believe that he was a fantastic player and he had a world-class attitude on the pitch. There were times when people questioned his commitment to football because of his '*off the field*' stuff'. No one had a better attitude or was more professional than David Beckham; it was just hard for some people to take the fact that someone could master a career on and off the pitch. It is a talent to understand the importance of image, community and charity work, because when the career is all said and done, very few individuals will be remembered for what they did in their career, but they may well be remembered for the humanitarian things attributed to them.

Legacy is more important than a little more money.

Talent often sign with the first agent who approaches them. I would strongly advise against this: Listen to what potential representatives say, have a good look around, speak to as many people as possible and then make a decision. Bringing such an influential person into your world without doing due diligence can cause irreparable harm. Most worryingly, some talent don't know how they have been represented until after their career has finished. I've been lucky enough to have been part of conversations with some of the biggest stars in football and sport after their careers ended; their stories were very interesting. One famous footballer (who had a troubled career) said that every time he had a problem or would complain about not being happy, his agent would get him a move; so throughout his career he never looked at himself or thought he was to blame for anything. He just kept moving clubs, playing well during the honeymoon period then, as regular as clockwork, falling out with the players, manager or staff. He went on to say that he could never have a conversation with his agent as he was always looking to make the next deal. Is this representation?

You can change clubs as many times as you want, but one thing never changes – you.

In The Zone

The relationships you have *In Your World* is key to your success as an individual; an honest relationship with the right people can help you immeasurably. Being honest with dishonest people will be your Achilles' heel. In sport, athletes carry secrets, insecurities and apprehensions; in many cases an athlete can limit their success by not being honest about their fears and insecurities. Everybody feels better after getting something off their chest and a tremendous weight can be lifted off an individual's shoulder if he/she can communicate their inner thoughts and fears. As previously mentioned, Frank Bruno faced a great internal struggle, which caused him to fight against his own demons before his fight with Mike Tyson.

Failing to prepare is preparing to fail.

The term *'in the zone'* is often used– a small sentence with a massive effect. Being in it can make you confident, fearless, and fully focused to achieve your goals. A lack of confidence and insecurity can affect what you achieve and how you perform. When I played table-tennis, I could look in someone's eyes and see if they were in the zone or not. Likewise, when I was in it, it didn't matter who was at the other end of the table; I just went for it. When I look back it wasn't easy to get in the zone completely. If there was something on my mind or I wasn't properly psyched up, I would invariably under-perform. Being in the zone is not a natural state of being, for any of us, but it is the way to achieve optimum performance.

Complete focus equals the utilisation of all our attributes.

Add to that excellent preparation and you have given yourself the opportunity to achieve your ultimate goals. People who achieve in sport, business, entertainment and other walks of life are in the zone.

They are focused; they look forward; they take the knocks and just keep on going and going. Success is like a continual 400 metre hurdles race; you've just got to keep jumping the hurdles and if you knock one over and fall, you've just got to get up and keep running. A '*pyramid*' is the best way to describe the battle to be successful. At the top there is a tiny space for the people who just don't give up and work-smart. Working-smart is so important because just working hard can only get you so far; so then you have to learn the '*game and play*' and learn it better than everyone else. My mum worked up to twelve hours a day in a pie factory and earned £15 per week; no one could say she didn't work hard. There are people who can make a couple of phone calls, put deals together and earn a small fortune. People don't normally achieve in a '*normal state*'; they achieve in a '*psyched up*' state and when someone is focused in that way, then major objectives are possible. I remember being on training camps and sitting in meetings watching videos of me or one of my teammates and seeing how animated we were; running around and shouting every point. All this whilst we sat in a room sipping a cup of tea in a very relaxed state.

Bruce Forsythe still admits to being a little nervous before going on stage; it's good to be like that, because it gives you an edge. He is one of our most successful entertainers ever and he still gets that buzz before his performances. That's because he loves his craft and still wants to perform to the highest level possible. Anxiety, apprehension, nervousness and stress can be all-consuming. For lots of people it takes over their mental state and makes performing impossible. Some people get so nervous before a performance that they are physically sick; even some athletes have been known to lock themselves in a toilet before a major competition. All of that can be countered by going through a simple routine to get '*in the zone*'. When I competed, music was a way to get myself psyched-up. I would listed to passionate, inspirational songs, which would get me in such a fevered state that if a Boeing 747 landed in front of me, I wouldn't have even noticed.

Sometimes, people work so hard to achieve something and then just before the moment of achievement, there is a nervousness, anxiety and apprehension – but that is normal. The key is to feel those things and then perform. And the reason why sportspeople use psychologists, is purely to do with performance. My view is that everyone is capable of higher levels of performance by finding ways of getting '*in the zone*'. I can remember specific matches, where for some unknown reason, I just played like a man possessed and beat players who ranked far higher than me. In all walks of life we need to be 'in the zone' for moments when we need to perform. That's because we all have it within us to perform at this heightened state, but we often need someone to psyche us up. Before moments when we would normally be nervous, some words of encouragement from a mentor or friend could help us perform. In my early twenties, I would speak to my mentor about buying a flat and moving out of home. He would always tell me that getting on the property ladder was one of the most important things I needed to do. Every now and again he would ask me if I'd done anything about it. Then one day he called me in the morning and asked me if I'd been to an estate agents. I said no. Well, his next few sentences went something like: 'Get your arse out of bed, go down to the estate agents and ask to see a few flats. Then put a deposit down on the one you like. I'll be phoning you in the afternoon to make sure you've done it.' He put the fear of God in me and I was so psyched up that by 2pm, I had bought my first flat. I literally do not remember the whole process; it was like I was in a trance. In sport, the right people can add a large percentage to a performance. Different characters need a different type of approach. The common denominator has to be that you achieve a state of complete focus and a winning mentality. Achieving that often means tapping into someone's subconscious. That can be achieved by the attitude and comments displayed by the people around the sportsperson and the '*psyche-up*' talk directly before the performance. Our subconscious controls us, and sometimes it's difficult for coaches to know how their talent are going to perform.

Wimbledon 2013 saw the wonderful Sabine Lisicki play some amazing tennis; beating world No.1 Serena Williams. She became the darling of Wimbledon because of the dazzling tennis and her obvious humility. After her semi-final win over world No.4 Radwanska, she cried tears of joy. All the way through to the final she was the underdog; fighting to win her matches, but in the final, she was the favourite in many people's eyes. That change in mental approach, affected her badly; probably because it was her first Wimbledon final and the occasion and environment got to her. The British public had really taken to her, but she performed badly and made many unforced errors and double-faults. She needed to admit that she was nervous, worried or even scared to play in the final as the favourite, then someone close to her could have addressed her psychological state. The fact was that the public were a bit bemused because she only started playing when she was a set and 5-1 down in the second set. She then played with a freedom, that if she had done so from the start, she would have won the match. I've seen this many times in sport; once the burden of winning is almost gone, a person can play with a freedom they were scared to do from the start. The women's singles 2013 – was won by Marion Bartholi – who played with great focus and determination. She played as if the centre court was her home, and that is part of getting people '*in the zone*'. A major part to getting someone in it, is to make them feel comfortable in any given environment. Bartholi was '*in the zone*' and Lisicki wasn't; that is mainly what performance boils down to.

In Cuckoo Land?

Plenty of people live in their *own world* and that is interpreted by most of us as someone being '*a little crazy*' because they are '*living in cuckoo land*'. This book focuses on the importance of the people *In Your World,* but some people live in their own mind-set or own world, and just expect everyone else to play along. To achieve success, continued success and even greatness, people need to think in a different way to the norm. To even think you can be the best at something or believe you can be the person to achieve above all others, means you have to think differently to everyone else. Some people believe they don't need anyone because of the belief in their own ability and are prepared to work hard to levels they know others won't do. The legend, that is Daley Thompson, trained on Christmas Day, because he wanted to have an edge on his competitors. Others live in their own world, which is an irrational, non-productive, unadvisable world. It's actually scary how many people don't listen to anybody and because of their own '*world of magnificence*'. We've all listened to someone speaking and thought: '*What the hell is this person going on about?*' It wouldn't be so bad if they used it in a constructive way or were actually on the right path to success. Being in your own world can make you impregnable. It keeps you focused on obtainable goals. You create an environment where you do not listen to anybody, so nobody can influence you. That's all good if you are on the right track, but if the thought process is misguided then you can be on the road to disaster. It's always intrigued me how people get to be in a world of their own. I've realised that some people are so insecure about what other people think of them that they create a persona and kid themselves into believing that they are amazing and that they are better than everyone else. That develops into giving the impression they are thick skinned, tough and at the top of their game, but really they are constantly seeking approval and listening to see what people think of them. A common phrase from someone like that is: '*I don't care what people think.*' But really they d0 as their whole world is what status they have with others.

Others are in their own world because they are desperate to have attention, status and acknowledgement; but the difference is, they are willing to put in the hard work. The fear of not having status or achievement scares them so much that they cocoon themselves in a mind-set that is driven sometimes to the extreme. They believe that advice will weaken them or show signs of weakness.

'*Cuckoo Land,*' is a very interesting world; it is a land where people are living on an island that has no entrance points. By this I mean they have no interest in sense or reason and will only let people into Cuckoo Land who also want to live in the clouds. The actual term '*Cloud Cuckoo Land,*' refers to a state of absurdly over-optimistic fantasy or an unrealistically idealistic state where everything is perfect. Someone who is said to live there is a person who thinks that things that are completely impossible might happen, rather than understanding how things really are. It also hints that the person referred to is naïve and unaware of realities or deranged in holding such an optimistic belief in that world. There's nothing wrong with having a little '*Cuckoo*' about us, because first, we have to dream to achieve great things – but the problem arises when people just expect things to happen without hard work and sacrifice. Many people, who have achieved great things, may have been told that they live in 'Cuckoo Land.' This being because at a young age they saw something or were inspired by an event and decided they wanted to play at Wimbledon, be an astronaut and walk on the moon or be prime minister for example. Well, a little bit of '*cuckoo*' teamed with having the work ethic and desire can make the seemingly impossible, possible. It is not '*normal*' to achieve amazing things, so obviously, you have to think differently to the masses. Anyone who has the same mind-set as everyone one else, cannot become the *lily in the grass field.* It is always difficult for people to express their imaginative views in a group, team or family because others may tell them that they are living in '*Cuckoo Land.*' So, a little bit of '*cuckoo*' can help in the pursuit of success and greatness, but being totally submerged in it brings unhealthy problems.

Others are in their own world because they are desperate to have attention, and believing you don't need to work hard or be proactive to succeed. Sometimes we hear people say '*what will be will be.*' Well if you sit on your bum in your bedroom and watch TV all day then, '*what will be will be.*' You will not achieve anything. But, if you are proactive, get out there, meet people and are prepared to work hard then 'what will be will be.' You will be giving yourself more of an opportunity to meet the right people who will give you the right advice and possibly be part of your team.

The Great World Builders

In sport, some of the great '*world builders*' are tennis players; they create their world, by forming a team including a coach, physical trainer, agent, manager, sports psychologist, girlfriend and many others. They are insulated by their world and protected from negative influences. If you have never watched a whole tennis match, watch one. Watch how badly the players want to win and watch the fist- pumping and encouragement that comes from their team. Tennis players do absolutely everything to build a team with the common goal of success. The question beckons: Do we do everything possible to build the right team for success?

Sir Clive Woodward understood the importance of individuality and team mentality. So what he did was make sure his staff improved each person individually and also installed the '*warrior spirit*'. Combining '*individual*' coaching with '*team*' coaching is one of the hardest things a coach can do. It is much less work to focus on general statements aimed at the whole team. Team members want individual attention; they want to know what to work on, what their role is in the team and the appreciation of that role. In any team there are the people who get the attention and the glory. There are also the '*water carriers*'. A term used in football for players who work solely for the team. The coach has to make sure that the 'water carriers' get personal acknowledgement and appreciation. These guys don't need the headlines, just a quiet word in the ear. Woodward created a winning culture, which was terribly difficult to do. The result was a World Cup win for England's rugby team in 2003. Winning cultures must have the commitment to win. It's about the attitude they display. Woodward breaks this down into three parts:

1. Obsession with the task: Individuals focus on attention to detail and have an uncompromising level of excellence.

2. Responsibility: A readiness to take tasks on as their job and make sure they are seen through.
3. Enjoyment: Team members have to ask themselves whether their colleagues enjoy working with them, and why.

When I played table-tennis, I never felt that my world was conducive to me becoming a really top player; there were often negative vibes around and team members wouldn't help each other. In team competitions and tournaments, the mentality of the team/group is 90% of how good the performance will be. People often talk about marginal gains, but there are many things that do not only wipe away a marginal gain, but give other teams an edge. The mentality of a team is set by the manager and the coaches; the team members take notice of every little thing that is said or done. Respect is a huge thing in a camp; a manager's decisions, actions and what he says has major ramifications on the team. If certain individuals are selected, and that isn't justified, then it can have a negative, marginal loss in the camp. Other things like, lack of leadership, favouritism and negative messages all add to the negative marginal, loss count and before you know it, the team is performing marginally below par. Another important aspect is for the manager to make sure that he/she is above backstabbing, gossiping and bitching. In a claustrophobic environment, individuals can say and do things they wouldn't do normally. Certain things can become magnified and seemingly important in the claustrophobic tournament world. Managers have the difficult task of creating a positive environment where everything is geared towards winning and the team are constantly reminded about the bigger picture. Tennis at the top level is so tough, competitive and mentally draining as the margins are so small. Out of the top 100 there is such a small difference in the levels of tennis, most players can get to 4 – 5 games in a set; some even win sets, but more often than not, the same players win all the majors.

There's a small difference in talent and ability and a huge difference in who wins the big points, and that is all about mentality. The way someone thinks often comes from their world. It takes a very strong person to be forthright in their views with negative people around them. Everybody in a tennis player's world is there to help, support and push the player to achieve the best they can. Djokovic is the ultimate team builder; he knows the importance of his team and he always gives glowing tributes to them after his successes. When he added Boris Becker to his team, he also kept his other loyal members. His intelligence in identifying who he needs around him is outstanding. The Becker addition came from nowhere; having seen Becker around town (London) and spoken to him on a couple of occasions, it was quite a coup for Djokovic to convince him to travel the world as his coach. If one of the greatest tennis players who ever lived, feels that they needs to add someone or something to their team, how can others feel that they know it all? Becker joined the team alongside long time coaches, Marian Vajda, Miljan Amanovic and Gebhard Phil-Gritsch. One of the great things about having the right people in your team is that they will help identify what is needed to make the team stronger. In 2013, Vajda realised that Djokovic needed a new coach and helped him make the choice of Becker. This was a surprise to a lot of people in tennis, as Becker was an unproven coach. Another coach would not have wanted to bring in such a strong personality, but Vajda wanted the absolute best for Djokovic and there was no ego involved in the decision-making. Vajda stayed as part of the coaching team and allowed Becker to take charge and improve certain parts of Djokovic's game. The decision to bring Becker in has been a masterstroke. Djokovic has gone on to win numerous grand slams. Mostly, the person best placed to identify what is needed to improve a team, is someone already in your team who doesn't have an ego that is bigger than the bigger picture. No matter how good you are at something, there is always someone out there who will give you information you didn't have and a new perspective.

Whereas footballers don't generally build their worlds, football club managers do; they are enthusiastic team builders. Managers have to surround themselves with people who will help them become successful; their team would include coaches, scouts and agents, amongst others. The partner/wife they end up with is normally someone who is happy or accepts being a so-called '*football widow*'. This is because managers spend most of their time doing their job and during the football season have no flexibility or free time. Even in the summer when the season ends, they are planning for the next campaign. As any world builders, you can have people around who are going to push you and challenge you to perform to the highest level. Andy Murray is one of those who continually works to have coaches and other people around him who will challenge him. The comfort zone is not an option for one of our greatest ever tennis players. Sometimes '*world builders*' will surround themselves with the so-called '*yes men*'. This is because they do not want to be challenged; they want to be protected and are scared of either losing their position or having someone in their world take their place. World builders who do not want to be challenged, create a team with a reinforced glass ceiling. So nobody grows, not even the world builder. There's only one thing worse than telling someone to leave your world because they are not growing, and that's keeping them in your world with them not growing. The winners are often the people who are not scared to surround themselves with creative, smart and strong people. Richard Branson is one of those people who saw the bigger picture and hired the best people to build his world and '*brand*'.

The Unspoken Truth

This chapter addresses stuff often never spoken about, but is prevalent in all team, family and friend situations. If it is not identified, it can spread like a type of cancer and result in teammates wanting their own team to lose, family wanting each other to fail and friends hating the success of each other. In terms of sport, it will sound crazy to the general public, mad, even stupid but in every sporting team where you have individuals not in the starting line-up or left feeling that they have been badly treated, they might not only want their team to lose, but they could cause serious problems behind the scenes. Resentment develops and breeds very easily in sporting teams; it can fester and cause segregation and underlying negative tensions. Team members can be segregated to an extent where they get stuck in their thought process and take an active role in being a negative influence on the team. Sometimes it can be more important to them, than taking a positive view to get in the team and be part of success. You see, ultimately, sports people are selfish and even if they are in a team situation, they care about themselves first. The school of thought that a sportsperson cares more about the team than themselves is nonsense. It is the politically correct thing to say, but in reality, every sportsperson wants success for themselves first, ahead of any team situation. The ideal scenario for most sports talent is for them to perform well and for the team to win. It takes a very special leader to create a situation where everybody pulls together. The team is not just about the talent and performance, it's the substitutes, medical staff, back-room people and office workers. A smart-team builder will create a world where everybody pulls together. It's a really tough thing to do, because you can never keep everybody happy. There are individuals who are just destructive. There are people who enjoy negativity with no positive view on any situation and those guys have to be identified and let go. Negative individuals get much more satisfaction from failure than success; the glass is always half-empty and the whole world is against them.

An extreme version of this individual is someone who will commit sabotage just to feel better. Individuals can feel so badly '*wronged*' that he/she will develop a desire to hurt their own team or company. They start to try and convince team members that if they perform and do well they are helping the manager, boss or leader. This of course does not totally convince team members not to perform, but it does insert negativity into their minds. In companies, members of the workforce can be bitter towards the more affluent employees. It is a mistake not to let everybody share in the success of a team or company. Again, smart leaders have a structure where everybody feels they are part of any success. Ultimately, no individual is more important than a team and there are genuine team players and people who enjoy the whole team ethic and love the whole comrade thing. In some instances, the subs, reserves and squad members are as important as the regular starters; this is because no team wins trophies and titles without a squad and a team often relies on members that are not necessarily first team starters, but play important roles at different times of the season. If a leader wants a squad member to play for and perform for the leader and team, then they have to be treated fairly at all times. The key to having non-starters bringing a positive effect to a team, is for them to feel like an important and valued member of the squad. How to motivate squad members to push for a first team place, is not only difficult but often not given enough attention. A '*them*' and '*us*' situation can develop very quickly if separate meetings, training sessions and '*assessments*' occur in the wrong way. Financially, it's lazy to just give obvious bonuses to the starting players and ones who get a piece of the action. Long-term and for team spirit, financial benefits should go to the whole squad. I accept that team leaders will have concerns when giving rewards to the entire squad, as there are members who will not respond in the right manner. But, in that case, they shouldn't be in the squad in the first place. It's hard to believe, but on every bench there are players who want their team to lose or to concede goals so they can enter the pitch.

An extreme version of this individual is someone who will commit sabotage just to feel better. Individuals can feel so badly '*wronged*' that he/she will develop a their team, but deep down they are hurting because they're not involved.

When teams go away for tournaments, like I did for World, European, Commonwealth and Olympics Games, half the squad sometimes don't compete and that can be a very painful experience. I was part of teams abroad, knowing I would never get a chance to play unless my whole squad was kidnapped. So, I developed a friend's network at tournaments and along with competing, I thoroughly enjoyed catching up with people from different countries; it kept me sane. One of the really tough things for people not in the starting line ups, is to perform when called upon. A type of lethargy can set in and it can be difficult to slot in for ten to fifteen minutes, or part of a match. If the managers and coaches don't have a completely rational, impartial and competitive structure, then not only will squad members not prepare themselves mentally for action, but it could add a touch of complacency to the guys in the starting team. It is nevertheless a major achievement for someone to come in off the bench and perform, for all the reasons I've just spoken about. Back in 1990, we competed in the European Championships in Gothenburg, Sweden. I didn't play a game until we lost in the semi-final, then I played for third place against the old Yugoslavia. Our tournament was over and I was then given a game. The Yugoslavian team consisted of players ranked much higher than me: Primorac, Lupelescu and Kalinic. They had all played every game in the team competition, so as we say in the sport, they were '*played-in*'. What I'm going to say next typifies the importance of who's *In Your World* and what they say to you. I went into the tournament cold and played out of my skin, beating Lupelescu and Kalinic. After beating Lupelescu, I collapsed on the floor with joy. I'd beaten players ranked numerous places above me in Europe and the World.

The then chairman of the ETTA (English Table Tennis Association) came up to me and said: '*You were fresh and it showed in that match.*' It was a congratulations; not for performing under difficult circumstances, but for having an edge from not playing. You can sit on the bench thinking: '*What's the point in going on? It's a no win situation.*' Then, you can be judged for not performing. This happens more often than not. Footballers labelled as substitutes can find themselves in a no-win situation. A scenario is that there could be ten minutes left in a match and the substitute (striker) comes on, gives a great performance and scores. Then, the manager tells him: '*Well done; you're a good substitute.*' But, if the same player comes on and plays badly, the response from the manager could be: '*That's why they are a substitute.*' So whatever the player does, it doesn't get them into the team. The bottom line is that a player can't really show much in a ten-minute spell, but the way that the player is treated has larger ramifications on the team and all the lower levels in a club structure. Every player should have aspirations to step-up to a higher level; and being a substitute at a higher level is a realistic way of getting into a higher team. If managers/coaches create a healthy environment of competition, then young players will thrive and be motivated. Apart from the starting eleven, all the players behind the substitutes are in a pecking order. A good environment for the development of players gives hope and a light at the end of the tunnel for all those who aspire to get on the substitutes bench. There should be stepping-stones for players. Substitutes cannot and should not be put in a no-win situation, as it will demotivate the ones following behind. So, it is really important that coaches and management acknowledge the importance of squad members and give positive acknowledgement when someone performs from the bench. It gives all the other bench members hope and encouragement. I remember going to the World Cup - England vs. Argentina in 1998. After the gruelling game, which we lost on penalties, friends and family then went to the team coach and waited for the players.

Outside I saw a couple of the players I knew, who hadn't played. They looked exhausted and drained. One of them said that he was gutted about the result but was glad it was all over. He just wanted to go home. He was exhausted and frustrated at being around the team and seeing no opportunity or chance to play. He looked relieved to be leaving. It is truly a gift to be a manager of a team with the ability to keep everyone motivated and believing in the chance of an opportunity. One of my lawyers once said to me:

'*When people feel there is no hope then they become dangerous.*'

People in a team/work situation will become a negative force if they believe there is no hope. Whilst being a team game, it is also about individuals and if people don't play, they're not happy. Sports like table-tennis, badminton and volleyball, involve team members sitting very close to the action. People out on the field of play can benefit from true support and that gives them an extra boost. Sports like football have team members on the bench and in the stands. The managers have to win the '*battle of the bench*' in order to create a winning team. Players on the bench have to feel that they are both playing a part in the team and have a chance of playing. What's the point of having young players and reserves if they are never going to play? The guys in the stand can create a group of negativity and try to disrupt the squad, because they feel so far away from them. Some of the most dispirited sportspeople are the ones who travel for major tournaments and then do not compete at all. If they are not managed properly, they can fall so deeply into a hole that even if they were called upon, their performance wouldn't be great. These members can surround themselves with negativity, form cliques and try to create problems for the management. I played in teams with great team spirits and teams with bad team spirits. I played in teams where sometimes I wouldn't look at the bench because I knew that some people wanted me to lose.

Outside I saw a couple of the players I knew, who hadn't played. They looked be higher than his/her teammate on the national and international rankings.

I can honestly say that wanting a teammate to lose a match was endemic in some teams I was part of. We won European and World Cup silvers and could have won a lot more. The best team spirit I can remember, in twelve years of being part of the national team, was in Kenya in 1993 at the Commonwealth Games with Michael O'Driscoll, Chris Oldfield, Nicola Deaton, Sally Marling and my good friend Nick Mason. We supported each other, screamed from the side-lines when our teammates were playing and enjoyed spending time together when we weren't competing. I have fond memories of that trip and often think about it. At different times, I look back and think: '*Why was the team spirit so good?*' It's quite simple; the characters in the team were the right blend and we all liked and had genuine respect for each other. I believe that you don't necessarily need to like someone but you have to respect them, otherwise you can't be a legitimate comrade or colleague – whereas the people on that trip were good people with no competitive insecurities. What strikes me is that, regardless of what personalities are in a team, leaders can insist on certain standards that selfish and self-centred people have to abide by. Individuals who are totally selfish, but who can have a positive sporting impact on the team have to be carefully managed and guided. They believe that when the team does well, it is because of them, and when it fails, it's because of others. That's how they think and you cannot fundamentally change them, so it's best to get the performances out of them. In the world of a team leader they must be respected and the opportunities for all must be fair. This sounds obvious, but if competition is not fair it sets the wrong standards and again takes the edge off the team. Alex Ferguson always made a point of speaking to all his squad members. He also explained to players why they were not playing in a particular match.

Outside I saw a couple of the players I knew, who hadn't played. They looked win for the team. That ethic comes from the top; if the players don't respect the leader or they feel that the situation is not fair, then it creates a negative atmosphere, and in turn, less chance of winning. We all remember when Ferguson said he sold Andrew Cole because, '*he wouldn't make a good sub.*' That was an interesting statement, because Ferguson had always had squad members and players who knew they would be subs but were happy to be part of a winning squad. Andrew Cole was always one of the first names on the Man' United team sheet, but when things changed Ferguson knew that Cole would be unhappy and that might be a problem. Sjolkshar, on the other hand was Ferguson's super-sub, who never complained, and was happy to be part of the squad. Managers sometimes make the mistake of having favourites who other team members are unhappy about; this obviously causes problems and sometimes makes members focus on other things rather than their craft. Politics, is often a word used in sport when it comes to selection. Sports people have to know that they will be judged solely for their talent, work ethic and professionalism. If that is not the case, then some individuals may take their eyes off the ball and try to play a political game or they may not push themselves 100% to achieve a place in the team. In a perfect world where the leaders set the right standards and competition is fierce, the group will achieve optimum results and team spirit. Team Spirit is also something that is often spoken about. Lots of people don't understand why certain teams under-perform and have seemingly bad team spirits. Leaders have to create a team of people who complement each other and have a bond that is unbreakable as a team. Sports people are generally selfish, but it is up to their leaders to instil a strong team ethic. The great Arsenal team of the late nineties and early noughties - Pires, Henry, Bergkamp etc, had a team ethic not seen before in football. Pires would dribble around four players, be one-on-one with the goalkeeper and then pass it to Henry for a tap in and Bergkamp would set up goal after goal.

The team genuinely played for each other. Footballers often say: '*The most important thing is that the team won.*' But how many would let someone else get the glory? How many would be in a position to score but pass the ball to a teammate to tap in? That team respected each other and the boss. They believed in the team ethic and put it into practice. A scenario which many people will find hard to believe is that a manager or coach of a team, who holds a position of absolute strength, can sometimes not be massively bothered if their team performs because they want the owners out, or they want new players or they want to show that the team just isn't good enough. Writing this section was particularly difficult, because it's hard to accept that your own team members would not want you to win. But whilst football and some other sports are awash with money, and sometimes, fragmented team spirits, soldiers stand tall in terms of their values. You see, people in our military are not paid fortunes but they fight for each other, stand up for one another, and fight as a team and often put their body on the line for their comrades. The team spirit of a soldier is unquestionable. This is because they truly believe in the cause – fighting for their country. They stand proud and respect all their colleagues, because they know what's on the line. Sporting teams that have a fraction of the fighting team spirit that our military people have, will achieve great things. The one thing a football fan hates is to see, is a player not fighting for the cause and quite rightly so. A prerequisite of a footballer, or any sportsperson is to leave everything out on the field or arena. There should be no excuse for not giving 100 % and fighting for their team. Imagine if our military decided that they weren't going to bother fighting for the cause or they were going to stop putting in as much effort – we'd all be in trouble.

Secret Lives

More people than you think have secret lives; sometimes to the detriment of themselves. Leading a life that friends and family don't know about or doing something in secret that has a detrimental effect is a huge burden to carry. Absolutely everybody has secrets about themselves that they do not divulge either wholly or in part. The question to ask is: '*Am I going to regret the part of my life where I am non-productive and incapable of constructing a future?*' Having a secret like depression for instance makes someone incapable of constructing a future. Depression is something that can take a long time to actually show itself fully to a person and no one can be at fault for not identifying the symptoms early enough. But when those involved became aware of this increasingly diagnosed illness, it is imperative to seek help. If someone is fortunate enough to have a person in their world who identifies the problem, then help can be sought a lot quicker. Secret depression can leave friends, family and colleagues bewildered: '*Why are they never happy no matter what they get?*' Or '*Why do they disappear for days?*' Some find the workplace or sports arena a place of relief; an environment where they can forget about how they actually feel. Others put on a front and find it energy consuming. Some people have the ability to shut down their feelings and what is really going on with them. This is of course dangerous, because it is suppressing emotions that could one day explode. Having said that, there is a school of thought that some people become successful because of something that hurt them in the past, which ignites a determination and focus to succeed. Many successful people were bullied as kids and never spoke about it until they had achieved a level of triumph that was a victory over the people who hurt them. Michael Phelps is the most decorated Olympian of all time, winning twenty-two medals in swimming, eighteen of those medals were gold; an all-time record.

As a kid he had big ears and a lisp and bullies made his life absolute hell. Phelps used the hurt as an inspiration and now has opened up about those days and even goes back to where he grew up and sees the same bullies. They obviously want to be his friend now; that's how ironic life can be. It is important for the likes of Phelps to be a voice for all those who were bullied, lost their confidence and were unable to fulfil their potential. People not being able to express themselves in their personal lives can be an unbearable burden. It is unimaginable what it must be like to hide who you truly are. Not being able to express your true self can be a catalyst to thrive in self-expression in the sports arena. Not being able to live your life how you want can be like being in a cage. Acceptance is a major issue; those who have secret lives are desperate scared of becoming alienated from friends, family and/or the public. But what is worse, living a lie or seeing who your true friends are when you reveal who you really are? Everybody deserves to live their life in a way they want, as long as nobody gets hurt. We are in the twenty-first century and some people in the public eye do not feel comfortable to come out as being gay for instance. In football it still seems to be a taboo. Football is the new '*rock and roll*'. Footballers are the superstars in entertainment, so suffice to say, if anyone comes out, then it will help all of those in the closet so to speak. Anyone, who is brave enough to make such a statement, should be supported by the public, friends and family. Sections of the general public might think that because someone is rich and famous, they don't have problems and shouldn't receive empathy. But nothing is worse than not being able to be who you are and live in a way you want to; it's called freedom. Gareth Thomas, one of the most capped Welsh rugby union players of all time, revealed he was gay in 2009. His decision to go public made him, not only the first openly gay professional rugby player (who was still playing the game at the time), but also one of few professional sportsmen to admit to being homosexual. The fact that so few sportsmen have come out since then shows what a difficult decision Thomas faced.

As a kid he had big ears and a lisp and bullies made his life absolute hell. Phelps because they had become his family and the closest people to him. But, like all people living a lie, it can become overwhelming. Thomas was gripped by fear and anxiety and he admitted to not being able to sleep. He had two choices; carry on the lie and be miserable or find the strength to come out, tell the truth and free himself from the shackles. Breaking point came after one particular match in which Thomas felt he hadn't been able to give his all on the pitch. He started crying and couldn't stop. His coach asked him what was wrong and Thomas seized the opportunity to tell the truth. Instead of his big fear of everybody turning their backs on him, he felt overwhelming protection from everyone. What his coach said to him after the moment of truth changed his life, he said: '*You can't go through it alone, and these people love you.*' That kind of support should encourage anyone leading a secret life to have faith in the fact that there are people, in your life, who will surprise you with their love and support. Thomas reached out to his team and they gave him complete support. He now feels strong and lives with the knowledge that there's nothing that will ever defeat him and in times of difficulty he can always turn to his team for help and assistance. A substantial percentage of the public will be leading a secret life or have a vice that no one close to them knows about. The only people in the loop will be other participants, who also don't want anyone to know. Everybody knows that having a vice in moderation is not going to hurt anybody, but doing it in excess will. People fall into an excessive participation in vices for different reasons and depression is a common reason. The key to not letting it ruin your life and the lives of others is to tell someone who cares and will not be a soft touch. Confiding in people who don't really care will not change anything. They will say stuff like '*sort your life out*' then go and make a cup of tea. Gambling is one of the scariest vices, because you can literally lose everything. It is also a vice that is very difficult to reverse in the latter stages of the downhill slide.

Gambling is obviously popular with some footballers; this is down to boredom and/or seeking a '*buzz*'. Former West Ham United footballer George Parris, has given me permission to tell his story in a bid to help those with a secret gambling addiction. He started playing cards with friends at sleepovers when he was just eleven years old. Then he got involved in '*card schools*' as a youth and reserve team player. In the early 1980s (in his late teens), he started going into betting shops and gambling on horses and dogs. Into his 20s, things escalated and he was going into betting shops most afternoons and running up debts on credit cards. Parris was now playing for West Ham United with a secret gambling addiction. Only the betting shops knew the amounts he was losing and he admits to being deluded, himself, when it came to how much this was; in fact he would kid himself into thinking he was winning. In his late 20s he got married and moved to the midlands to play for Birmingham City FC. During that period his secret gambling got completely out of hand and they had to sell the house due to debts and moved to Brighton FC. They rented a flat there. Parris took his gambling to new heights and after walking out of a bookies, having lost everything including all his family's money, he contemplated taking his own life: '*I drove up to Newhaven and remember looking out over the bridge there and thinking, what do I do?*' It was at this point, when he had lost everything, that he realised the gravity of the situation. Thankfully he went home and told his wife that all their savings were gone because of gambling. People with secret addictions believe that it has nothing to do with anyone else and fail to address the fact that eventually there will be repercussions on loved ones. Ironically, Parris says that he doesn't know whether gambling affected his performances on the pitch. He was in complete denial and his life became one big lie. He lost count of how many times he said to his wife: '*Just popping out to get a bottle of milk,*' and then not returning for hours. He would make up a story that usually had something to do with getting stopped by the police.

To be fair to George, he tried to confront the issue over several years, but five years later he relapsed and started gambling secretly again. The lowest point of his addiction came when he withdrew all the money from his young son's building society account for '*one last bet*', which subsequently lost. He then started attending the *Sporting Chance Clinic* for regular counselling sessions and still has a relationship with them now. Gambling can have no physical symptoms unlike taking drugs or being an alcoholic. Some sportspeople say that the pressure of their profession drives them to drink, take drugs or gamble. A study in 2014 claimed that one in four footballers suffer from depression or anxiety problems; mostly do so in secret. International players' union FIFPro carried out the research that showed 26% of players reported they had mental health problems with that figure rising to 39% among retired players. FIFPro's chief medical officer Dr Vincent Gouttebarge said: '*Contrary to popular belief, the life of a professional footballer has some dark sides.*' The public read about the millions footballers earn and the '*fantastic*' lifestyles they lead, so few have sympathy or empathy for young men that seem to have everything. But whilst money gives you the opportunity to buy material things, fame can put you in a cage. By this I mean not being able to go out for a walk in the park and enjoy the anonymity that most people take for granted. The common belief is that money buys you happiness and people cannot be depressed when they have money. The study by FIFPro, found that along with mental illness being more prevalent in football than in other populations, it also happened more to those upon retirement. Speak to any footballer and they will tell you there's nothing quite like preparing for a match then running out onto the pitch on a Saturday afternoon. Being a professional footballer gives focus, purpose and that amazing feeling of being part of a team. This is another reason why footballers need to think long term when constructing a team to look after them during and after their careers.

There should be some kind of development in business, community, media or philanthropy running alongside their careers so they don't feel like they fall off a cliff when their careers are over. Footballers can concentrate on their '*on-pitch*' careers whilst professionals take care of the '*off-pitch*' interests. As they get older they can take more interest in what they will do after football.

There is also a school of thought, that people with money and fame are ungrateful, which is quite simply wrong. There is nothing worse than acting like you are happy when deep down you are hurting. So it's understandable why many keep their depression a secret, but the hope is that they have enough trust in someone around them to admit that something isn't right. It can be really confusing to seemingly have everything you've ever wanted but to still have a deep feeling of unhappiness. Depression can often be after losing something or somebody meaningful. One of the world's most famous and successful talk-show hosts – Ellen DeGeneres admitted that losing everything sent her into depression. Her sitcom on ABC was cancelled in 1998 and she was no longer making money. She also felt treated disrespectfully, for no other reason than being gay and after working on the show for five years, DeGeneres admitted going into: '*A deep, deep depression.*' Constant disappointment and not seeing a light at the end of the tunnel can also cause a dark cloud to hover over people. Singing superstar – Nicki Minaj, kept getting '*doors slammed in her face*' when trying to make it as a performer, she said: '*It was just one dead end after another.*' She got so depressed that she contemplated a very dark thought: '*What would happen if I didn't wake up?*' Superstars like Brad Pitt, Angelina Jolie, Halle Berry and Gwyneth Paltrow have all admitted suffering real low points in their lives. They all suffered in secret then came out and told the world after beating the dark demons. They are great examples of people who fought back and went on to achieve so much.

Success

What is success? How do we judge success and who is best placed to do so? Successful people have and develop a certain mind-set and whatever they do they achieve levels of success. Those who do not naturally have or develop the right mind-set, rely on others to help and nurture them in the right direction. A positive mind-set can be like trying to speak a very complicated language to some and like eating and drinking to others. It's an intriguing mystery trying to understand why some people always see the glass half-full and others half-empty. It isn't necessarily to do with whether you come from a poor or rich background or an educated or uneducated one. The likes of Richard Branson, Alan Sugar and others started from humble beginnings. People talk about luck, but luck comes to those who try and conduct themselves in a certain way. Because we all want recognition, we often let others judge whether success has been achieved. I competed in table-tennis, at the highest level for over a decade, and enjoyed some fantastic times both individually and with my team. But no matter how well my team or I did in various competitions, we would receive scraps in terms of press exposure. So, it was difficult to feel that we were achieving great things when there was very little recognition from the press and public. What I have realised over the years is that success has to be judged by oneself. You have to be the one that judges what you want to achieve and whether you are successful. Earlier I spoke about Steven Gerrard and Alan Shearer, who might not have won as many trophies as their peers but are considered successful and will have legend status for generations. Others may have won more trophies and medals but might not necessarily receive recognition from the press or public. Basically, the press and public will give recognition to people if they, in turn, give something to the public. That '*something*' is communicating with the public via the media.

By doing that, the public '*buy*' into an individual and show that by supporting things the individual does, like merchandise and attending events where they are performing. If a singer can't sing but the public buys their music, then they are successful. A sportsperson, who is a great brand and has the public's support, is deemed, by the public, more of a success than the person who has the medals and titles but doesn't communicate. This is because large sections of the public take no notice of sport and they will only know a few individuals who they deem to be successful. Even in a sport like football, millions of women have no interest and only know a few players. But women are the powerbrokers and anyone who thinks otherwise is misguided. Let's take football for instance, success '*off the pitch*' depends on the brand: a footballer's followers and successful endorsements. At boardroom level, companies' decisions are taken on the character and brand of individuals. Women have the influence on who is deemed a good brand, whether they are physically in the boardroom or speaking to their partners or family members in private environments. A mother would not let their sons wear products endorsed by someone who is a bad role model, whereas a father may look at it and say: '*He's a bad boy but a great footballer.*' A footballer, who is publicly a good husband and father, will get the female vote and that translates itself into support on all fronts. So, it's fair to say that everyone wants to achieve some form of success whether at work, at home or in general wellbeing. I believe that the single most important thing in the search for success, is how we distribute our passion and energy. We all have a certain amount of energy but do not always distribute it wisely. The positive energy we bring and leave in any situation will eventually have an impact on our future. If you walk into any room and bring a positive energy, then people will feel good, and when you leave the room you will leave an energy, and that will make people remember you. Job interviews and casting couches are obviously places where people expect a performance and positive energy. But if you bring that to a social gathering or informal surroundings, it tends to have a stronger effect on people.

Comedians often distribute their energy by saving it all for the performance and hardly any for their private lives. How often have you heard someone say that they met a comedian in person and they were not that funny? There is always a payback for using up your energy in one particular way and for those who pursue success in their profession – the payback is in their personal lives. Football managers have no choice but to use a lot of energy in their career because the profession is all-consuming. It's often draining and can leave little time to get involved in family and personal issues. It's fair to say that most successful people distribute their energy in a way that is conducive to success in their careers. When you see a sportsperson being interviewed, they will often not give a lot of energy to the situation because it is believed that media stuff doesn't help them perform and is just something that comes with the territory. All of their energy is saved for training and performing; then the rest periods are as important as the above, so during periods of rest an athlete doesn't want to exert energy on media stuff. There are of course the exceptions like David Beckham, Usain Bolt and Victoria Azarenka. Bolt is unbelievable; he obviously exerts amounts of energy training and performing, but finds even more for the public with all the media stuff he does and the commercial ventures he is involved with. His personality is all about energy. He gives so much on and off the track and that is why he's one of the most marketable talents the world has ever seen. On the other hand we have seen truly great athletes who did or do not believe in giving energy outside of training and performance. The big irony here is, that no matter what you achieve as a sportsperson, the media will not give suitable recognition or plaudits to anyone who doesn't play the '*media-game*' or those who don't communicate to the public via the media. Some examples that spring to mind are: Lennox Lewis, Paula Radcliffe and my good friend Linford Christie. Linford never bought into the whole media thing and so didn't have that communication with the public. He was someone who dragged himself up from the streets of South London, trained like an animal and won Olympic gold in arguably the hardest discipline in sport – the 100 metres.

Comedians often distribute their energy by saving it all for the performance and last decade? He should be awarded a knighthood. There should be a statue of him beside a running track. But no, he has not received the respect due to him, because of his lack of relationship with the media. To a certain extent, he was and still is a fairly shy person; he disliked and felt uncomfortable doing interviews. Lennox Lewis was another intrinsically shy person, who went on to become one of our most successful heavyweight boxers of all time. A guy who was born in Forest Gate, London, moved to Canada at the age of seven then won Olympic gold in Seoul 1988 and moved back to England to pursue his dream of becoming World Champion. Again, where is the recognition for this guy? Where is his knighthood?

There is nothing scarier than setting the bar low and not reaching it.

Inner Mind of an Athlete

Top performers in elite sport share common traits: a determined and often unparalleled focus, positive people around them and a winning mind-set. Becoming the best at what you do involves hours of tedious repetition and perfecting skills that can be viewed from the outside as talent. As the world's best sports people get to the very top of their game, it is tiny changes that can be made. For instance, looking to attain marginal gains in sport psychology could mean the difference between success and failure. Dr Steve Peters is an English psychiatrist who works in elite sport. He has helped Chris Hoy, Ronnie O'Sullivan and sprint champion Adam Gemili, as well as working closely with Liverpool FC. Peters uses special coping strategies, designed to handle both success and failure, as athletes look to the huge pressures of World Cups and Olympic Games. In track and field in particular, athletes deal with such fine margins that stress and anxiety can be inevitable. Peters' focus is on forgetting the past and doing one's best and delivering what one can on a given day. As young British Sprinter, Adam Gemili sat in the blocks in the European final in Zurich in 2014, he faced three other men who had run nineteen seconds over the distance (all with faster personal bests). However, Peters emphasises that all Gemili can do is execute his race plan; moving through each stage of the race and ignoring the other lanes, mind games and possible false starts. Peters helped Gemili (and many others) discover the machine in his head, and apply a system to help deal with the pressures of competition day. Peters focuses on using the 15% that makes the difference between a good athlete and the greatest. This final 15% can be nutrition, biomechanical changes and most relevant here, psychology. Chris Hoy accepted that there were mental areas he could improve; showing a common attribute in champions – a need, a burning desire to be at 100% all of the time. Hoy wanted to get a bit more out of his training and Peters helped him learn mental skills that would enable Hoy to be at 100% when training and competing.

Once you get to the very top, tiny improvements make all the difference and it is those who are able to push for more and find the final percentage who win, keeping winning and consequently become the greatest. Peters uses the metaphor of the Chimp (the limbic part of the brain) as something we need to manage. Using the parietal part of our brain, we can control animal instincts and desires (fear, aggression, nervousness and other emotions). An athlete can then use this on competition day, when it is vital for them to be at their very finest. It is the winners, the champions and the record-breakers of the world, who are able to control the limbic part of the brain; becoming both physically and mentally 100% and able to perform to the very best of their ability on a consistent basis. We can look elsewhere in psychology to Carol Dweck, who proposes the idea that we can grow our brain's capacity to learn and solve problems. Dweck describes two ways to think about a problem that is slightly too hard for us to solve. The first is that you are not smart enough to solve it, and the second is that you just have not solved it yet. Dweck refers to a school in Chicago, where students had to pass a certain number of courses to graduate; however, if they did not pass a course, they were not labelled a failure but instead were given the grade '*not yet*'. Failing gives us a sense of worthlessness and disappointment, but attaining the grade '*not yet*' puts us on a learning curve – a path to future success. Dweck conducted research by giving ten year-olds problems which were slightly too difficult. Some of the students responded positively, embracing the challenge and showing an understanding that their abilities can be developed; these had what Dweck refers to as the 'growth mind-set'. Others responded rather negatively; fearing failure and feeling their intelligence had been up for judgment. Dweck considered these students to have a 'fixed mind-set'. Those with a fixed mind-set run from difficulty and when neurologists studied these students' brains, they showed little electrical activity when confronted with an error.

Once you get to the very top, tiny improvements make all the difference and it is those who are able to push for more and find the final percentage who win, The greatest sportsmen and women share another common trait – the growth mind-set. Those with this mind-set, dream big dreams. This mind-set is common among both entrepreneurs and Olympic Champions, who do not fear failure but battle problems with resilience and understand greatness as progressive. In people with this mind-set we see more effort, better strategy and greater perseverance. They push out of their comfort zone to face a new challenge and the neurons in their brain form new, stronger connections. Thus, over time, they will become better and more successful. It is these people who achieve great things in sport. Of course it is possible to teach the growth mind-set, but it is important to note it as a common denominator among the sporting elite. The growth mind-set helps an athlete pick themselves up after their worst defeats and succeed in a comeback to their greatest achievements. It helps an athlete believe they can beat the competition; pushing landmark barriers of what was previously thought impossible. It was Mike Powell knocking on the door of the nine-metre mark in the long jump, or Usain Bolt aiming to go underneath nineteen seconds for the 200 metres. The growth mind-set can be a result of nature, or it can be nurtured, but it is key to sporting success and one of few things both Tyson Fury and Jessica Ennis share. By looking at what some of the best Psychologists have to say on what attributes contribute to sporting success, we can see how the mind is central to achieving greatness. But an important question is whether anyone can achieve greatness or whether we need some sort of genetic head start? In David Epstein's *The Sports Gene,* Epstein recalls the story of Laszlo Polgar, who seemed to prove that being successful, talented and skilful at something is a process of nurture. He raised his three daughters to be chess prodigies; two of them became the best and second best women chess players in the world; a true pioneer in the thinking that talent is made, not born.

Once you get to the very top, tiny improvements make all the difference and it is those who are able to push for more and find the final percentage who win, given field, so long as practice began before they were three and practice became specialised by the age of six. Whilst his first two daughters are exceptional chess players (first-born Susan became Olympic and World Champion), Laszlo's third daughter Judit is considered the greatest female chess player of all time. A Grandmaster at the age of fifteen, Judit broke legendary Bobby Fischer's world record to become the youngest ever to achieve grandmaster-status, and proved with her estimated fifteen-thousand practice hours of inexorable repetition what it really takes to achieve excellence. It is clear that hard work pays off and that endless dedication and perseverance can separate the good from the best in elite sport. But a huge question, which is sometimes raised, is why there are often inexplicable amounts of successful people from one place, all taking part in the same sport? Why are East Africans so good at distance running? And why does Jamaica seem to win so many sprint medals at the Olympics? Genetics is the first answer we hear. East Africa's ancestry in cattle-herding, suggests those who were good at running long distances with cattle attracted women, thus reproducing and passing down the distance-runner gene. Ben Johnson and Usain Bolt similarly share ancestry in the Maroons – West-African descendent warrior-slaves, who over-threw the British Army in North-Western Jamaica during the eighteenth century. David Epstein regards the Maroons as genetically suited to an explosive, anaerobic event such as sprinting. Whilst genetics plays its part in explaining why small places produce large amounts of talent, New York Times best-selling author Daniel Coyle goes a step further in unveiling what is really going on. Coyle studies '*talent hotbeds*'; little places that produce a statistically incredible number of what we call talented performers.

These are places where talent seems to bloom and Coyle analyses these so-called '*hotbeds*' to answer the question of how someone becomes excellent at something. Coyle tried the skill of keepie-uppies with a golf club and a golf ball; he attempted to bounce the tiny ball off of the head of the club as many times as possible, in as many entertaining ways. He found that, with no golfing background, he failed miserably at the start, but gradually got better. After enough practice hours, Coyle became efficient at the task in hand and impressively bounced the ball in a variety of confident and creative ways for long periods. To someone unaware of the hours of practice Coyle had accumulated, it would seem that Coyle had a niche talent. This was obviously not the case. As we grow up we are told a beautiful story of babies born with mystic gifts. Innate and supremely special, these gifts, along with hard work and practice, make the greatest sporting celebrities of our era – Tiger Woods, Serena Williams, Mike Tyson and many others. The story goes that they were all magic babies who grew up destined to become stars. This story is entertaining, however, it is also fictional. Coyle describes talent as a person doing exactly the right thing at exactly the right time; this could be a sprinter running the 100m in under ten seconds, or a brain surgeon performing an intricate procedure.

'Going through life thinking you can create great performance by natural gifts, hard work and talent is exactly like going through life thinking you can create a Ferrari by combining steel, red paint and Italians' – Coyle.

When we see a hurdler's hamstring glide over the barrier and then contract a moment before impact we use language like '*muscle memory*'. Muscles, unfortunately, do not have memory; our skills exist in the human brain. Talent is not a mystic birth-right, but instead something constructed in our brain by intense practice. It is operating on the very edge of one's ability that increases learning velocity tenfold.

Struggling, failing and trying again is how one gets better at something, and eventually perfects a skill that masquerades as a magical talent. Leeds-based football coach, Simon Clifford studied what it was exactly that made Brazilian footballers so good. There seemed to be something more than merely winning five world cups – young Brazilian children appeared to be incredibly skilful; their touch so impressive. Clifford went to Brazil and found children playing in cramped indoor spaces, competing in a version of our game called Futebol de Salao. They played in a small area with a small ball. As passing is tighter and defensive pressure is greater, one has to be more precise. There is no room to play the beloved long ball. As a result of the game's close, pressurised nature, one is constantly making mistakes, thus struggling, and acquiring greater skill. Clifford brought Futebol de Salao back to Yorkshire and made his U14 team play it ceaselessly, until they became so good they beat both the Scottish and English U14 national sides. It is clear by Clifford's research, that it is not the genes of the Brazilian children that made them naturally skilful, but the fast-paced, closely-played way they practiced the game; allowing them to continue *'reaching and repeating'*, *'failing and getting better'* and subsequently building faster, more fluent brains able to play more intricate passes at speed. Neurobiologist Dr Douglas Fields explains what is happening when an individual gets better at a skill. He refers to myelin, the protein-sheath around nerve fibres, and suggests that it responds to practice. As an individual practices a movement, electricity is being sent through it, and the myelin responds by adding another layer. Every time the young Brazilian footballers would attempt to control the ball in a tight space, they would fail and then repeat the action; layers were being built, providing more insulation and ensuring the electrical signal speed increased massively. At this neurological level, one can see how practising meaningfully creates and masters talent. Those who are like a Ronaldo or a Messi of the world, eliminate passive learning, embrace struggle and failure and keep trying to perfect a skill.

Struggling, failing and trying again is how one gets better at something, and idea that practising the skill is drudgework and so continue with the monotonous repetition until they go from good, to brilliant and then to the best in the world. It is their choice to remain relentless in their quest to be the best and continue to train, however repetitive the task may seem. The best football coaches understand the importance of this and celebrate the heroism of repetition. No footballer or team is doing magical training and nobody is benefiting from doing something another person cannot do. Successful coaches see an idea, practice or skill and copy or imitate it; there is greatness in the mundane, and repetition and imitation are highly regarded in elite sport. Imitation can be as important as innovation, both at grass roots and at the top level. Coaching plays an integral role in making a sporting champion. In track and field, we see the presence of a successful, or somewhat legendary coach, lift an athlete in the warm-up area and make the difference between winning and losing. A great coach can have a positive impact on an athlete without even saying anything, and their presence alone can be the pickup needed after a poor first round attempt at a championship. A coach, who was able to do this for a close friend of mine and a list of many others, was British sprint coach Lloyd Cowan MBE. Coach to a great number of national sprint champions, as well as Commonwealth hurdles champion, Andy Turner and World and Olympic Champion Christine Ohuruogu, Cowan stands at well over six foot tall and carries a buoyant positivity; yet carries it in almost a nonchalant way. A giant of a figure in the warm-up arena, Lloyd's presence during block starts at the National Campionships, or a small pep talk whilst walking towards the call up area before a final, can make a marginal difference in mental preparation for a race. Merely having a coaching figure watching over your mundane drills, mixing a supplement or accelerating out in a warm-up, projects comfort – an air of calm that is needed in such a pressure situation.

Struggling, failing and trying again is how one gets better at something, and especially whilst she was, controversially, excluded from competing for a year after three missed drug tests (bans and injuries can be the loneliest times for any athlete). And after winning back-to-back World and Olympic titles in 2007 and 2008, he played a key role in getting Christine back into the mind frame that winning the World Title again in 2013 was a possibility; following years of injured and off-form seasons. In the 2013 World 400m final, reigning champion Amantle Montsho, later banned for stimulant methylhexaneamine, lead to the home straight with Ohuruogu, a few metres down. She said:

'I just remember thinking 'Lloyd is going to kill me.' He gave me specific instructions, and as usual, I didn't listen. But as Lloyd would do, I stayed calm. I knew in the last 50m that the others would start dying. In the last 50m I would die less than they do.'

This idea that Christine had – that the others would decelerate at a greater rate than she would – was something that Lloyd would make his athletes believe in training and was perhaps the reason she was able to win the 2013 world title. Cowan's entire training philosophy, although somewhat unorthodox, focused more on speed-endurance and decelerating slower than one's opponent as opposed to acceleration, which is the key to speed and sprinting itself. Moreover, the moment of inception was months, even years, before that world final. Somewhere buried in the thousands of hours of practice Cowan and Ohuruogu put together, was a point where Christine believed that she would out-sprint her opponents in the final segment of the race. Great coaches are fantastic at making an athlete believe in something, and believing in Lloyd's modus operandi – decelerating more efficiently than one's opponents – seemed to have won Ohuruogu another world title. Great coaches stick with their athletes through the many lows that spectators fail to see at an Olympic Games or World Championships and great athletes stick with their coaches long after their great successes.

When Great Britain won the bid for the London Olympics we wanted the best coaches possible, to ensure our athletes had the greatest chance for gold. UK Athletics brought in coaching Guru, Dan Pfaff, tutor to forty-nine Olympians and five world-record holders. The result? One of our greatest moments from the Games; the surprise gold medal in the long jump on Super Saturday. It came in the form, of then-Pfaff-coached, Greg Rutherford. When considering what it takes to achieve greatness at championship level, Pfaff considers a number of important observations over his forty years of coaching. Pfaff notes that an athlete must be comfortable with taking calculated risks; a common trait among the sporting elite because top performers realise that risk drives positive change. This could involve strategy, mechanics or training methods, but risk avoidance and the familiarity of comfort zones can stop one's progress – it is essential to get used to being uncomfortable. Pfaff also observed that top performers detached themselves from perfectionism; believing in a perfect performance could slowly become negative and disturb both competition and practice. Analysing world record efforts can often show a number of flaws, and there may not ever be the perfect jump, run or throw. Other important traits, common among the athletes Pfaff coached, were communication and enjoyment. An important thing to remember is that communication is essential to building relationships; the ability to express a thought, mood and desire can ignite the relationship between coach and athlete and build important, reciprocal relationships with those closest. Similarly, enjoyment is fundamental in all endeavours. Enjoying the activity is what keeps top athletes going after the financial rewards make less difference, and once they have already made it to the very top. Finally, Pfaff noted that champions embrace failure, stay resilient through adversity and accept criticism better than those who do not quite make it to the top. Top performers never tire of their mundane tasks and strive for excellence in other areas of their life, off the track or pitch.

Interestingly, this concurs with many sports writers, Coyle and Epstein especially; that the world's sporting elite embrace the monotonous repetition of practice and do not fear failure. These are integral traits that athletes need to acquire through choice, and when examining top performers from different sports it is these same traits that continue to appear. Ex-British table-tennis player, and my teammate of many years - Matthew Syed, suggests that believing some of us are meant to be great and others are mediocre is damaging to both us, and society. Getting great at something depends on the quantity and quality of our practices and experience. Syed considers his success circumstantial and not a God-given talent. Specifically that he had the good fortune of a table-tennis table at home; a skilled older brother; a fantastic local coach and a top-notch local club. It was these set of circumstances that made him successful and not a magical birth-given gift. Syed talks about his experience in table tennis, where the acoustics are incredibly fast. When we see top table tennis players in action, we are impressed at the super-quick speeds at which they are able to return the ball to their opponent. In Syed's insightful book *Bounce*, he talks of the difference between his ability to return anyone's table-tennis serve at great speed, and being hopeless at returning an elite tennis player's serve. He was excellent at the former, yet miserable at the other. This raises the question of what it is about Serena Williams or Andy Murray that makes them able to return a serve at great speed. Purely anecdotal, but a worthy story to answer this question. When close friend and upcoming sprinter, Antonio Infantino, won the British Indoor 200m title in 2015, his reaction time was 0.12 seconds. In just over a tenth of a second, his brain had registered the gun firing, and his feet had pushed off of the starting blocks; propelling his body forwards at a forty-five-degree angle towards victory. To those watching in the stands, it seemed a lightning-quick response. But to him it was almost subconscious, a set of movements practised so many times over the past twelve years that it was second-nature.

Yet, a week later, back in the office, Antonio and a few colleagues tested their reaction times, by trying to clock a stopwatch at precisely 9.58 seconds (Bolt's 100m world record). He managed 9.60 after three attempts, yet one of his colleagues quite easily stopped it at 9.58 on his second go. It seemed it wasn't that he had particularly good reaction times, it was just many years of high quality, self-motivated practice that allowed him to explode out of the blocks so quickly. And so it is not that Serena Williams or Andy Murray have super-human vision or reactions, but it is their training that enables them to return a serve. Specifically, it is hours of practice that gives them access to a pattern-recognition, as their opponent moves their body before they have served the ball. Again, here what is key is the accumulative hours of meaningful practice at a given task or skill. It is those who are most determined and find enjoyment in such monotony that get to the top in sport. And those who try to take shortcuts or give up, who often fall by the wayside. The role of confidence in sport performance is essential to success. High confidence in Track and Field can make the difference between winning and losing in a major final. Athletics is a sport that deals with exceptionally fine margins. To take the 2015 World 100m final as an example; most sports fans can name the always buoyant, self-assured winner Usain Bolt, who beat a '*choking*' Justin Gatlin to victory by just one hundredth of a second in 9.79s. Less people however, are aware of (joint-bronze medallist) Andre De Grasse, the Canadian twenty-year old, who was third in 9.92s, a mere 0.13 of a second behind the international super star that is Usain Bolt. Just over a tenth of a second was the difference between legend and almost complete anonymity. (De Grasse, at the time, was an unsponsored amateur attending university). With such fine margins and an intense, competitive environment, the world's top athletes need an unparalleled focus on themselves as well as the task in hand. This can often mean a relative neglect of the people close to them on competition day.

Competing can often be a series of automatic, outcome-focused responses, sticking to a plan and with a sole emphasis on victory. It is those who can keep positive. Enjoyment, happiness, relaxation and excitement combined with confident body language and committed, maximum effort can make up the few hundredths of a second between winning and losing. And it is the world's best who get it right, time after time. There is however, something more than positive psychology and skill acquisition through repetition that makes champions. It's a common trait shared by many elite athletes and concerns; a somewhat delusional and egotistic nature to the athlete's personality. Firstly, what people see on the television or in an athletic stadium is merely the tip of the iceberg for athletes. Thousands of hours of hard training have gone in to what supporters and fans are watching. Moreover, hundreds of fails, countless lows and a great number of injuries have thwarted any athlete in a given event. And after so many continual failures at something, a person begins to construct a slightly deluded view of themselves and their situation. This is the reason we have athletes who try and try, but never make it out of domestic level on to the international scene. It is also the reason that athletes stick at it, and finally break through. Secondly, athletes need to be somewhat selfish and narcissistic in order to succeed. They have to make choices based purely on their own needs and not let the disappointment of agents and coaches influence their career decisions. Being out on a track in front of thousands of people can be the loneliest place in the world; isolated in a pressure-cooker environment where only the individual themselves can succeed or fail. The combination of delusion and egotism contributes to the making of a champion. The athlete can be deluded in the sense that after each fail, they still believe they are going to become the best at what they do, and egotistical in a belief they are the best, and only a relentless focus on themselves can get them to where they want to be. It's the choices of an athlete who makes them the greatest at what they do.

This can mean having the right people around them, making changes in sport-psychology or choosing to accept monotony and repeating movements that neurologically acquire skills that others perceive as innate talent; these choices are not just *In Your World,* but in your mind and it's here that sporting success starts and ends.

Dream Makers and Stealers

Everybody has a big picture, a dream or an aspiration. The people *In Your World* can have a major effect on whether you achieve those dreams. You see, there are many more '*dream stealers*' than '*dream makers*' (people who will help you achieve your dreams). *Dream stealers* come in many forms and guises; it could be your boss, friend, family member or acquaintance. Sometimes *dream stealers* are those who have given up on their own dreams and want to talk you out of yours, because it would be too painful seeing a friend, colleague or family member succeed. This can also be the case for people who simply don't have dreams and can't be bothered to chase something that is a risk. The problem here is that the people saying you can't do it are normally louder than the people who talk about their dreams. An intriguing question is why are people so scared to talk about their dreams and what they want to achieve? By identifying *dream stealers* you can actually stop negativity getting into your psyche because negative messages are often disguised in what people say. When we are talking to friends, family and colleagues about aspirations, we want to believe what they say, so the stuff gets embedded in our psyche. The danger with that is our subconscious is thirty times as powerful as our conscious mind. So whilst we might not recognise what is being said, there will be an unenthusiastic tone that will leave us feeling negative. There are '*loving*' *dream Stealers* that love and want to protect you; they want you to be safe, not get hurt and have a secure job, parents spring to mind. Although my parents would have liked me to be a doctor or lawyer, they didn't stand in my way when I started playing table-tennis and when I turned professional my mum was 100% behind me. My mum loved table-tennis, because I did. She also loved it when I played football (up to the age of sixteen). She would come to my Sunday league games and try to give me food at half-time. She would come to table-tennis '*finals night*' and sit there watching and supporting me, with a bag full of food in case I was peckish in between matches.

My mum didn't understand table-tennis; all she asked me was: '*Did you have a good time? Did you win?*' She even asked me the same questions when I was at the Olympics in 1988. I obviously said: '*I had a great time but didn't win.*' I knew my mum loved me and would support whatever I did, so on I went, playing table-tennis. Although I didn't earn much money, I achieved honours and experiences that money can't buy. I am biased towards mothers because I am so close to mine and mums are simply the best in the world. My mum was a *dream maker*, by just giving me support and not trying to stop me doing what I loved. Because of my love for mums I found Davina McCall's story both harrowing and inspirational. Without my mum's love and support I wouldn't have achieved half of what I did. The word '*inspirational*', is often used, but Davina McCall is that and more. She is an extraordinary human being; I can hear you say: '*I know*'. She is one of our most loved TV stars but her story is just so inspiring. The support of a mother for a daughter is a very special relationship and can empower talented girls to achieve their dreams. Davina didn't have the support of her mother; in fact they had a strained relationship. Davina was abandoned by her mother, when she was three and raised by loving grandparents, with occasional help from her father, Andrew McCall; a graphic designer, who visited at weekends. So, Davina's environment became the love and influence from her Grandparents. The great thing about Grandparents is that they are often used to being the second tier support and when they are pushed to the front line, they can be even more understanding than their own children. During her late teens she moved to live with her father and his second wife in London. She became hooked on heroin and cocaine; an addiction she could not overcome until her mid-20s. In the past, she blamed her mother – a reformed alcoholic who claims to have stopped drinking in 1998 – for the frailties, which led to her drug habit. But whatever our parents give us, or whatever the relationship we have is, we can all still achieve our dreams.

My mum didn't understand table-tennis; all she asked me was: '*Did you have a* achieve their dreams, there are the Davina McCall stories sprinkled in the mix.

When Davina was in her mid-teens, her mother was living in Paris and when she went to see her mum, she was treated like a friend rather than a daughter. Reeking of alcohol and dressed in electric blue floor-length fake fur, she would haul Davina to decadent parties, and expect her to mingle with her bohemian friends. Reliving those days, Davina has likened them to an *Ab' Fab'* double act: She was '*Saffy*' to her mother's '*Edina*'. Yet beneath the humour, the awfulness of acting as a stooge for her drunken, flirtatious mother always comes through. So, it's fair to say that the lack of inspiration from parents can demotivate and leave you with a serious lack of ambition. But, the awful, negative experiences that Davina went through, actually made her determined to make a success of her life; and she has. Her mother did things that would normally steal the dreams of a young girl, but some of us have the strength of character to fight against negative influences. Davina is living proof that regardless of people trying to steal your dreams you can still succeed if you want it badly enough. With the help of Narcotics Anonymous and family friend Eric Clapton, who she briefly dated, she kicked her drug habit and landed a presenting slot on MTV. In the early '90s, she landed a show called *God's Gift* – a dating show. It was on every Wednesday late at night and I remember thinking: '*This girl is absolutely brilliant!*' There was no doubt in my mind that she was going to be successful and probably no doubt in her mind either. I'm so pleased to see her doing well because she was meant to be a star and although the person that should have been there for her, wasn't, she found a way to succeed. Davina experienced the lack of support that could have easily seen her use it as an excuse not to succeed or not do anything with her life, but she did the contrary and that is why our next generation of girls can look to her for inspiration. Davina's experiences no doubt made her angry, frustrated and hurt, but she used her anger in the right way.

Being hurt and angry by how someone has treated you can give you a fierce desire, which is much stronger than someone patting you on the back and saying: '*Well done.*' I have so much respect for this lady and I hope that girls and boys out there who feel the hurt and pain that Davina did, can also bounce back and do something positive with their lives. One of the great dream makers is Judy Murray, and yes, she is another mum. Part of Andy Murray's feeling of invincibility and strength comes from knowing his mum is there in the background dealing with important issues. The unwavering support, honesty and love a parent gives, cannot be compared. So when a parent can contribute to a career and become a dream maker, it just doesn't get any better than that. Dream stealers don't have a hope in Andy's world. His team are all dream makers; headed by the infallible Judy. Because of the hard work Judy Murray and the team have put into building their world. It has become a '*dream factory*' – because success is everywhere. Personal relationships flourish and everyone ups their game. Andy and Jamie Murray are riding the crest of a wave and long may it continue. The mind-set of dream makers, is that you only have one choice and that's to find a way. Dream makers will tell you that failure is just a blip and others will say it's a sign that you shouldn't even be trying. Dream makers are a wonderful group of people who will selflessly help others reach their potential because they enjoy helping others. Some people know that they may not have the desire or inclination to achieve success, but will still be positive with others. If someone says to you: '*Go chase your dreams,*' then that says a huge amount about that person. The right people will help you remove mental obstacles and help visualise the path to success. When you are thinking about what you want to achieve, the question is: '*Why not?*'

What do you have to lose? You lose more if you don't start and try.

Whilst writing this book, I caught the underground train to London from my office. I sat opposite two Asian guys.

One was older, well dressed and had an air of authority, dignity and class. Next to him was a somewhat younger man dressed casual/smart and hanging onto every word the older gentleman said. The younger man would ask a question and the older man would answer in a manner of a teacher with a pupil.

It became obvious to me that it was father and son. I started a conversation with them and remarked how good it was to see father and son having the kind of relationship I never had with my father. The son was in awe of his father and so he should be; his father is a well-respected professor and lecturer. After a short-while the son asked me what I did and I spoke a little about football and other stuff. The son got excited and started speaking about football and how he was a talented youngster playing at one of the top clubs in the midlands whilst playing for his school and Sunday league team. He explained that he really wanted to be a footballer but his father said he should study and become a doctor – and a doctor he was. He went on to say that his father was right and that football was a precarious profession and that being a doctor was the best thing he could have done. What the father then said was something that reveals everything about a '*loving dream stealer*'. He told me that when his son was playing football, he went to see all the managers of the teams and explained that although his son liked football, his studies were much more important and that football shouldn't interfere with his academic aspirations. He went into depth about how he went to each club and made sure everybody concerned knew that they shouldn't expect his son to make football his profession. Amazing, most parents would be desperate for their son to become a footballer; but this great man, who I must say was very impressive, stole his son's dream in one way but ensured he focused on a secure ambition on the other. Most importantly, the son was most grateful to his father for focusing his mind on the big academic picture.

There are good people in your life who want the best for you, but have an element of dream stealing in their thoughts and advice, because although they genuinely want the best for you, they often worry that you may be making a mistake, instead of thinking about what you may gain. Most mums and dads want the best for their kids and most importantly they want them to be safe and secure. The so-called '*Pushy Parents*' often push their kids into different avenues because they are trying to live their lives through them. Because of a change in thought processes over the generations and a lack of understanding when it comes to certain professions, parents can be negative about their kids going on an adventure or chasing a profession that is presumed insecure.

Sometimes, parents will do everything for their kids except let them be who they want to be. Parents can give us so much. They can give the right love, support and guidance. In some families, tremendous pressure is put on the kids to follow a set path, regardless where their real talent lies. There is often a lack of communication between young people and parents. The negative response from parents is often to do with a lack of understanding; if parents are sat down and the route that their child wants to go down is explained to them and they then see the passion, they might be more understanding. Those who choose to take an unconventional career path find it difficult explaining the journey they want to take because they don't fully understand it themselves. What they often have is an example of someone who has been successful and a burning desire to fulfil the ambition. The world changes through generations, but communication always remains key to the understanding of how we all want to live our lives. Battle lines don't need to be drawn up because a son or daughter wants to pursue a career or do something that is outside the box so to speak. Mums and dads feel a lot more comfortable knowing their children are in solid careers that they understand. What we must all remember, is that parents just want the best for their kids and once they completely understand a situation, they can be more supportive. Parents also like timeframes.

They want to know how long you're going to give this '*dream*' and will you get a proper job if it doesn't work? They also want to know '*Plan B*', but often people who are driven, focused and passionate about their chosen career path don't have one. Having a Plan B is deemed a sign of weakness or acceptance of possible failure. Most family members don't mean to dream steal in a bad way; if there was a '*secure dream*', they would be happy. Good parents never stop being parents; they worry most of the time and base a lot of conversation on what their kids are doing. If they don't understand what their kids are doing, then they don't feel part of the whole situation. In sport it can be an owner, agent, manager even teammate, but sometimes dream stealers are just people around you who don't want you to leave their circle, go off and travel the world, as they are too scared to lose you. A female friend of mine was going out with a guy, who she loved, but felt there was an adventure in her. She was offered a job in Canada for a year and she really wanted to go but was worried about what he boyfriend would say. He told her: '*You go-ahead and I'll be waiting for you when you get back.*' Simple, but wonderful. She did come back and they have been happily married for years. Life is an adventure and so it should be; you may love someone but have different dreams. You never really have someone completely with you, if they are not reaching for their true dreams. A couple may be together, have some similar dreams and some totally different ones. If you can empower your partner to achieve their dreams, then you have that person wholly and completely. When I first started my company a girl worked in reception for me, and one day I noticed she was a little upset. I asked her what was wrong and she said that her friends were going to see the Chippendales (male exotic dancers) and her boyfriend wouldn't let her go. We may laugh at this, and whilst watching a group of men show off their pecs may not be a girl's dream, the story is an example of someone trying to control their partner's life.

If he would have said: '*Go and enjoy it. I'm off to the gym,*' she might have said: '*I'm not going; I can't be bothered.*' but at least it would have been her decision. Support but don't control. She would probably have gone and had the experience and that is what life is about – experiences, we should all support people close to us.

Everyone should be able to enjoy life's experiences and make their own decisions.

Unfortunately, some couples and friends steal each other's dreams; sometimes because of a little ignorance or lack of understanding.

Go places, meet people, do things.

For every person who travels the world there are another hundred or so that have wanted to do it but have been dissuaded: 'Backpacking – Yuck! Why do you want to do that?' Or 'You might not get a job when you get back.'

Not everybody has a character as strong as Beckham; most people will find it difficult to do something that no one around them understands. Most people are happy to stay with what they know; some people want to try different things but just do not have the accessibility or finance. Those who do, have no excuse. Life is a dream-factory and it's amazing what you can achieve together. If a group of students decided they wanted to travel the world but didn't have the finance you would be amazed how generous the community would be if they did some fund raising activities. The best advice I can give to anyone thinking about being part of a great experience, is to just do it. The worst that can happen is that you have another experience under your belt. No, actually, the worst thing that can happen is to not do it and spend the rest of your life wondering.

Don't be scared to try; an imperfect life is a perfect life.

If he would have said: '*Go and enjoy it. I'm off to the gym,*' she might have said: '*I'm not going; I can't be bothered.*' but at least it would have been her decision. things you dreamt about. Those things that keep you awake at night, like thinking how amazing it would be to play for Manchester United; own a great company or even become the Prime Minister – remember, Margaret Thatcher's parents were grocers from Grantham. Dream stealers pounce on people at their weakest moments and instead of helping them through these moments, they seize them like vultures and their prey.

Once a dream is stolen and a different path is taken, it's so hard to recover.

Every day and every moment of a young performer's life is their day; nobody has the right to steal their dreams by being an enabler. Even if they hate you for a day, a week or a year, you can sleep at night knowing you didn't get them to do something reckless. Strong characters will react to dream stealers in a way that pushes them to achieve an '*I'll show them*' mentality. Winners in life often react to adversity in a positive way; someone patting them on the back, won't put fire in their bellies like someone saying '*you can't do it.*' Encouraging talent to react in that way, helps them to fulfil their potential and fuels the fire. So much time is wasted in the workplace by individuals not being motivated and lacking a big picture. We all have to be reminded what the big picture *is*. People with experience, knowledge and a broad mind are seldom dream stealers. If you can surround yourself with people like that, you have a better chance of being inspired. Some people do not have the experience or accessibility to give worldly advice, but if they have an open-mind to the possibilities out there, then that, in itself, can help them give others a positive outlook. Lack of experience, travel and knowledge can be contributors to some folk being narrow-minded and in some cases that is understandable. But, it is unforgiveable for someone with a lack of vision to try and tell others that something isn't possible for reasons, they themselves, can't substantiate.

All across the UK and the world, there are talented people with desire and nowhere to turn. Nothing is impossible, but success is difficult and throughout the ups and downs a mentor or advisor with vision can help immeasurably. In football, it's often really hard to focus on the big picture because so many things can happen in a week, never mind a career. But, there is a common denominator with the guys who make it to the top: They have very few agents or personal advisors. This is because people who come into your life on a short-term basis, are not going to take a long-term view and are often dream stealers. Agents who turn heads of talented footballers are often major dream stealers; this is because they have no interest in the bigger picture, but just the next deal around the corner. To become successful in football or any walk of life, you have to develop character, '*stickability*' and win your battles along the way. If you don't learn how to win your battles you can never become great.

We all know the saying: A winner never quits and a quitter never wins.

Dream stealers convince footballers, and those in other professions, to not win any character winning battles but to take the easy way out and worry about the future when it comes. Great players like Lampard, Beckham, Gerrard, Owen and Rooney have all had very few advisers; in some cases just one. There are plenty of dream builders in this world; you just have to find them or be lucky enough for them to find you. When you have the right people around you, it's not rocket science to work out who they are. Good Karma is an amazing thing to have and people with good karma will want you to succeed. We are all selfish to a certain extent and we all do what makes us happy. The lucky people are the ones who like helping others and are selfless. Although they do what they do because it makes them feel good, at least it's a positive outcome. Others are '*happy hoovers*" – they feel great when others are having a bad time. They go around sucking the happiness out of anyone who has a glint of a smile on their face. Ever heard the saying misery loves company?

Well people who are miserable love making others miserable as well. Not only that, millions of people watch TV shows like *EastEnders* and *Coronation Street*, which are doused in misery. It seems lots of us watch shows like that and feel better afterwards. A kind of: '*My life is not so bad after all.*' But, instead of feeling safe stuck in a '*misery matrix*', why not make it your life's mission to get the absolute most out of your life and career? No dream stealers, only dream makers. David Beckham is someone who has lived the dream. There is no place for dream stealers in Beckham's world.

David Beckham

David Beckham is someone I admire greatly; he has shown it is possible to love and be successful at your craft, whilst being smart enough to develop your brand. Who could have predicted that Beckham's career would have developed into such an amazing global brand? Well, he knew and he made it happen by associating with dream builders and not dream stealers. His choices all through his career have been carefully planned and executed. The move to the MLS in July 2007 was a masterstroke, because it gave him a platform in Los Angeles and the US to develop his brand to super-star status. Allegedly, when Beckham was asked what type of brand he wanted, he replied: '*Tom Cruise.*' Within football circles, there would have been nobody that could help David Beckham achieve a similar status to Tom Cruise – one of Hollywood's biggest stars. Beckham knew that, so, he had to make a big decision and decide who could help him. Because it was such a ground breaking move and had as much to do with his brand, as football, '*the big business – small world', that is football* would not approve. Critics had watched with amazement as Beckham still managed to make England squads whilst playing in the States. Lots of people questioned why he made such a move and why he did not want to play football at the highest level in Europe. The answer was that he was going to make history by developing the game in the biggest economy in the *world* – America. How many people could think outside the box and help the Beckhams achieve their dreams? How many people believed that it was possible to be a global brand and still give 100% to your craft? Most people are influenced by others and football has its standard unwritten rules. Beckham ripped up those rules. He did what seemed a lot of branding and PR stuff, which created its own pressure. As soon as Beckham lost form or didn't play well it was inevitable the blame would be placed at his door for doing too much outside of football. Another amazing thing about his success in the states is, that football had no status there and yet he has managed to have the same popularity as some of Hollywood's biggest names.

Beckham is someone that had dreams – big dreams. In order to satisfy his ambitions he had to build a world that would help him achieve everything he wanted. Beckham's mind-set and vision is rare, especially in football. No one is going to preach branding, marketing and worldwide status. Any one taking that kind of approach would be frowned upon because all young players are told to focus on their football and not to get side-tracked by doing too much off-field activities. But Beckham proved that doing off-field activities would not affect his football. He also proved the doubters wrong. Let's not forget how much criticism he received for being seen in the news pages and not just the sports ones. Beckham was the lily in the grass field. He wasn't scared to wear a sarong and can you imagine how much stick he got for that? Once a strong following is established you have power; add to that family values, patriotism and a fantastic partner and the brand is worth millions. He and his advisors realised that if you are continually in the press, then you are building a seriously strong brand with huge marketing deals to follow. Meeting Victoria was a major piece of luck, but marrying her and starting a family was genuine love that also added to the Beckham dynasty. When you are married to someone like Victoria, your world becomes stronger, smarter and a fantastic family unit. There are plenty of partners trying to advise their spouses about various matters. It is an absolute disaster if that person doesn't know what they're talking about. This is because people in the public eye and in sport or entertainment will listen and often trust their partner's opinion, even if it's nonsense. Successful business people are often more equipped to decide what is good or bad advice; this is because the journey in business is a long and winding road. Beckham's world is one created by him; he has taken control of his life and taken the path he wanted to. He will be remembered as a very good footballer, but his legacy will be his humanitarian and ambassadorial efforts. Watch this space as he will continue to be creative, transcend boundaries and remain one of the most famous men on the planet, even when others have long be forgotten.

After The Love Has Gone

There's a saying that goes: The true character of someone, is how they treat people who can do nothing for them. That is one of the best sentences I have ever heard because the only true friends you will ever have are the ones that have no conditions on your relationship. In an ideal world, the people *In Your World* would have an unconditional relationship with you. Your partner would want to be with you regardless of what uncertainties life throws; your friends would support you through thick and thin and your work colleagues would give you encouragement when you are not performing. The problem a lot of people have is over-using what they have, to the point that when they don't have it, they're lost and often depressed. For instance, someone who is good-looking when they are young and uses that fact to get on, can often just focus on their appearance and not how they communicate. But, when their looks have faded, they will be faced with the fact they haven't learnt how to communicate with anyone properly. And this can be a really lonely place. We have had boom years followed by bust years and in those periods, lots of people made and lost lots of money. When you have something that people want you will be befriended in such a way that it seems real. When the bust years happen, your true friends are there with you and any flaky people gradually disappear. Footballers and others who attain wealth and fame can also get by on everyone wanting to do everything for them and for years and years they don't know who their friends are. Even the so-called hangers-on genuinely believe that they are friends. Footballers often have the unenviable task of trying to sort out who the hangers-on are and who the real people are. But honestly, who wouldn't want to have all the riches, fame and attention that footballers, pop stars and entertainment stars get? The problem is that it is like concentrated orange – too much in too short a period. If the whole fame and money thing was diluted just a bit more, then the whole experience would be more rational.

I've been lucky enough to have had some very interesting conversations with footballers, who I never represented, but whose careers were over; they look back and tell me that they no longer have any contact with the guys who made millions from them. Why? Because they were never really friends. Their relationship was conditional on the footballer making money. How sad. A great example of this was Bobby Moore; our biggest football hero ever as World Cup winner in 1966 and captain of England. Whilst he played football, and especially, the 'post' World Cup success he was adored and people couldn't do enough for him. But, as soon as his career waned, no one would give him a job. He was left in the wilderness. It's hard to believe that the Football Association or any of the clubs he played for couldn't find a role for him in their set-up. This is a guy who fought cancer from his early twenties and went on to be a legend. If that can happen to Bobby Moore then, it can happen to anyone. We've all seen the pictures of Paul Gascoigne and Kenny Samson struggling to cope with life after football. I fear for our talented young sports people, entrepreneurs and leaders, because if they don't take responsibility for who is around them, who they listen to and what advice they are getting, not only will they not fulfil their potential but life after the high-performance years, will be very difficult. A major problem here is that youth, success and attention might seem like they will last forever, when they are in fact transitory. And with that there isn't any importance placed on finding the right people to build for the future. When someone is doing well, it is imperative to have people around them building on their success and laying foundations for the future. But unfortunately for our talented youngsters, the wrong people around them can always move onto the next gravy train and when that happens our talented youngsters are now older '*has-beens*', who were not advised or guided in the right way. There are so many great advisors, mentors and teachers out there in every walk of life, so, we all, need to keep looking for them.

All about the Money?

Over the years, I learnt very quickly about how to deal with money and the implications it can have on people's lives – which is mainly negative. The value of money was very clear to me when I watched my beloved mum coming home from work after a twelve hour shift from the pie factory earning £5 a day. What was important to her was paying the bills and putting food on the table. If she had a pound or two she would share it amongst the kids. Whilst my mum was being so prudent with money, my dad, God bless him, was doing the opposite. He'd get paid on the Friday and it would be gone by Sunday, from being down the pub and bookies. When I played table-tennis there was little money about. In fact when on England duty we would earn money from the governing body in *'units'* of £5. If you were on four units like I was, that would be £20 a day whilst on training camps and international duty. The amount of discussions that went on about units were interesting, because the national coach gave out the units in accordance to where you stood in the team. What was interesting was that it wasn't so much about the actual money, but the value the coach and governing body saw in you. So for instance, I was on four units but someone who ranked a place or two above me was on twelve and you would automatically think, is he worth three times more than me? That is a dangerous precedent, as teammates or colleagues in business can be seriously demotivated by inconsistent distribution of money. I've listened to many people tell me: 'It's all about the money so earn as much as you can.' Well, the first thing to say about that, is if you chase money solely, it will put on some running shoes and run from you so fast that you will need Usain Bolt's legs to catch it. Also, having that thought process gives you a short-term view on everything. Every time someone offers you a little more money you're going to take it, without weighing up the true value of the situation and the long-term view. If it's obvious to everyone that you are *'all about the money'* then you are owned by it.

There's a saying: Penny wise; pound foolish. You can want a little more money so badly that you actually do yourself a disservice in the long-run. Also, some people put money before everyone, but what do they want the money for? To support charities? For humanitarian work? To put their children through private school? Because we would all understand people who want to do something positive, but unfortunately the desire for money is often to do with self-promotion - cars, watches, shoes, and material things. So you can end up having the drive for money and taking your eyes off what's important; your craft and focus on the improvement of yourself and ambitions. You can end up with things that will gradually be worth nothing. You can give one person a pound and they will turn it into three pounds and you can give another person a pound and they will turn it into zero. Football is awash with money and it is absolutely frightening how much can be spent on depreciating assets. The crazy thing is that how much a player earns is seldom reflected by what they end up with. A player who has a decent career, playing in the Championship; earning an average of half million a year over a ten year period could set himself up for life with some smart investments and control over the desire to buy things with no residual value. On the other hand, a player could earn an average of one million pounds per year over a ten-year period and end up with nothing by buying badly. Like: Buying new cars then selling them back to dealers or purchasing new houses that have very little chance of increasing in value and so on. So you can see that the guy who has a half-decent career, a stable family relationship, good investments and no interest in buying lots of new cars, can have financial stability. One of the worst things that money can do is stop people from communicating properly. It can make people think that they don't need to communicate with anyone because they can buy what they want. Money can also attract the wrong kind of people, who themselves are not interested in communicating but to enjoy the affluence. The only true relationships we can have are unconditional ones, where we put aside money, power, influence, looks and intelligence.

There's a saying: Penny wise; pound foolish. You can want a little more money earn vast sums of money, but still have the desire to train, perform, achieve and improve. It's not an easy thing to do otherwise there would be lots more Gerrards, Lampards, Ferdinands and Campbells. When someone achieves success that results in substantial wealth, the people *in their Worlds* play a vital part in proceedings. It is so important to have people around you who don't get carried away with the change in financial standing. Having friends or family who have the 'spend, spend, spend' mentality is an absolute nightmare. Sometimes the perception of a footballer from the people in their world is that: '*They aren't doing much to earn the money*' and then it can become the mentality that the footballer has 'won the lottery' because their jobs aren't valued so they are seen as lucky. However, to actually become a top footballer, playing in the Premier League is extremely difficult with the odds stacked against those who try. So, footballers are paid what they earn because they are the talent in a multi-billion pound industry. Players need to learn the value of money for themselves and consider the future – what happens if they get a long-term injury? For as long as I can remember money was never my God and that is why when it came to negotiating contracts in football, it never phased me. But money has ruined many careers, relationships and families.

Brand

Your brand is who you are in the eyes of the public and people who don't know you. As mentioned earlier, Beckham understood the importance of his brand: Excellence at your craft, conducting yourself in the correct manner and being a 'family man'. For Beckham, being a 'family man' is something that comes naturally; he quite obviously loves his wife, kids and family and he also is happy to share some of that with the public. The public will buy into and support well-known people who are 'family people'. Family is the foundation of life and that's why companies also buy into this ethos in a big way. The public also buy into '*couple's PR*' because relationships are a huge topic of conversation and they are also something that most people want – a good relationship. High-profile relationships are important to the public because we are intrigued by certain couples and often put them on a pedestal. So, being a brand is not rocket science, it gives you credibility, makes you a role model and can make your bank balance a lot bigger for a longer period. Not every person in the public eye cares sufficiently about their brand, nor do they understand the importance of communicating with the public. Some see building a brand as a hassle and a pointless exercise in trying to reach unobtainable standards. Twitter is an innovation tinged with irony because many individuals who don't buy into the whole branding thing, try to communicate with the public and wonder why they often get things wrong. Random messages without any thought will alert the public in a negative way. For those who have good advice and understand the whole branding concept, twitter is a huge additional tool in their brand development and communication with the public. But, the question remains: Why don't some high-profile people care about their brand? In fact, for someone to care about their brand, they need to surround themselves with people who understand the importance of branding. If representatives of talent don't have the expertise or care about their client's brand then that person will come across very badly to the public.

In Your World you have to care about the perception people have about you and most importantly, the people around you must care about the perception people will have about you. Branding may not be rocket science but it is hard work. Lots of advisers and representatives can't be bothered to do it. Why? Because it sometimes means having difficult conversations with clients and doing things where no one gets paid in the short-term. Talent, who have a good brand, can transcend their craft, have influence on different platforms and even have different careers after sport. Talent, when performing at a good level have the possibility to be a brand. To be honest the public buy into certain things:

- Family
- Relationship of a couple
- Communication
- Love of one's country

The ingredients to becoming a brand may be simple, but most people competing or performing just do not have the energy or time to donate to it. Most athletes and performers want to train/work hard then rest at every opportunity possible. They give every ounce of their energy to training and performing; that's why you often see athletes/performers speaking in press conferences without much energy or purpose. It takes mental and physical energy doing anything other than practice or performance. Talent often get extremely irritated by having to do too much outside of their training schedules, which is why there has to be a genuine interest in the brand stuff or a determination to do it. Very few want to keep doing press, photo-shoots and personal appearances after a hard day of training or rehearsals. This leaves the door wide open for those who want to have the profile as they do all the photo-shoots, press and personal appearances. How often have you heard someone ask why a certain person is famous, seemingly for no apparent reason?

It's because they may not be great at any particular craft, but they are willing to do every brand opportunity going. Let's go back to the main ingredients of being a brand. Couple's PR is quite simply the biggest form of PR all over the world as the public have a fascination with relationships. Two people at the top of their game is great, but just one person with a willing partner can get fabulous recognition and huge endorsement deals. In fact, a partner who was deemed the '*unknown one*' in a relationship can quickly lose that tag and the public can almost forget how they became famous. The famous relationship between David Copperfield (American Magician) and Claudia Schiffer (Supermodel) back in the '90s, was one of the first examples of how couple's PR can achieve huge profiles and do great business. Schiffer was a very well-known model in Europe and Copperfield was a super-star magician in the States. Neither had an amazing profile in their partner's backyard. But once they started dating they were huge news. Pictures and stories appeared in both continents. The repercussion was that Schiffer achieved great contracts in the US and Copperfield sold out shows in Europe. The great thing about them was that they were both at the top of their respective crafts, but joining forces made them powerhouses. It takes exceptional individuals to have a relationship and hold the family together with the glare of a spotlight on them 24/7. That is why I have the utmost respect for couples like Victoria and David, because they are human beings and have problems just like everybody else but they hold the family together.

Great Leaders - Dream Teams

This section focuses mainly on football mangers and explores the worlds they created in order to achieve success and their own ambitions. Wenger, Ferguson, Mourinho, Guardiola and Del Bosque are some of the greatest managers who ever lived and the way they created their worlds is fascinating. Being a football manager is one profession where you have to be totally selfish in every aspect of your world. A manager's wife has to be selfless and understanding to the extreme. Friends and family come second to the huge demands of 24/7 football; and then there's the coaching staff. What type of people do these guys have around them and why? Then there are the players. Why is it that players sometimes play for the manager and at other times players just don't seem that motivated? How do you manage thirty professional footballers who: '*just want to play football*?' One thing is for sure, a manager has to create his own world and these great managers all did it differently.

Arsène Wenger

Wenger is known for being a father figure. In Wenger's world he treats his players as family, and he talks football, family and life. Wenger's world is one where footballers develop not only as players, but also as people. He lives by a moral conduct and is respected by the right people for his morals and ethics. People should ultimately be judged by the way they conduct themselves and not by what they achieve. Wenger has won almost everything in the game but his exceptional standing in football is that he has never broken a contract. You may think: '*Why is that a big deal?*' But he is not a hypocrite and to earn ultimate respect from people you have to have strong morals on big issues. That is why you will never see Wenger criticising a player who is honouring his contract and getting into a strong position with the club. Some people in football will criticise a player for not signing a new contract because it suits them to do that. Many players at Arsenal, in recent years, have decided not to sign new contracts and ended up with a year or so left. Nasri, Walcott and Van Persie spring to mind. Wenger has never criticised them publicly for honouring their contracts – because he is not a hypocrite. Even Mathieu Flamini left on a Bosman free transfer then came back and signed for Arsenal again after a stint in Italy with AC Milan. The players know that he is fair and focuses totally on his craft. He loves to develop players and if a footballer shows a desire to improve and has the right attitude he will back them to the hilt. His support of his players is unwavering to the extent that in a period he would say: '*I didn't see it*' (the incident) rather than criticise his players. This was him being totally loyal to his players and refusing to be put in a situation where he would have to acknowledge that a player had let him and the team down.

The great managers instil trust, belief and respect in their players.

That ensures unwavering loyalty, understanding and success on and off the pitch.

The manager can even become something of a father figure, a leader and someone who players will push boundaries for. It is the art form of man management. Arsène Wenger has developed that quality throughout his managerial career and it has brought him loyalty and trophies.
I remember the first conversations I had with Wenger before Sol joined Arsenal. He had a genuine interest in other people's lives and spoke with great wisdom. If you are in Wenger's world, you benefit not only from his wisdom but his moral standpoints and amazing knowledge of football. He is truly a professor of football. I know I have already used this quote, but to me it is so important. It's something that Wenger said to me during our conversations; something I will never forget – in fact I have found it to be a golden rule for life:

'There are smart people and stupid people. Smart people know their priorities.'

I've spoken about how footballers should lead their lives. Many people in life do not know their priorities; they do not know what the important things in life are. Wenger may be mad on football, but his priorities are with family and when you have that principle you can go and take on the world. Whilst there is always speculation about Wenger's position as manager, he has never broken a contract. Not too many journalists care for that because it's not a good story. Some managers believe the way to have respect from the players is not to be too close and to have space between them. Wenger gets his respect by the way he conducts himself - his coaching and his open-door policy. Players know they can go and speak with him about anything; they also know that he is a very tough character. Thierry Henry was a player who benefitted from Wenger tremendously. They would sit and talk football and life before and after training. The biggest compliment to Wenger is that even when players want to leave the club, they discuss it openly with him. Both Thierry Henry and Patrick Vieira sat with Wenger and discussed leaving the club. That is of course not the norm because players can become alienated from their mangers when they want to leave. Wenger's reputation, coaching and management has brought glowing references from even the biggest names within the game.

Thierry Henry, Patrick Vieira, Cesc Fabregas and Robin van Persie and many more talk as if they are Wenger's disciples. Henry and Fabregas describe Wenger as something of a father figure; a manager who gave them their big chance to flourish and shine. It brings about a sense of loyalty. If and when players do leave Wenger, they often get a sense of guilt that they are departing from their mentor's care. Fabregas was drafted into the first team at sixteen. Van Persie was given his chance after gaining a reputation as a troublesome teenager growing up in Holland. Henry converted from winger to Arsenal's most successful and prolific striker of all time. If you listen to the tributes, then it is clear that they regard Wenger as someone to look up to; the biggest influence on their career and the reason why it was so hard for some of them to leave. There is genuine affection and loyalty in their words. Ex-Arsenal captain Cesc Fabregas, who swapped the Emirates for Barcelona, said:

'Wenger was like a father to me. He did so much for me and without him I wouldn't be here now. I spoke to him before I left and it was so hard. At one point I couldn't even talk because I was so sad. It was hard to say goodbye and hard to leave. He has done more for me than anyone and he is the best person I have met in football.'

Former Arsenal midfielder Alex Song said:

'I am who I am thanks to him. When I came to England, he was a big help to me. I was very young, just seventeen, not twenty-five like I am now. Wenger was like a father to me. It was very hard for me at first because I had left my family behind in France, and so he treated me like a son.'

Arsenal midfielder Santi Cazorla, part of the all-conquering Spain set-up, said:

'He's a father figure for all of us. He's spent so much time here that he's gained this respect. If you've been here for so long it means your CV must be so good. He's very close with the players, very natural and he has this passion that he wants Arsenal to keep winning.'

Wenger has a reputation for being cool in the dressing room. When he loses his temper, the players really need to sit up and take notice. On the training ground, it is more about being given freedom to play – a license to entertain and enjoy their football. Henry was wayward in his finishing when he arrived at Arsenal; albeit he had already won the 1998 World Cup with France. Despite having won the highest honour in the game, Henry arrived from Juventus with something to prove. It had been a difficult spell in Italy; he did not enjoy it and he arrived at Arsenal with his confidence low and with a feeling of uncertainty in his mind. But Wenger gave him freedom on the pitch. He stuck with him even when, as Henry recalled, his shots were hitting the clock high above The Clock End at Highbury, rather than the back of the net. Wenger's methods are about short, sharp and precise training and sessions that the players enjoy. He is notorious for working on his own team's strengths, encouraging forward play and not paying much attention to defending. As long as his own team scores one more than the opposition then he is satisfied. In fact, some players have been critical in the past that not more work is done on defending, team shape and discipline. But that has always been his philosophy: A playing-style, which his players buy into, enjoy and revel in. They want to play for Wenger and for the teams that he builds. The majority of players who have signed for Arsenal generally arrive with a story of how they wanted to sign for Wenger, learn from him and play under him. A classic example of this was told out by Arsenal's Welsh midfielder Aaron Ramsey who, when he was seventeen, had the pick of the Premier League's top clubs. Manchester United were battling it out with Arsenal for the Cardiff City youngster's signature and yet it was Wenger's personal touch that persuaded Ramsey to join Arsenal. Wenger was at Euro 2008, but left nothing to chance; chartering a private jet to fly Ramsey out to the tournament, to meet him and to charm him. Recalling why he chose Arsenal and spelling out Wenger's qualities, Ramsey gives a fascinating insight into Wenger's methods and ability to nurture the best young players. '*The main factor was meeting with Arsène Wenger and to hear what his plans were for me,*' said Ramsey, recalling his decision to join Arsenal over United.
Here are some insights from Ramsey, which highlight all of Wenger's qualities:

'He has brought through so many youngsters and given them opportunities and turned them into great players. That was the main factor really.'

'He gives you confidence. He is very approachable and will talk to you on how you are doing. He is great like that - on how you can improve.'

'He gives you that freedom on the pitch to express yourself and to do that. I have definitely grown up as a player.'

'We are a team with good players. You just have to trust him with what he has been doing. He has been there for so many years and been so successful.'

'The players are behind him 100 per cent. Even though we have been inconsistent we want to win something for him as much as ourselves and the fans.'

Wenger's personal touch also shines through in the story of how Ramsey decided to join. It is a familiar story throughout a raft of young players. Philippe Senderos, the former Arsenal defender, once recalled how Wenger turned up at his house when he was still at school in Switzerland to persuade him to sign. After that, how could he refuse? It was exactly the same for Ramsey back in 2008. Ramsey recalled:

'I was overwhelmed. I was seventeen and one of the best managers in the world wants to meet me face-to-face and the way that they did it. They flew me over there on a private jet.'

'It was quite overwhelming at the time and it was definitely a factor.'

'It was a hard choice to make at my age but I have no regrets with what I chose. I think I chose the right one. It was a difficult decision.'

'I felt more wanted at Arsenal and felt that the plan was better for me and they give youngsters more opportunities. Plus, with Manchester United, they had a lot of midfielders as well at the time.'

Those stories have been mirrored throughout Wenger's reign. Another involved Alex Oxlade-Chamberlain. Arsenal signed him in the summer of 2011, but only after competition from various clubs, including Liverpool and Manchester United. Oxlade-Chamberlain, together with his dad, former England winger, Mark Chamberlain, did a few tours of clubs and met the staff. When it came to Arsenal, Wenger had father and son in his office and spelt out exactly how he saw Alex's role in the first team; using the fingers on his hand to explain Oxlade-Chamberlain would be central to his plans with Theo Walcott wide right, Jack Wilshere also in the middle. Wenger knew all about his father's career, the history and the background. There had been thought and planning. His charm completely won them over and filled them with a confidence, which persuaded him to join. During Oxlade-Chamberlain's first season, frustration crept in at a lack of first team opportunities. Rather like with Walcott, Wenger wanted to hold him back, develop and nurture him slowly. But when the time came, Wenger thrust Oxlade-Chamberlain into the first team, even for bigger games against AC Milan and Manchester United at the Emirates. It was those outings, which gave England manager, Roy Hodgson the belief and confidence to take the youngster to Euro 2012. If they are good enough in Wenger's eyes, then they are definitely old enough. Similarly, Fabregas was given his debut at sixteen. It instilled a belief in the young Spaniard that he had made the right choice to leave his boyhood club, Barcelona, in search of a more guaranteed path into first team football. Wenger's faults, in fact, lie perhaps in showing too much loyalty and faith in players. He will not sign players for fear of blocking the path of youngsters already at the club. How many big club managers have that mentality? No one seems to give him credit for that; he develops his young players at all costs whilst some other clubs just keep buying the so-called '*finished Article*'. That raises the question, as to who that best serves? Surely Wenger's first loyalty is to bring success to Arsenal? But if he decides not to sign a player because it will block the path of a young talent then that must be at the detriment of the team. It is a carefully trodden path. Wenger has missed out on players on occasion because of his unswerving loyalty to those already at the club. But it does promote an incredible sense of loyalty from those who keep their place. One classic example is Abou Diaby.

A supremely talented and yet injury-prone player. His injury problems stem from a horror challenge soon after Diaby had joined Arsenal from Auxerre in the January transfer window of 2006. In a meaningless end-of-season game with the clock ticking down, Sunderland's Dan Smith launched a terrible lunge on Diaby, which left the French midfielder in agony and his career in tatters. It was a long road back. Arguably, Diaby has never fully recovered and it will always be debated as to whether he has fulfilled his full, natural and immense potential. There was injury after injury and wasted season after wasted season. Yet Wenger admitted that he showed more loyalty to Diaby than he might have done because, he partly, felt responsible for the original injury. Wenger views his players as under his care. In Diaby's case, Wenger was almost blinkered.

Before the start of the 2012/13 season, Arsenal sold Alex Song to Barcelona. Song's time had come and gone. Another player plucked from obscurity and turned into a big star. But it left Arsenal short in midfield. Rather than signing a physical and powerful holding midfielder to anchor the Arsenal team, Wenger decided to stick with Diaby rather than block off his path. In the early part of the season, it worked a dream. Arsenal played well, Diaby starred and yet injury inevitably struck again. It was supposed to be a make-or-break season. It ended in break again as Diaby suffered a terrible knee ligament injury in training towards the end of the campaign. While Wenger remained loyal to Diaby, was it at the expense of the team? It could easily be argued that it was. But that is Wenger's philosophy and veering away from that vision would quickly see a change in that loyalty. Wenger has built generations of different teams. When he first arrived at Arsenal in 1996, the Frenchman inherited a team with a resolute defence; a squad with a drinking culture and one which had grown stale after winning trophies under George Graham.

Graham, who was dismissed after a bung scandal, had assembled a team based on a solid back four, with keeper David Seaman behind Lee Dixon, Steve Bould, Tony Adams and Nigel Winterburn. Martin Keown was also a defensive rock. Arsenal, however, had almost gone out of control.

They had also slipped into decline; a decline not arrested by Bruce Rioch's brief spell in charge. Paul Merson and Adams all had much publicised off-the-field problems. Adams confessed to alcoholism and Merson confessed to using drugs. It was a dressing room full of challenges and big characters. Then suddenly, there was a tall, thin, bespectacled Frenchman, trying to win over a sceptical group of players. They mocked Wenger when he first arrived; doing silly French impressions behind his back, unsure of his reputation in the wake of a few famous '*Arsène Who?*'' headlines. But Wenger proved himself to be a leader in his field. He did not need to be a dictator. He won over the players with new methods. Wenger introduced new short, sharp and specifically targeted training sessions. The players did more work on possession, style and skill. These sessions kept the players interested and engaged. Wenger also began to improve player's nutrition; supplementing with Creatine - an organic acid used to improve muscle size and power output, whilst enhancing recovery.

Diets included food rich in chlorophyll like broccoli, thus alkalising and high in energy. The players would eat together at the training ground; it was part of team bonding. New stretching exercises worked and the players felt as if Wenger was extending their careers. Adams famously even had a wisdom tooth removed to ease a long-standing back problem and Wenger obviously had a specialist he knew in France. They were also playing good football. They stormed to the Double in 1998; they played attractive stuff and Wenger built the first of several generations of teams. That 1998 team kept the famous back four. Henry had arrived by the Double of 2002 and Wenger's best team of 2003/04 were nicknamed '*The Invincibles*'. They won the Premier League title without losing a game. Wenger had assembled a team of strong, powerful players. '*Man Mountains*' like Kolo Toure, Sol Campbell, Vieira and Henry. They never knew when they were beaten. They were about power, pace and brilliance. Not to be afraid of change, Wenger broke up that team and went in a different direction. They began to have smaller, more skilful players with more intricate passing movements. Arsenal played the '*Tiki Taka*' model almost before Barcelona. But Wenger's new methods only had limited success.

The FA Cup was won in 2005 and yet they lost the Champions League final a year later. Wenger's stubbornness shone through. His loyalty season after season of near misses ended with Wenger insisting the players would come good with trophies. Arsenal fans became frustrated with the wait. Yet there have been moments of ruthlessness. Gilberto Silva losing the captaincy - and finding out after reading about it online - and then being sold. Many would argue far too soon. Patrick Vieira was also sold and after years of transfer sags and flirting with Real Madrid; Vieira did not want to leave when he eventually went in 2005. In fact, Vieira was talking of a new contract at Arsenal when suddenly the club's former vice-chairman, David Dein, informed him that Juventus were interested. And they wouldn't stand in his way. It had been Wenger, studying statistics on player performance levels, who believed Vieira was on his way down and decided to move him on. Similarly, a year later, Wenger's relationship with Robert Pires, perhaps never recovered when he sacrificed the French midfielder after Jens Lehmann was sent off in the 2006 Champions League final. Pires, a member of Wenger's famous 'Invincibles' team of 2003/04, said:

'The final in Paris was the worst moment in my career. Two days after the final we spoke about two things. I said I was going to sign for Villarreal and I wanted to know why I was substituted. He was sorry but he saw that with me in the team we would play more defensively; it was complicated with only ten against Barcelona.'

'Leaving was the most difficult decision of my career. I thought I would end my career there, but I could see in the final against Barcelona, Wenger had lost his confidence in me. The fact that I was only allowed to play eighteen minutes in that final remains painful. I'll never agree with him that he made the right decision.'

The one time Wenger criticised a player in public, happened with Argentinian defender, Nelson Vivas, who shouldered the blame for Arsenal slipping up at Leeds in 1999.

There was no way back for Vivas and yet Wenger has not criticised players since. Even when they have done the dirty and left him. Finally, and perhaps most intriguingly, comes another example of Wenger's man-management and ability to keep a happy and largely contented dressing room. It is a bizarre logic from a man who earns £7.5m-a-year as Arsenal manager. That is a huge salary, but Wenger oversees the whole running of the club. He is the most important figure at the club. Wenger employs a '*socialist*' wage structure among his squad. No one player – no matter how big a star or name – is allowed to earn far more than another who shares the same dressing room. Therefore, you will never find resentment or anger from a player as he hangs up his shirt on a peg in the dressing room next to a teammate, knowing he earns four or five times as much. Wenger firmly believes in those values to keep the players together. The Frenchman explained recently why he believes no one should earn a lot more than anyone else. Wenger said:

'We pay well. We pay very well. I've spent all my life making sure people who work for us are paid well and I believe if you can do it, you do it. My principle is to pay something that makes sense and is defendable in front of every single player. We make exceptions sometimes but they are not maybe so high. If you want to keep making profit you have to respect that. We have no players on £200,000 a week and I think other clubs will come down to us with financial fair play. We have a more socialist model.'

There are many methods and theories on man-management. There is no right or wrong way, particularly in football. But Wenger has a philosophy and consistency, which has, down the years, ensured the players always remain fiercely loyal, determined and, above all, ready to go into war for their manager. There is no doubt that Wenger's best qualities are his man-management which, given his standing in the game, often does not rely on too many words. Some former players will say that he does not like confrontation, he will often say very little, even to the point of blanking players who are not in his team. But that will make players even more determined to win back his respect. His presence commands respect. And when he does speak, players tend to listen.

Two contrasting approaches have been illustrated by different Arsenal players: Their emerging left back Kieran Gibbs and record signing Mesut Ozil. For one, Wenger did not need to say anything. For the other, a phone conversation and some important words did the job. In the case of Kieran Gibbs, he spoke recently how Wenger does not need to say very much but when he does the words matter. '*He has got something special,*' said Gibbs in an interview conducted with him for Rabona magazine.

'*When you're first coming into the team, he's got an ability to make you feel like you deserve to be there. He doesn't have to do a lot because of who he is. If he tells you something, whatever he tells you, if he pays you compliments then you think: it's Arsène Wenger telling me this ... You go home and you think: Wow, Arsène Wenger has told me this. You think he must be right and you take it on board. He's not a manager who is constantly on your back, he just lets you take it in and learn for yourself. He always tells you to play free, do what you feel that the game deserves. That has helped me a lot. I'm quite like that. If someone tells me to do something, and they tell you in a certain way, I react differently to if someone tells you just to get on with it and let you learn. He tends to just throw you in and learn by yourself. I'm my own biggest critic so I will know what I need to do and what I don't need to do. He can read someone's personality as well. He will leave you when you need to be left and tell you when you need to be told.*'

In contrast, when Arsenal pulled off the signing of the summer, the £42m deal for German playmaker, Ozil, it was clear that he went to the Emirates because of Wenger. And, specifically, Wenger's phone call – conducted in German – with a clear message of how he saw Ozil in his team, his vision for the club and expectations and ambition, persuaded him to leave Real Madrid for Arsenal. '*Somehow this telephone call just flicked a switch in me.*' Ozil told the press when he joined.

'*I thought: What he is telling me is what I have missed at Real: transparency, trust, respect. He told me exactly how he sees me [as a player]; how he wants to use me; what he expects from me and what he hopes I will contribute.*

I want to win titles and will do everything in order to do that. That is my mentality. We will do everything to get as far as possible in all the competitions. I learned that at Real. I go into every competition wanting to win.'

The ambition is clear. Even to the point that Ozil says the size of the deal is irrelevant. '*The transfer fee has nothing to do with me. I would have joined Arsenal on a free.'* That is the Wenger factor; the art of man-management and being able to command respect with words and with your own standing within the game.

Del Bosque, Guardiola & Mourinho

Back in 2009 with the Barcelona future of Eidur Gudjohnsen in doubt, the Icelandic striker met with manager Pep Guardiola.'*What do you want from me?*' the player asked. Pep's answer was immediate, to the point, and unequivocal. '*Your life,*' he said. Harsh maybe, but from Pep's point of view, why should he not expect from his players? It was precisely the same commitment, obsession and dedication that he himself had given – a passion that would take him to the very brink of destruction. Guardiola is an obsessive person and *in his world* everyone one else has to be obsessive too. Pep, like Jose Mourinho and Vicente Del Bosque, expect the very best. The roads they took may have been different but invariably all of them led to the winners' podium. The statistics alone are mind-boggling. If one includes all tournaments, the great managerial triumvirate that is Guardiola, Mourinho and Del Bosque, have amassed in their careers no fewer than forty-five trophies between them, since they entered the bear-pit that is football management. For a thumbnail analysis of the differences in their characters, look at the differences in their victory celebrations. At one end of the spectrum you have the brash, loud, and aggressive, in your face Mourinho who has almost made a second career out of celebrations guaranteed to wind up his opponents. Remember as far back as 2004, when he raced down the Manchester United touchline following the equaliser that saw his Porto side knock the English side out of the Champions League at the last sixteen stage. Fast-Forward to the Camp Nou for the Special One's greatest ever defeat; a 1-0 reversal against Barcelona that was enough to send his Inter side into the Champions League final, following a 3-1 victory in the first leg in Italy. Mourinho's incursion onto the field at the end of the game almost started a riot, and it was only a combination of Victor Valdes and the switching on of the sprinklers that eventually got him off the pitch! Now contrast that with the quiet, unassuming almost embarrassed celebrations practiced by the ever-dignified, Vicente Del Bosque who allowed himself a moment of unbridled joy after Iniesta scored the goal that was to bring the World Cup to Spain for the first time; before suddenly, nervously composing himself when he realised that the attention of the world was on him.

And then somewhere in the middle, there's the enigma that is Pep Guardiola. No less passionate and capable of showing his feelings – especially in victory – than the brash Portuguese manager, but somehow more measured, dignified and inherently more respectful of his situation and his opponents and also not afraid to wear his heart on his sleeve; as he showed after victory in the 2009 World Club Championship, when he dissolved into tears, after securing victory against Estudiantes. To date, the opportunities to witness such celebrations have been numerous. The three managers, between them, have won a total of twelve league titles, six domestic cup finals, six Champions Leagues and one UEFA cup. While Del Bosque also has the small matter of a World Cup and a European Championship (won during his tenure as his country's national coach.) Guardiola and Mourinho have achieved the full house of major trophies, namely League, Cup and Champions League in the same season; Mourinho with Inter and Guardiola with Barcelona. Mourinho, is the only one of the three so far to have won trophies with non-Spanish sides and victories with Porto and Inter Milan place him in an elite list of four managers, namely, Ernst Happel (Feyenoord, Hamburg), Ottmar Hitzfeld (Dortmund, Bayern Munich) and Jupp Heynckes (Real Madrid, Bayern Munich) to have won the Champions League/European Cup with more than one club. But what is it that makes these managers so great? What sets them apart from so many of the others and is there a common denominator that determines their success?

What makes them winners? One of the major things that unites Del Bosque, Guardiola and Mourinho is, of course, a passionate, unconditional and irrefutable love; some might say obsession, for the beautiful game. Guardiola is often heard saying: '*A manager's work is never done,*' which is his way of saying that football dominates his life – sometimes to the expense of those closest to him.

'What's wrong?' Asked one of Pep's colleagues when he saw him looking glum.
'Yesterday, I should have gone to see my daughter in a ballet and I couldn't.'
'Why not?' asked the friend.
'Because I was watching videos of our opponents.'

Mourinho, and in a quieter but no less purposeful way, and Del Bosque, are no different. Once again the difference is in the detail. To use a medical analogy, while Jose will often use a sledgehammer, Pep prefers the scalpel, while Del Bosque's approach is perhaps more holistic. All three are invariably the first to arrive for training, and the last to leave. But if there is one thing that all three men have in common, it is the presence of an unshakeable family unit around them. It is from the closeness and rock-like stability of their family lives that all three men operate. Mourinho, whilst dedicated to football, has publicly proclaimed that: '*The most important thing is my family and being a good father.*' When Guardiola walked away from Barcelona, one of the major reasons cited by him was a need to reconnect with his family who he felt were paying the price for his footballing obsession. Twenty-four years ago, Del Bosque's wife, Trini, gave birth to Alvaro, the second of their three children. Seven weeks later, their son was diagnosed with Down's Syndrome.

'*It was relatively traumatic when we were told,*' said Del Bosque.'*When he was born, the first thing you ask yourself is, why us?* If it affects other people, why not us? It could happen to anyone.'

'*A couple days later we asked ourselves, why couldn't it happen to us? Now we ask ourselves, what would we do without Alvaro?*'

You sense that for Del Bosque, important as football is, when compared to his family-life, it is perhaps ultimately only a game. Similarly with Pep, but in his case a game that invades just about every moment of his life and is a reference to every conversation he ever has. For Mourinho, despite the strength of his family life, despite everything he says, it's all about three things: Winning, winning and being loved.

Vicente Del Bosque

The footballing world has, throughout the years, been littered with decisions so perverse and so illogical, that their only purpose would seem to be bringing into question the sanity of the decision maker. On the 23rd of June 2003, with large numbers of Real Madrid fans still nursing hangovers following the 3-1 victory over Athletic Bilbao that earned the Merengues their 29th La Liga title, Vicente del Bosque was sacked despite a four year tenure that had seen him bring two La Liga titles, two Champions Leagues, one European Super Cup and one World Club Cup to the Santiago Bernabeu. Madrid fans celebrating around the Cibeles fountain would have done well to enjoy their latest triumph. It would be their last opportunity to celebrate the arrival of any major piece of silverware for four years. Five managers would come and go before Los Blancos would win another La Liga. Fabio Capello finally brought home Madrid's 30th La Liga title in 2007 and guess what his reward for that was? You've got it; he was also sacked. Ultimately Del Bosque's greatest strength had, in the eyes of the powers that be, been interpreted as his greatest weakness. Never in the history of football has the innate humility, decency, politeness, avuncularity and just plain goodness of a man been so perceived as an inherent flaw. Del Bosque wasn't so much damned by faint praise as kicked in the teeth with it. Nice guys come last, they say, except of course that Del Bosque had proved that actually sometimes nice guys do win. This '*nice guy*' in fact stands alone as the only manager in the history of the game to have won the three major trophies available to him; namely the Champions League, European International Championship and World Cup. But when Florentino Perez and his fellow assassin, general manager, Jorge Valdano announced they wanted a more modern 'librillo' (notebook), what they meant was they wanted someone with a different image – an image they considered more in line with what they considered Real Madrid to be. The new image came in the shape of the dashingly good-looking, sun-tanned, smart-suited, multi-lingual, Carlos Queiroz who ticked all the boxes. Except for one that is, because apart from one Super Copa (Spain's version of the Community Shield) he won nothing. But what made him the great manager that he was?

Born on 23 December 1950 in the town of Salamanca, Del Bosque, apart from loan spells at Cordoba and Castellon, just about all his club footballing life in Spain was involved with Real Madrid, either as a player or a manager. An organised, efficient rather than spectacular defensive midfielder, he went about the business of playing in the same way he managed: Quietly, solidly and with the utmost respect to all those that he came across along the way.

'*Leadership,*' he said, '*must be likeable, affable, cordial and above all emotional. The fashion of authoritarian leadership is gone. Football is about life. You can't be angry all the time.*'

And he summed up his approach to his players in just eight words. '*A leader is admired; a boss is feared.*' While he was admired by his players for his quiet, dignified, patient approach, the illusion propagated by some is that he is simply a good bloke from the sticks and he managed to create a positive group-dynamic amongst some of the greatest players ever to lace up a pair of football boots, without having a single tactical bone in his body; is as inaccurate as it is insulting. A whole host of brave and innovative tactical decisions, many of them unpopular at the time, showed him to be as tactically astute as the very best in the business. You have to go back as far as the 19th of April 2000, to the Champions League quarter final second leg against Manchester United at Old Trafford; when a piece of tactical brilliance from Del Bosque saw the English club fail to retain the title they had won in Barcelona the previous year. United had gone for, and got, a goalless draw in the first leg at the Bernabeu and were strong favourites to finish the job back in England. Del Bosque's decision to play with just three at the back was a masterstroke that took United totally by surprise. Victories over Bayern Munich in the semis and an easy 3-0 victory over Valencia in the finals, earned Madrid their ninth and, to date, last Champions League. The decision to play Sergi Busquets for all but twenty-eight minutes of the tournament as the main defensive midfielder, when many didn't even consider him good enough for the Barcelona first team, proved pivotal in Spain's conquest of the World Cup.

The introduction of Llorente against Portugal, when most people were screaming for Fabregas and then the introduction of Fabregas in the final, were also decisions that radically affected the results of the game and the ultimate destination of the trophy. And with supposed footballing experts who should have known better, moaning and groaning about '*boring Spain*', during the 2012 European Championships; he showed the doubters with his false number nine tactic; that the number you have on the back of your shirt doesn't necessarily determine how and where you should play. As of the 17th of June 2013, Del Bosque had an international record of seventy-three matches played, with sixty-one wins, six draws and six defeats, with 178 goals scored and forty-eight conceded and a win rate of 83.3%; which by anybody's reckoning must make him one of the most tactical geniuses of all time, or the luckiest man since Lazarus! In March 2011, Del Bosque was brought back into the Madrid fold when he was awarded honorary membership alongside a tennis player (Rafael Nadal) and an opera singer (Placido Domingo). '*Del Bosque is loved because he represents values of moderation, prudence and cohesion,*' said Santiago Segurola, one of Spain's foremost football writers.

'*He is a very interesting figure because he is a Madridista to death. He served the club for over thirty years. He coached the team, won leagues and Champions Leagues and the World Cup; but he is accepted more by the rest of the world than he is by the core of Real Madrid.*'

'*When Florentino Perez awarded him the honorary medal, the normal thing would have been to present it to him in the middle of the pitch at the Bernabeu and people would have risen to applaud a Madridista, but this didn't happen. I think that Real Madrid is a club that divides.*'

Lesser men might have told Señor Perez what to do with his honorary membership. Del Bosque is a better man that that and showed no anger; instead he was quoted in Marca as saying:

'I don't want anyone to feel like they have an obligation towards me. Madrid has given me everything. I'm a man who is very grateful towards Madrid. They don't owe me anything.'

Del Bosque brought the curtain down on an illustrious and dignified career after the 2014 World Cup in Rio. Barring the footballing shock of all time, his Spanish side qualified for the tournament where they tried to retain the World Cup they won in 2010. What were the odds on him becoming the only manager since Italy's Vittorio Pozzo in 1934 and 1938 to win twice for his country?

Jose Mourinho and Pep Guardiola

Great sport has always brought with it great rivalry. Football may well be a team game, but nothing excites the public more than the thrill of one against one; mano-a mano. When Jose Mourinho was appointed manager of Real Madrid before the start of the 2010-11 season, the battle lines were immediately drawn up. Mourinho was a man on a mission; namely to put an end to Barcelona's, and specifically Pep Guardiola's runaway success. And the dapper, charismatic, magnetic Portuguese style icon had every reason to believe he could do it. Originally an assistant manager at the Camp Nou under Bobby Robson and Louis Van Gaal, he had been passed over for the main job and had exacted his revenge when he returned to Catalonia just months earlier to mastermind Inter's victory over Barcelona in the semi-finals of the Champions League. Mourinho would show the watching-world how to stop Barcelona from playing by '*parking the bus*' – a tactic that served as a template in the future for any side seeking to thwart Barcelona's attacking prowess; to hold on to a 1-0 defeat but a 3-2 win on aggregate. '*It is the most wonderful defeat of my life,*' he said shortly after the game. Mourinho was back in town and, as far as the media were concerned, this town wasn't big enough for the both of them. Such was the media involvement in the Guardiola/Mourinho contest, that the teams were almost relegated to minor players in each unfolding drama that saw Guardiola's team pitted against Mourinho's team. Pep Guardiola and Jose Mourinho may have totally different styles of leadership and contrasting personalities, but they do have one very important thing in common: They both love football; in addition to this, they of course, also love winning and are successful in the leadership of their teams. '*Two Picassos in the same period,*' was how the Italian legend Arrigo Sacchi – no slouch himself on the managerial front – described the two managers. If Pep's greatest virtue has been his sense of caution, then Mourinho's is pure excess. While the Portuguese manager will spend time massaging his players' egos, defending the indefensible while simultaneously condemning any sleight, real or imagined, against his own team and players, Guardiola bases his methods on developing his players' confidence through opportunities and motivation; more manager, than massager, of egos.

Their individual style of leadership reflects their personalities.
Mourinho loved his self-appointed nickname, '*the special one*', even though at his second spell at Chelsea he preferred to call himself '*the happy one*'. Time will tell. Special or happy or perhaps both, one thing's for sure, Mourinho is footballing Marmite; you either love him or loathe him. Shortly after his appointment at Chelsea the unflinching, uncompromising Mourinho, as irascible as he can be charming, explained what he expected from his players at Stamford Bridge next season and in so doing effectively detailed just why the wheels fell off at the Bernabeu.

'If you are a top professional; if you are not a selfish person; if you put the club in front of yourself and if you are here to work 100%, for me, for your fellow players and for the club, we will have a wonderful relationship.'

'If you are selfish, if you don't care about the club, if you don't care about the image, if you don't care about the fans, then we are in big trouble. So it depends on you if the relationship is fantastic or not.'

'Sometimes you have groups that take to this in a very easy way; sometimes you have groups when this becomes like a doctrine and then it's easy. But sometimes you have a couple of guys who do not accept these kinds of rules and this is where you have some kind of problematic relationship. When a problematic relationship exists, if it is you and one player or you and two players, then the club in that moment, either supports the problematic players or it supports the manager.'

'If the club supports the manager, the two little guys are out. Easy.'

Contrast this with Guardiola's emotional address to his players on his first day of training at the world-famous, St Andrews in Scotland. In what was effectively his first day at the office, as he set out his stall, he transferred his philosophy to the group.

'Gentlemen, you can imagine what a huge motivation it is for me to be here, to coach this team. Above all I love this club, I would never make a decision that would harm or go against the club. Everything I am going to do is based on my love for FC Barcelona. And we need and want order and discipline.
I've been part of this club for many years and I am aware of the mistakes that have been made in the past. I will defend you to the death, but I can also say that I will be very demanding of you all; just like I will be with myself.'

'I will only ask this of you. I won't tell you off, if you misplace a pass or miss a header that costs us a goal, as long as I know you are giving 100%.
I could forgive you any mistake, but I won't forgive you if you don't give your heart and soul to Barcelona.'

'This is Barca, gentlemen; this is what is asked of us and this is what I will ask of you. You have to give your all.'

'And let's stick together when times are hard. Make sure that nothing gets leaked to the press. I don't want anybody to fight a battle on his own. Let's be united. Have faith in me. As a former player, I have been in your shoes; I know what you are going through, what you are feeling.'

'The style comes dictated by the history of this club and we will be faithful to it. When we have the ball, we can't lose it. And when that happens, run and get it back. That's it basically.'

The squad was seduced and not for the last time. Far from it. Just as the field of politics perceives the world in different ways, so did the respective styles of Barcelona and Madrid with Guardiola and Mourinho; they at the helm demonstrated two different ways of understanding the beautiful game. Madrid has always been characterised by an energetic style of play: Strong, fast and competitive. Barcelona discovered a style made in Holland, with fast, effective passing and offensive play. And whilst in the past, it was frequently presented as a *David and Goliath,* story with Barcelona relishing their roles as underdogs and Madrid more than happy to enjoy their big-cheese status.

What was being witnessed was a fight between two champions slugging it out, toe-to-toe and round after round. In the white corner was, Mourinho the mercenary, fighting for the national institution that is Madrid; and in the maroon and blue corner was, Guardiola, battling for the hopes and aspirations of not just Barcelona, but also for his beloved Catalonia. Pep Guardiola surrounded himself with players from the youth team who shared the same values: Teamwork, good passing, good behaviour on and off the pitch as well as some signings that understood the philosophy. Players who did not share his vision of the world, like Eto'o and Ibrahimovic were soon moved on. By the end of his first season as first team manager, he had brought the league, cup and Champions league back to Catalonia. Towards the end, beaten up, battered, bruised and totally exhausted, he realised he could get no more from his charges; so he walked away. The Portuguese coach, right from his successful league and Champions League winning days at Porto had always been used to leading a team of players whose loyalty to their manager was unconditional. League and cup successes followed at Chelsea, and then at Inter, where he managed the clean sweep of league, cup and Champions League. Anyone who doubted him was brushed aside. Victory was not the main thing; it was everything. And to an extent it worked. Barcelona's three year stranglehold on La Liga was finally broken when Mourinho brought the title back to the Bernabeu for the first time since 2008; a fact he is always eager to bring up early in the conversations when the press discuss his achievements and failings during his stay at Madrid. However, what he failed to do is earn the Castillian side what it wanted most; it's tenth Champions League/European Cup title. Although in true Mourinho style, he tried to turn this apparent failure into a triumph by announcing that he had taken '*Los Blancos*' to three successive Champions League semi-finals. So what of the future? Amidst much fanfare Mourinho, returned to Chelsea where he felt he had some unfinished business. Back to his spiritual home where he felt that people loved him and back into the warm embrace of Roman Abramovich, apparently prepared to forgive the Russian oligarch's indiscretions, where he spent months trying to win the hand of the very man that Jose had been slugging it out with over two brutal seasons, a very reticent Pep Guardiola. Forgive maybe, but forget? Is this true love, or a marriage of convenience?

Only time tells us and alas it didn't work out, Chelsea went on a terrible run and the love affair was over between Mourinho and Abromovich, this time probably permanent. Guardiola meanwhile (batteries suitably recharged after his sabbatical in the US) will be brushing up on his German as he takes the reins at Bayern Munich; without question the most successful side of 2013. Having left the pressure cooker of Barcelona to avoid the demands of having to win it all again, Guardiola now finds himself at a club where the previous incumbent, Jupp Heynckes did precisely the same at Munich as Pep had done at Barcelona winning the German League, Cup and Champions League. Knowing then what he knows now, would he still have taken the job? Only he knows that. Whatever happens, it's pretty safe to assume that we haven't heard the last of Jose Mourinho and Pep Guardiola yet. As this book is going through its final draft, Guardiola is at Manchester City and Mourinho at their biggest rival, Manchester United. The Premier League will benefit from the fascinating battle that will follow for years to come.

THE WORLD OF SIR ALEX FERGUSON

Tell most people that they are a control freak and they would be insulted. To Sir Alex Ferguson it would have verged on a compliment. Control, throughout his twenty-seven years as manager of Manchester United, was a constant aspiration and for the last third of that tenure it became almost total. How he came to savour the word, triumphantly delivering it to audiences from Dublin, where he addressed students, and across the Atlantic to the Ivy League stronghold of Harvard, where he told academics seeking the secrets of his methodology: '

You can't ever lose control. Not when you are dealing with thirty top professionals who are all millionaires. And, if anyone steps outside of my control, that's them dead.'

He meant players, of course. Players such as David Beckham, whose insubordination extended to a refusal to remove a beanie hat during a United team meal, and Ruud van Nistelrooy, who, when informed that he would not be coming off the bench in a cup final, called Ferguson a four-letter anatomical noun. But he didn't actually kill them. Indeed many a player would crave the punishment of a transfer to Real Madrid, which was duly visited upon Beckham and Van Nistelrooy. But they had been banished from Old Trafford and that, to Ferguson, was all that mattered. Any player who challenged the manager of that club – or indeed Aberdeen, the most significant of those at which he worked in Scotland before arriving in Manchester in November 1986 – had either to lose face or go. It was Ferguson's guiding principle: Fundamental, in his view, to the acquisition of three national championships in Scotland and thirteen in England, countless other domestic trophies and a 'European Cup Winners Cup' with first Aberdeen and then United before the Champions League title was brought to Old Trafford in 1999 and brought back in 2008. Ferguson went to Manchester believing he could make success substantially self-perpetuating because, with the first taste of it, came his coveted control.

He had seen this happen at Aberdeen, where the ensuing momentum interrupted the Celtic/Rangers duopoly over Scottish football, and he always intended it to recur on the bigger stage. If anyone ruled England, when Ferguson took over at United, Liverpool did and a few years later, before he had won his first title, they figured in the outlining of his vision of a legacy. '*Only one club in the history of the game has been able to maintain success over two generations,*' he said. He meant Liverpool. '*Now that will be out of my remit,*' he added, erroneously: '*Because my lifespan here will probably stretch no more than another six or seven years – if I'm successful. I'm trying to be realistic. But, whatever I do, I have to lay down a really good foundation that will continue the success. All the work that goes on in this club is not about today but about tomorrow.*' That was in 1992. The reigning champions, George Graham's Arsenal, were about to be deposed by Leeds United under Howard Wilkinson. But Liverpool held the record for titles overall and their total – eighteen – seemed to put them firmly in charge. United had seven. When Ferguson handed over to David Moyes, Liverpool still had eighteen but United had twenty. United had that record. Ferguson had – to use the famous expression he could not remember ever employing – knocked Liverpool off their perch. In terms of European titles, Ferguson had merely narrowed the gap, for Liverpool still led 5-3, but in domestic terms it was indisputable that he had established – there is no other word for it – control. And not just over Liverpool. Ferguson's Manchester United ended up wresting back control from Arsenal, after they had won Doubles under Arsène Wenger, and Chelsea once the initial effect of Jose Mourinho in his first spell had worn off. The returns to prominence of Ferguson's United seemed inexorable in the years preceding his retirement; at the end of yet another triumphant Premier League season in 2013 – by now he was aged seventy-one- Ferguson even exerted a measure of control over his employers; the Glazer family of Florida, who recognised that the value of their investment was best preserved by ceding de facto authority to him. He all but anointed his successor – though he was careful to note in a subsequent autobiography that the decision to appoint Moyes had been '*unanimous*' – and went upstairs to the boardroom on his own lucrative terms.

But it was the power he exerted over players that will be remembered, with admiration, by all those who remain in the profession of football management. He adapted over the years. At first he was hands-on, using the force of his intensely competitive personality to motivate and cajole. By the time he had settled to his task at Aberdeen the fear factor was part of it; as Gordon Strachan recalled: *'I'd never seen anything like it in my life. My dad got angry – but it was nothing like this.'* An away match in Romania produced a case in point. Ferguson had asked the team to adopt new tactics and Strachan, in particular, struggled with his role, being constantly barked at by the manager.

'And then I did the silly thing. I had a go back. Just before half-time. I knew I was in trouble. All the other players knew too. It was a long, dark tunnel at Pitesti and I was walking alone. We got into the dressing room and he hadn't arrived yet. In situations like this, the boys would keep their heads down. He [Ferguson] would always be wearing these shiny black shoes and, sure enough, they appeared. They were moving about. And then they stopped – and they were pointing at me. I could feel the boys on either side of me edging away. And he came right up to me and slaughtered me. I stood up – I wasn't being brave, I just had to breathe and he turned away and with a hand, accidentally knocked a row of cups of tea in the direction of Willie Miller and Alex McLeish. He saw me smirking and that made him knock over this samovar. It was so big and iron-hard and must have been hot – it must have hurt.'

The second half saw Aberdeen improve and go through comfortably on aggregate; helped by a penalty converted by Strachan. *'If I miss this,'* he remembered thinking as he ran up to the spot, *'I'm a dead man.'* Ferguson didn't always have to rant to get a response, however, in his second season at Aberdeen, 1979/80, the club won the Scottish title and his credibility with the players was no longer questioned by any. It was at Aberdeen, too, where he learned the skill of delegation that was to stand him in such good stead when he took the more complicated assignment Manchester United became. He made a change of assistant, bringing to Pittodrie the assertive Archie Knox, with who, he was to have a long association both north and south of the border.

A few weeks later Knox complained: *'I don't know why you brought me here.'* Ferguson asked what he was talking about. *'I don't do anything,'* he replied; albeit in the stronger language that always passed between these men.

'I'm the f------ assistant manager! And you still do all the training sessions. It's ridiculous.' Only one other person was in the room. Teddy Scott was a much-loved part of the Pittodrie furniture; a faithful member of the coaching staff whose opinion, though seldom volunteered, always counted. Scott looked at Knox and then at Ferguson and said: *'He's right.'* Ferguson listened as Scott explained that, instead of barking instructions all the time, he should be observing the players' work, maintaining control. As soon as Ferguson heard his eureka word, he saw Scott's point. The next day Knox was put in charge of training and Billy Stark, who Ferguson later bought from his former club, St Mirren to replace the Manchester-bound Strachan, noticed the change in his behaviour. It would be more subtle. The players would be put through their paces by Knox, but all of a sudden someone would notice a Mercedes gliding into the car park of the training ground. They knew whose it was. They knew he was watching them. And he knew they knew. *'There was nothing he didn't know,'* said Stark. *'That was what he wanted to impose on you. It was all to do with his control thing.'* Ferguson's passion for psychology had been stimulated by friendship with the canny Jock Stein, who later chose him as assistant with the Scotland team (Ferguson became temporary manager at the 1986 World Cup after Stein had died of a heart attack towards the end of a crucial qualifier in Wales.) But mind games then became second nature to the boy from Govan. He played mind games with referees, the opposition and even – indeed especially - his own people. He told his Aberdeen players that the press, the referees – the whole establishment of Scottish football – were against them and this built a stockade mentality. It became his world and he didn't emerge from it until he retired. It could be said that his greatest achievement was to convince the players and staff of Manchester United – one of the world's biggest and richest clubs – that everyone was against them and so they'd have to fight and work a little harder for success. In this sense, he made a world of his own. And it was very much a world of work.

The example he set was phenomenal. While restructuring the youth-development system, he changed the first team with an increasing volume of purchases, almost always conducted in his presence. Jose Mourinho remembered being a relatively young man when he first met Ferguson in Barcelona. He was interpreting on the Catalan club's behalf during negotiations for the transfer of Jordi Cruyff and being impressed by the force with which the manager helped chairman Martin Edwards and other United officials to do the best possible deal. Back home, Ferguson would arrive at his office overlooking the pitch at the training ground soon after dawn, and any journalists seeking interviews would have to share his readiness to do the red-eye shift, because from 9am the knocks on the door would begin as the coaching staff asked for instructions about the day's sessions. And Ferguson would often arrive home after midnight; always to be met by his selfless wife Cathy, whose part in his single-minded quest for footballing success was finally acknowledged in his 2013 autobiography. The process of delegation was to widen as Ferguson, whose ability to live with changing times was inseparable from his managerial longevity. He hired experts in everything from diet to podiatry, but, asked once why he had not engaged a battery of psychologists, he replied: '*I do that myself.*' His excellence in the field was never more vividly demonstrated than in the case of Eric Cantona; the player who changed a good team into a great one and made United perennial champions. Ferguson signed him in November 1992 after a tipoff from Gerard Houllier, then manager of the French national team, and a little concerned that Cantona was suffering from a personality clash with Howard Wilkinson – the boss of reigning champions Leeds United. One day Ferguson happened to be in the Manchester United chairman's office when a call came from Leeds about Denis Irwin. Irwin was not for sale but Ferguson passed Edwards a note asking him to inquire about Cantona. The Leeds director on the line, Bill Fotherby, indicated that a deal might be possible and the rest is history. Suddenly, with Cantona in the team, United's scoring rate doubled. Ferguson had already sorted out the defence by pairing Steve Bruce with Gary Pallister and by the end of the season, he had replaced Wilkinson as manager of the champions.

Cantona, the catalyst supreme, was asked some years later what Ferguson had done to make a hitherto restless soul feel so effectively at home and replied: "*He gave me freedom to be involved completely and not feel in jail. That's psychology – man to man.*"

By then Ferguson had adopted a ploy that became almost his trademark – the pointing at the watch. In his autobiography he said it was less to alert the referee than to discomfort the opposition while they were trying to hang on against United in the latter stages of matches. But towards the end of the first successful title campaign, there was the home game with Sheffield Wednesday that will forever be remembered for Bruce's two goals. Wednesday had taken the lead midway through the second half with a penalty given by John Hilditch, who had begun the afternoon as a linesman but then deputised for the injured Michael Peck in the middle. It had been a simple decision – Paul Ince had tripped Chris Waddle – but its implications seemed to stun Old Trafford. Might the title slip away yet again? Ferguson could not afford such negative thoughts. He had to think positively. As time began to run out, he was glad he had been chipping away at Hilditch before Peck limped off, reminding the then linesman of how many stoppages there had been. With just five minutes of normal time to go, Bruce got his head to a corner. 1-1. And the bombardment went on. But Wednesday survived until six minutes into stoppage time, when Bruce rose again to get the winner. Amid scenes of unbridled joy, Ferguson ran to the touchline and his assistant, Brian Kidd, continued to the pitch, where he sank to his knees and glanced at the heavens, knowing that Old Trafford's wait was all but over. A dynasty was born – and with it the phrase '*Fergie time*'.

Ferguson's football world had always stretched beyond Britain's borders. Versed in the European game from his time as a striker with Dunfermline Athletic; in a fine side whose scalps included Everton and West Bromwich Albion, he had fallen for the sounds and smells of Spanish football in particular. And towards the end of his time in charge of Aberdeen, he confided to friends that he would leave this happy ship only for Manchester United or Barcelona.

So imagine his pleasure at completing a Spanish double in the Cup-Winners' Cup when, having overcome Real Madrid in the 1983 final with Aberdeen. He guided United to triumph over Barcelona eight years later. That was after the FA Cup had been landed in 1990, at the culmination of the campaign sparked by the Mark Robins goal at Nottingham Forest that was said – exaggeratedly – to have kept Ferguson in a job. The European trophy confirmed that Ferguson's methods were taking the first team in the right direction; while chairman Edwards and fellow directors led by Sir Bobby Charlton knew that in the background there were kids who would be all right. Ferguson had told them, way back when he was offered the job in November 1986, that it would be a long haul and the first Premier title – in 1992/3 – signified the journey's end and a new start. The production of young players had always been fundamental to Ferguson's grand design and around that time of the title celebration, word began to sweep football that United had a youth team capable of dominating the English game for years. The only trouble, according to Alan Hansen's declaration on *Match of The Day,* was that: '*You win nothing with kids.*'

United were to win plenty with Paul Scholes, David Beckham, Gary and Phil Neville, Nicky Butt and perhaps the most spectacular capture of Ferguson's youth revolution, Ryan Giggs; who the manager and his staff had persuaded on board after he had been training with rivals Manchester City. Ferguson had a natural gift for making decisions, in both the long and short terms. His short game had been brilliantly illustrated by the ruthless axing of goalkeeper Jim Leighton after a 3-3 draw with Crystal Palace in the original final of the 1990 FA Cup. The replay was won with Les Sealey between the posts – and the securing of Cantona. And now the long game kicked in. Such was the advance of Beckham, Giggs and company, that the loss of Cantona could be almost seamlessly survived as the trophies piled up. Ferguson's control was unchallenged now and, when Keane went after criticising teammates once too often, business was as usual. Ferguson's mantra was that the manager had to be the most important man at the club and he could enforce it as he liked; eventually allowing Beckham to drift to Madrid as yet another superstar emerged in Cristiano Ronaldo.

Only Wayne Rooney succeeded in rocking the boat and it may not have been wholly coincidental that, when the Merseysider's mutual discontent with the manager became persistent, Ferguson took his own decision to step up to the boardroom. The strain of maintaining control could be handed over to Moyes.

When he subsequently published his 2013 autobiography, the split with Keane was graphically described and, when Keane retorted that: '*He doesn't know the meaning of the word.*' The Irishman meant loyalty. That might have stung, for loyalty had always been part of the Ferguson creed. Those who stayed inside his tent were rewarded. Those who ventured outside were scorned. For some he stretched further than others. Cantona was indulged, notably on a celebrated occasion, when, after the squad had been ordered to wear club blazers and ties at a function at Manchester Town Hall, the Frenchman turned up in a shell-suit. No one said a thing as they waited for Ferguson to arrive. When he did, he merely glanced at the odd one out and muttered to aides: '*Oh, that Cantona – what a man!*' This was because Cantona never really let him down. Even after the incident at Crystal Palace, when he was handed a long ban for kicking a home fan, who had jeered him, he came back as good as ever and repaid the debt on the field. Ferguson saw a bit of himself – the early rebel who led a strike at a tool-making factory in Glasgow – in Cantona and even Keane. He built a club in his own image. He might have increased the staff tenfold as football, ever richer, thirsted for the myriad little advantages that specialists could bring. But he never really changed; the fact his closest friends included folk from his Govan childhood, emphasised that. He remained the same man. It was just that Manchester United became his wider world. There might have been better tacticians; there might have been equally artful managers of men; there might have been just as sharp judges of a players and there might – though it is unlikely – have been executives of such boundless energy. Others might have equalled the intellect that caused at least one Prime Minister – Tony Blair – to seek his counsel. Others might have been able to command a room. But Ferguson had the lot and it was his range that created the most enduringly successful institution in the history of English football. In his world, there could be only one winner.

Ronaldo and Messi

They are two of the greatest footballers ever seen and have remarkable similarities in their stories, but are very different people. Having the common sense to have continuity in who is around you is not rocket science; being a footballing genius is. They both left their homes at a very early age to pursue their dream of playing professional football. At just twelve/thirteen years of age, both these mercurial talents left the safety and comfort of an environment they knew. Ronaldo left Madeira, Portugal and travelled to Sporting Lisbon. Messi left Argentina with his family and travelled all the way to Barcelona. A child, thrown into a world alien to them, will need the support of their immediate world (family); in order to help them cope with the change. Even though Messi travelled to Spain with both parents and his sister, his mother and sibling went back to Argentina as they didn't adjust well to life in Catalonia. Ronaldo on the other hand, went by himself; hence the reason he is a little more self-focused than Messi. Both of these guys missed out on their youth and adolescence. They didn't do the normal things kids do, like hanging out with mates and having carefree fun. They went from being young children to fully-fledged football-playing adults, without going through natural growing up and adolescence. Both became *'man-kids'* and they had to grow up very quickly as at an early age they had the responsibility of looking after their families. At the age of eighteen both were the breadwinners and both were keeping families well looked after. That itself can be a burden or an inspiration; the latter was the repercussion. Something that kept them both sane, was sticking to their traditions no matter what anyone said or if other kids made fun of them. Messi was the most Argentinian of Argentinians and spoke with a broad accent. Although some kids would make fun of it, his father was around to remind him of his roots and they would happily converse at home in the tongue Messi was accustomed to; this was important. Messi also bandaged his feet before putting his boots on. People thought there was something wrong with his feet, but it was something he learnt in Argentina and he kept doing it regardless of the funny looks he would get. His father, strong as an ox, encouraged his son to continue doing everything Messi felt comfortable with.

Ronaldo had a strong Madeiran accent and kids his age would find it funny, but no one was laughing when he was running rings round everyone and scoring countless goals. In Ronaldo's mind and world, he has had to do everything himself (to an extent) and that is why he seems a bit more selfish than Messi. Messi and Ronaldo are both obsessed with playing football and this is where they have the most in common. They are first to arrive at the training ground and last to leave. But what will surprise you is that when a talent is the best in the world at their craft, there is a cloud that consistently hovers over them. It is something that they all know is out of their control. Ronaldo and Messi live in the constant world of fear and uncertainty. Because no matter how good they are and no matter how much money they make, they never know what's going to happen tomorrow. The big fear is injury.

Now, here is my theory of the *'tripod'*:

So imagine that Messi is a camera and underneath him is a tripod.
In order for that camera to take a great picture, all three legs of the tripod have to be fixed, stable and in the right place. If one leg wobbles then the picture doesn't happen. So, to be the greatest player in the world, all three legs of the tripod must be there: 1) Talent 2) Dedication 3) Luck and timing. If any leg of the tripod collapses then the worlds don't collide to create a symphony of legacy. From day one, Messi has had his father, Jorge Horácio, around him to guide the mercurial talent through the early and tough years and has played a huge part in keeping Messi's feet firmly on the ground. One of the things that ties the family roots is the love of Argentinian food. One of the first things Jorge did when arriving in Barcelona, was to find Argentinian restaurants, and to this day the family still enjoy their native food as a regular tradition. Ronaldo's father, Dinis, died in 2005 and from that time he has hailed the role Alex Ferguson played in his life as a father figure. But it is his mother who has been the constant from day one. She is the person who reminds him of his humble beginnings and gives him the unconditional love and support. Ronaldo's mother, Maria Dolores dos Santos Aveiro, admitted that she considered having a termination when she found out she was expecting the global superstar.

Times were so tough in those days that Maria didn't know whether to bring another child into the world. His agent – Jorge Mendes has also played a strong role father figure role.
Ronaldo had already been at Manchester United since 2003, when his father suffered liver failure and was admitted to a London hospital. A poignant exchange between Ronaldo and Ferguson cemented the respect Ronaldo had for Ferguson as a father figure: '*When my daddy was dying, he was in a hospital in London, and it was not good. I said to (Sir Alex) Ferguson: 'Coach I want to go.'*
It was a crucial moment of the season.
Ronaldo said at the time. 'Ferguson responded with: *'Football doesn't mean anything compared with your dad. If you want to go, go.'*
Ronaldo was deeply appreciative of that. The crucial aspect of a father figure is the respect factor. People like Ronaldo and Messi live in a world of crazy adulation, unthinkable wealth and access to whatever they want so they need someone who is a constant and a person they can respect. Ferguson gave Ronaldo tough love and helped make the Portuguese talent one of the best players in the world. When an individual receives so much adulation, there is a craving for normality; a need to just have people around who know them and not just the persona. By having someone in their lives, who they can look up to and know are of resolute and strong character helps keep them focused and grounded. People in general (especially young talent) need someone to answer to; it's easy for young footballers to go off the rails. What would most young men do with millions of adoring fans and even more millions in the bank? We can't blame footballers for thinking they were or are indestructible.

Boxers

Craftsmen of the pugilistic art, have the irony of having to rely solely on themselves in the ring, but can have a disastrous existence if they do not have the right people around them. Some of the world's greats have admitted to fighting demons and depression; along with having to cope with crazy mood swings. It's fair to say that some boxers rely on the sport and the intense discipline it demands in order to keep a sense of stability in their lives. Boxing is a brutal existence and like gambling, boxers have to know when to stop. Their trainers and advisors must make the unenviable decision of knowing when to throw the towel in, both inside and outside the ring.

Respected boxing writer Pat Sheehan said: *'If you want loyalty from a boxer then buy a dog.'*

It's a phrase whispered by boxing promoters, who are sick to the back teeth of fighters walking out on them just as they start to earn the big money. Just as a promoter starts to think he is about to get a decent return on his investment, he is blown out and another promoter, who is promising more money, walks away with his arm around the boxer's shoulder. *'Sign here please son.'* This in some respects is similar to football; there is always someone trying to turn the heads of sportspeople; normally because of money and the opportunity to earn lots quickly. Those people are not interested in building up the footballer or boxer, but instead, in turning the heads of the individual when there is money to be made. Building up a fighter to world title potential, is a combination of financial backing and weaving your way around the fighting politics, plus of course a significant amount of skill and bravery inside the ring. And not necessarily in that order. The team a young boxer puts around him before a punch has even been thrown, is arguably the most crucial step any fighter will make in his short career. A boxer's most intimate choice for his team is his trainer. This will be the person who knows his charge is going to get hit and at times seriously hurt. But he must ignore the pain being felt and urge his fighter forward in search of a victory. There must be an unshakable and largely unquestionable loyalty between a fighter and the man in his corner, or it will very quickly fall apart.

There must also be total trust between the fighter and his manager because this is the crucial first stage of looking after what is earned in prize money.
And there needs to be a belief that the promoter, the man who takes most of the financial knocks when things go wrong, is looking after the fighter's best interests and not his own. So the team should read – boxer, trainer, manager, promoter. It sounds simple, but there is an awful lot of room for matters to go belly up whether the boxer wins or loses. There's no blue print for how a fighter chooses his team; it really is a case of what works for one, doesn't work for another; but he must take extreme caution or the millions available to the best in the world, will never materialise. What every boxer needs to admit to himself, when he starts out with dreams of becoming a world champion, is that the hardest sport in the world is business. And if they start to think that appointing close members of their family to look after their affairs is a sure fire way of getting it right ... they'd be wrong. The most recent high profile example of a boxer's family at war, centres around Ricky Hatton; who, it is claimed, no longer talks to his parents, Ray and Carol. '*Hitman*' Hatton, was one of the most adored fighters of all time in British boxing history. He became a two weight world champion; thrilling fans and taking so many of them to Las Vegas when he fought Floyd Mayweather and Manny Pacquiao that you would have thought you were having a stroll around Manchester's Piccadilly, instead of walking down the Strip. Billy Graham was Hatton's respected trainer, who worked without a contract. The shake of a hand between them was deemed good enough and Ricky never failed to pay up, but it still led to a bitter court case. Dad, Ray, looked after Hatton's business affairs and Frank Warren was the promoter in charge when Hatton won the world IBF light welterweight title for the first time in front of his screaming fans at the Manchester Arena. From those head-spinning heights, Ricky crashed to the bottom of the pile with allegations of drug-taking and serious booze-benders, which eventually saw Hatton admit himself to hospital in a bid to rid himself of his demons.
And what many regarded as a dream team simply fell apart. Graham was ditched as Hatton's trainer, with claims he could no longer do the hard work required in the gym; needing at times pain killers to blot out the pain from bad hand damage caused by pad work.

He took Hatton to court for around £1million in lost earnings after he was let go. Warren was shelved as promoter when Team Hatton took control of their future by negotiating directly with broadcasters. And, dad, Ray was hit by unsubstantiated claims of mismanaging his son's affairs, which led to a shocking scene at the back of Hatton's gym in Hyde, Cheshire, when father and son were filmed on CCTV having a fight.
Ray, Carol and Ricky allegedly haven't spoken for three years and he refuses to let them see their grandchildren. Mum, Carol described the situation in an interview with the Sunday Mirror and said: *'Ricky is more or less dead to us.'* It didn't quite come to blows when super-middle-weight king, Joe Calzaghe, who retired undefeated, decided it was time to ditch his trainer, who also happened to be his dad, Enzo. Only Joe forgot to tell his own flesh and blood he was out of the picture. His father discovered he was ditched when he read the story in the morning papers; he had trained his son for some time in an old blue shed at the end of his garden; the most unlikely place to give birth to a world champion, but it worked brilliantly until there was a big dip in Joe's fighting form when his record reached the 27-0 mark. Calzaghe senior recalled in his autobiography:

'The problem was Joe. I had gone from loving every second of what we were doing, to both of us dreading being in that gym together.' He also said: *'His attitude was poor. He acted as though he didn't care anymore.'*

'The Calzaghe father/son professional relationship was falling apart and I felt helpless to stop the rot.'

The reason Enzo was let go, was that some in the camp believed he had taken Joe as far as he could. Enzo was told his relationship with his boxer son was *'too close'*; an accusation proved totally wrong as Enzo remained in Joe's corner, despite the very pubic bust-up. Joe went on to unify the world super-middle-weight title, following his almost flawless performance against Jeff Lacy with a unanimous points win over Mikkel Kessler for the WBA, WBC and WBO titles at the Millennium Stadium in Cardiff. The most successful father/son relationship is surely the Mayweather's Floyd senior and junior, but even then it has not been without significant problems.

The split between flesh and blood reached such a peak, that Senior Mayweather agreed to train Hatton for his world title fight against his son Floyd. Just imagine that. A dad telling a rival how to beat up his son! But to prove blood is thicker than water he is now back training his son.

Amir Khan is a good example of chopping and changing trainers; maybe believing the grass is greener and he is now on his fourth in Virgil Hunter who was preceded by Oliver Harrison, Jorge Rubio, who lasted just one fight, and Freddie Roach. There is stability in the business side, however with Khan's dad, Shah looking after his son's matters, although family friend Asif Vali was recently axed from the team as business manager. Bad choices when appointing a team for a boxer leads one way; bad advice, zero motivation and professionalism being tossed out of the window by *'experts'* who don't know what they are doing. More importantly, without the right team you don't get the activity. The right team will progress a boxer in the right way, which enables them to learn and improve. The wrong team leads to inactivity and bad advice while any inactivity leads to zero learning. Time out of the ring provides the opportunity to stray. The most decisive relationship is boxer-trainer. But it goes beyond that. You could have the best trainer in the world, but if you don't get the fights that relationship doesn't matter anyway. Boxer-trainer is the most crucial part of the team, because it provides the basics of getting taught the ring skills. However if they are not progressed in the right way, in the promoter sense and the activity sense, then once more all the effort is a waste of time. Some promoters are more hands on than others. They will actively seek to be a recognised figure in the team and not just in the background tying up business deals. Promoters should instinctively know how many times a fighter should fight, whether they need a break, if they have picked up injuries or are struggling at their weight. They also need to look after a fighter's mental wellbeing, as well as their physical condition. As both combine to affect motivation and performance. One of the problems in boxing is that so much BS is spoken by people desperate to be part of that indefinable glamour which surrounds boxing. You can't fit bathrooms one day and the next declare yourself a promoter, although many have tried!

Promoters need experience of the marketing world, be business savvy and have bundles of what many consider is in short supply in the boxing world – common sense. Fighters need common sense when choosing their promoter, and of course, these days a promoter must have a TV contract. If a pro-boxer doesn't have those things behind him, he'll end up skint and with a career not worth a carrot. Frank Warren has taken the TV contract a step further and set up his own specialist, independent boxing channel, *Box Nation*, after deciding to go it alone and not rely on the likes of broadcast giant Sky TV. Promoters must chase the right purses for their stable, but can end up getting criticised when the boxer gives up home advantage to fight on foreign soil. If the boxer doesn't want to go, then he can dig his heels in and say no, but the main reason for fighting in someone else's back yard is that the money on offer is usually far in excess of what can be earned at home. Risk has to be balanced against reward. And then of course, if you are fighting away, your promoter's negotiating skills will be called into play, as he demands perhaps, a rematch clause or all neutral judges. One of the hottest debating points is whether a promoter can also be a fighter's manager; it's not allowed in the United States but it is here in the UK. It's been called a ridiculous position because how, for instance, can you be a fighter's manager and then negotiate the best deal with the promoter who also happens to be you! As in any business there are some unscrupulous operators, who are willing to take advantage of any naivety. If a youngster with lots of potential gets caught up in a long contract but promised bouts are not delivered, then it could be career over for them as they can't make any money. Some fighters are more knowledgeable about the business side than others – specifically ones who are self-managed. For instance the super-middle-weight World Champion, Carl Froch, has been around the business for a long while and knows how it works. He is now getting the rewards for his career and he doesn't need a manager to do it for him. Froch knows the value of international broadcast rights; he is aware of what sponsorship deals can add to his bank balance and is more than aware of what it costs to stage big shows and exactly what he brings to the table. He started early as an entrepreneur, buying his first house, which he still owns, with money borrowed on his credit card.

At the last count, Froch was up to around fifteen properties; not including the mansion he lives in with fiancé Rachael Cordingley. It's not the Frochs of the world who have to worry about the future, but the naive young professionals who are starting their careers. They are the ones who need managerial guidance. And it doesn't matter if a fighter's contract with a promoter is two pages long or twenty. If a fighter has a legitimate reason to walk away, then it doesn't matter how long the contract is; he can walk and the promoter once more has to pick up the pieces. There are huge costs to come out of a fighter's purse and it's not rocket science to work out that if they are only fighting twice a year and say picking up £5,000 a fight, then the wallet is hardly bulging by the time they have paid everybody out. The trainer might get 15% and the manager 20%; then there are training camp costs and the day-to-day expense of living. What's left? Not a lot. And that's if the fight goes ahead.

Kell Brook of Sheffield had to pull out of a world title shot against American Devon Alexander three times because of a succession of injuries to both fighters. Those three camps would have cost Brook around £50,000 and he had zero pay because the fight didn't take place. Picking up training injuries are the real tough part for fighters and it should somehow be budgeted into their plan for world domination, because when a bout falls through, there is no payday. It's not like other jobs where someone breaks their leg but can still go to work with their leg up and carry on earning. With boxing, if a boxer has an injury, they can't earn because they can't fight and the same applies if they don't have an opponent. There has been a trend of boxers forming promotional companies to maximise their earnings and Mayweather junior has done it brilliantly. His last fight was said to have generated around £75million, with the largest slice going to him. But it is only the super successful that it works for. One boxer, who believed he could do everything, as well as become World Heavyweight Champion, was Audley Harrison; the Sydney Olympic Games gold medallist. Harrison was in control of his own affairs from the outset, as the boss of *A' Force Promotions'* and his business received a massive shot in the arm when the BBC agreed to pay him £1million for his first ten fights.

He was boxer, manager, promoter and some say trainer, as he was alleged to have organised his own sessions doing exactly as he pleased rather than following instructions. It should have been the stuff of dreams except Harrison, as promoter, did not spend big money on undercards as it would hit his own earning potential as headline fighter. The result was that many considered the shows poor value for money with Harrison upsetting fans. But he is not the only boxer who couldn't deliver as a promoter. Former undisputed World Heavyweight Champion, Lennox Lewis tried it with *Lions Promotions* but his foray didn't last long and Joe Calzaghe's attempt at promoting never really got off the ground. Promoters have to be the flamboyant face of boxing, because the aim is to put bums on seats and convince TV companies their fighters are worth airing on the small screen. They don't come more gregarious than American Don King who re-wrote the rules when it came to being a promoter. King virtually ran the heavyweight division. He was looking after Joe Frazier ahead of the world title bout in Jamaica against George Foreman in 1973 and drove in a limo with Smokin' Joe to the National Stadium in Kingston. Frazier was knocked out in the second round and King unashamedly went straight to Foreman, gave him a big hug in the ring and left with him on a plane back to America to talk business. King whose electric shock hairstyle made him instantly recognisable was one of the sport's most controversial characters and even served time for manslaughter. He promoted among many others: Muhammad Ali, Mike Tyson, Tim Witherspoon, Larry Holmes and Lennox Lewis. King was also sued by all of those. One of the longest serving promoters is Bob Arum, of *Top Rank* in America, who graduated from Harvard and became a United States attorney under then Attorney General John F Kennedy in the Fifties. While he was a promoter, he also committed a host of felonies which included an alleged bribe of $10,000 paid to the then president of the IBF, Bob Lee, so Foreman could fight Axel Schulz instead of a top contender. Arum said, with a smile on his face, while promoting one fight: '*Yesterday I was lying. Today I am telling the truth!*' One new face on the scene is Anthony Joshua, the super heavyweight gold medallist from the London Games in 2012. Even when part of the GB Olympic team training at the English Institute of Sport in Sheffield, he would be asking reporters all sorts of questions about how the pro game worked.

He once asked: '*How do I become a promoter? Some of those guys seem to take all the money but without taking any of the punches!*'
From winning his Olympic gold medal, it was something like ten months before Joshua announced his promoter and trainer, admitting he took so long because he wanted to get it right. Joshua revealed:

'I really took time deciding who I wanted to sign for and I spoke to many, many promoters. It's so important to get the right team. I took my time and I finally got it all together going with Matchroom as my promoter and working with Tony Sims as my trainer/manager. The fighters get all the headlines and the limelight but there is a big team behind them who put in hours and hours of work. The business side of boxing is very important to me. I have a good family that help me. But taking care of the business side takes a lot of your time and I can't do it all by myself. And so it would seem, neither can any other boxer.'

Formula One

It often surprises people to learn this, but research shows that Formula One is clearly the second most popular sport in most European countries, after football. F1 tends to inspire intense passion among the faithful and quizzical bemusement among the unconverted. What is it about cars going around in circles? And how special are the drivers? They are sitting down to do this sport, after all. The fact is that Formula One has an appeal at many levels: close racing, the pure speed in qualifying, the politics, the personalities, the technology and the list is endless. But one of the most powerfully appealing things about F1 is the mentality of the drivers: The focus, the bravery, the determination, the ruthlessness and, let's face it, the insanity. These guys are a breed apart. Consider Robert Kubica, who suffered one of the worst accidents F1 has ever seen in the 2007 Canadian Grand Prix. Check it out on YouTube if you haven't seen it. He hit a concrete wall at 190 mph; the car rolled multiple times and destroyed itself while his body was subjected to a peak G force of 75g. Ten years earlier and he would have been killed without doubt. But the cars have been made much stronger. He walked out of hospital the next day. Reluctantly he was obliged by F1 doctors to miss the race the following weekend, but was back racing again twenty days after his near-death accident. Consider Kimi Raikkonen in the 2002 Belgian Grand Prix, at Spa. A car had blown its engine at the top of a steep hill. Its contour formed the daunting Eau Rouge corner. A curtain of white smoke formed a visual barrier on the crest of the hill; somewhere inside the fog was a stationary car. Locked in a furious duel with Michael Schumacher for pole position. Raikkonen did not lift off the throttle and plunged into the smoke at over 180 mph. What kind of person would do that? It's probably clear already that F1 drivers are not normal human beings. No elite sportspeople are of course. They have a special talent, which sets them apart and they live in a rarefied world of private jets, supermodel girlfriends, endorsements and worldwide fame. But F1 drivers' mentalities are also shaped by something else – risk. Ayrton Senna was the last driver to die in a Formula 1 car in 1994 and thankfully the cars are much safer today, as Kubica's example illustrates.

But still the ghosts of former heroes linger in the mind-set of the current stars. In the 1950s, '60s and '70s a racer's mentality was shaped by the reality that if you were a Grand Prix driver, you had a one in five chance of dying doing your sport. Much of the glamour, which is still associated with F1, comes from appreciating the beauty and brevity of a life lived on the limit. These are extreme people doing extreme things, with the ever-present chance of paying the ultimate price for a mistake. The cars are safer now, due to advances in materials and regulations, but risk shadows them wherever they go and this informs their mentality. They will seek the best possible deal from a team or a sponsor, not because it means they can get a better jet, but because this contract may be their last. This breeds a unique kind of single-mindedness, which top drivers possess. It is an important quality. With only twenty-two seats in Formula 1, it's extremely hard to get an opportunity to race at the top level, unless you come from a very wealthy family or are part of a sponsor or manufacturer's young driver programme.

Sebastian Vettel's path to F1 was made possible by BMW and by Red Bull, who backed him from early on. Lewis Hamilton was picked up by the McLaren team as a thirteen-year-old, and they funded him all the way to F1. Both came from ordinary working class families. But there are many other examples of talented drivers who climb the ladder in junior racing series, but then hit a glass ceiling because their funding will not extend to the F1 rate card. Typically drivers in mid-grid and back of the grid teams bring between five to ten million dollars a year in sponsorship and such is the squeeze financially with rising costs that teams often take these drivers, over talented ones, with no money. This is not true at the very top end of the sport but is certainly true for the rest of the field.

Michael Schumacher is an interesting case. His father was a bricklayer by trade in Germany and he could not afford to pay for karts for his son to learn in. However he was employed as a manager of the local kart track, and so Michael would drive the karts every evening after school and at weekends. He is probably an example of the '10,000 hours theory' of becoming an expert through repetitive practice.

His whole childhood revolved around driving. As he progressed and needed to travel further afield, Schumacher found local backers who would take him to races. Without this, he would have had no future as a driver. So he found himself, from the age of eleven, travelling around Europe with adults and strangers. He said: '*They lacked respect for my friends and my family and they were often underhand and not always straight.*' To make matters worse, he didn't have his own father for company. '*We couldn't afford it,*' said Schumacher.

'*He wasn't around like many fathers to support and explain and be there for good moments and bad. Was I a little adult at eleven? Yes. I had to learn to deal with all kinds of people.*'

Schumacher had to grow up quite quickly. He formed a protective shell around himself emotionally to deal with the often course realities of adult life. He carried this through his entire career: a tough exterior, a confident, ruthless face to show the world. When the reality was actually, he was quite a vulnerable and sensitive person. But it's how he coped with the situation and got what he wanted, which was a chance to shine as a driver. His single-mindedness and the hardships he had had to endure to get the top, meant that he left no stone unturned when seeking competitive advantage over his rivals. His attention to detail was legendary. Once he had money, he spoiled the people who worked closely around him with gifts. He wanted them to be happy so that they would do their best work for him. Being reliant on others in his formative years also left him with a lifelong feeling that he owed people and this also informed the way he went about his racing. He was so burdened with a feeling of responsibility, that he put a huge amount of pressure on himself to deliver wins and championships and this made him the winning machine he was: 91 Grands Prix victories and seven World Championships. Schumacher defined a benchmark that all other drivers have to try to match. Success in sport, isn't just about doing your job properly, it's also about never giving anything away to the opposition.

A brilliant footballer can dribble around three players and score a wonder goal, but if one of his defenders makes a mistake and gives the opposition the ball and they score, it nullifies the advantage. Schumacher brought this mentality to racing; never giving anything away; pushing everything to the limit all the time and in this he was supported by his team, with the key management figures all backing his vision. To be successful in F1 today you have to have this mentality and never let it slip.

Red Bull Racing has dominated since 2010 by doing just that. All built around Sebastian Vettel. There is a side to F1 drivers, which revels in the challenge and this probably has something to do with the fact that there is a machine involved in the process; something that needs to be mastered. In addition to the challenge of competing against other elite athletes, Juan Manuel Fangio, the five times World Champion from the 1950s once said:

'There are those who stay out of trouble and then there are the adventurers. We racing drivers are adventurers; the more difficult something is, the greater the attraction that comes from it.'

This speaks to the side of a racers' mind, which is prepared to do what Raikkonen did in 2002 or Kubica in 2007. Racers have to push the boundaries all the time to feel alive. When Schumacher retired from driving in 2006, he took up skydiving and motorcycle racing, where he broke a bone in his neck. Bored with life outside the cockpit, he came back to F1 for three years, but he was already forty and he couldn't match his former glories. Formula 1 is certainly a sport where you have to make things happen for yourself, both in terms of taking opportunities on the track and off it.

Ayrton Senna was the first of the drivers with the '*win at all costs*' mentality. He and Alain Prost had a bitter duel in the late 1980s, which led to them driving each other off the road to settle two successive World Championships.

Prost once said of Senna: '*He thinks he can't kill himself, because he believes in God and things like that.*' The spiritual side of Senna was something quite unique in the sport. But his mentality was to win at all costs and Schumacher took that on from him. Vettel and Alonso are the spiritual heirs to this today, but Alonso's Ferrari team keeps failing to come up with a fast enough car for him to challenge Vettel. A driver is dependent on a car, as much as a footballer is dependent on getting himself into a winning team, if he wants major honours. The informed view is that Formula One is around 75% the car and 25% the driver. So the best driver isn't going to win consistently in a poor car, but he might win one or two races. While having the best car is not a guarantee of success. The driver still needs to go out and get the maximum from it in both qualifying (which sets the grid positions for the start) and the race. There are some circuits, like Monaco, where the driver can make the difference, because pure performance in the car isn't so important; judgement of the speed and running close to the barriers carries a premium. But in general for a driver, getting yourself into a competitive team is essential. How the drivers go about getting the best for themselves differs dramatically. Typically an F1 driver will have a manager, who travels with him to races and promotional days, eats with him in the evening and generally hangs around in the background. The best managers tend to focus on one client at a time, so they can ensure the driver gets exactly what he needs. Schumacher had this relationship with Willi Weber; Jenson Button has Richard Goddard and Fernando Alonso has Luis Garcia. Lewis Hamilton is someone that is taking control of his world in a different way to a lot of sporting superstars. He is gradually relying on himself more and more. After being managed by his father, he took advice and signed with Simon Fuller's *19* group. This step was made to take him to the so called next level.

The aim was to have a long-term strategy and turn him into a brand like David Beckham. *19* wanted to link Motorsport to the worlds of music and entertainment. As part of this strategy, *19* moved Hamilton away from the McLaren team, which had nurtured him since childhood, to the Mercedes team, which was building up to challenge for top honours.

From Hamilton's point of view the move was important for him to move on and develop as a sportsman and as a person. At McLaren there was always a side of the relationship, which echoed his status as an apprentice, despite coming of age by winning the 2008 World Championship. But, after dismissing the services of his father, Anthony, he then split with his girlfriend and in late 2014 split from Simon Fuller's *19* management. These were crucial moves that went totally against the *'Beckham path'*.

Hamilton and Nicole Scherzinger became a *Power Couple.* This was great for both of their careers. There is a fascination with couples and their lives.
It's quite simple; there is a much bigger consumer base in female-led magazines as opposed to say, F1 editorials. If you combine the two then there is a crossover; in this case, Scherzinger got more profile with F1 fans and Hamilton with the female platform. It is a bit broader than as explained above, but well-known sportsmen become much stronger brands by teaming up with a successful lady. Some couples in the public eye hold their brand together, even if the relationship is not going that well. This is because of the money and power it brings to the brand and the individuals. But, in this case, Hamilton decided not to continue playing the fame game. There's an argument to say that Scherzinger needed him more than he needed her. But nevertheless, he has not had another girlfriend publicly, even though the public crave the *'couples'* profile. So Hamilton came to the conclusion that he needed to clear the decks and trust his own judgement. 2015 saw him negotiate his own deal with Mercedes, and be quite public about that fact. Although he has five publicists named on the *Celebrity Intelligence* platform and is on the client list at *William Morris Endeavour Entertainment* (Los Angeles), he fundamentally represents himself. Now, no one controls his world apart from himself. Along the way Lewis Hamilton has had several mentors and advisers. He, unlike many other elite performers, doesn't believe that there is anyone, at the moment, who can add to his world. Lewis Hamilton is undoubtedly a very strong character; he is also someone who is incredibly single-minded.

His work life is Mercedes and his family life is highlighted by his love for his brother. He is well on the way to being an F1 great and he is certainly doing things his way and the days of anyone telling him what to do are long gone. The challenge now is to find the individuals who will be in his world towards the end of (and post) his career.

In contrast, Sebastian Vettel, although the youngest World Champion, never tried to have high profile management; he has no publicists and is not on any client list of the major American companies. If anyone wants to book Vettel for anything, they have to contact the Ferrari press office or speak to his lawyer. Only a handful of drivers have followed this route, such as Gerhard Berger and Damon Hill. But it speaks volumes about a drivers' self-reliance, that he is prepared to do that with the most important asset he has – his career. So, who does a driver take advice from? Strangely for such a complex sport, drivers do not have coaches. In golf or tennis it's inconceivable for an elite competitor not to have a coach. Football and rugby teams are based around coaches. Formula One drivers are different. That's not to say that there aren't any driver coaches – there are. Many drivers get some coaching on the way up; young driver programmes usually have a coaching component to them; teaching them about racing lines and race craft. They spend some time with a professional driver coach like Rob Wilson or John Stevens, but do they bring them into F1 and take them to every race? Certainly not. Coaching is not part of the culture of F1. But why is this? It's not because the drivers are perfect, nor because there aren't enough people who've done it in the past. There are hundreds of ex F1 drivers, many, have little to do. No doubt some of them would make excellent coaches. It may be partly a macho-thing, F1 definitely has that side to it, where it might be perceived as weakness if a driver '*needs help*'. Partly, it has to do with the ever-changing nature of the cars. After he retired, Schumacher said that he would have a short shelf life as an adviser to Ferrari and Felipe Massa in particular, as the cars would soon be quite different from what he raced. And the last fraction of a second is in the fine details of how you drive the car.

But Schumacher certainly helped Massa and the little Brazilian almost beat Lewis Hamilton to the 2008 World Championship. But the closest relationship a driver has is with his engineer, who works with him on setting the car up and then is the main voice in his ear over the radio when he is on the circuit. F1 is so engineering-led, that any suggestions for remedial work tend to come from the race engineers, as they go through their debrief session. It's hard to imagine where a coach would fit into that dynamic. So the engineers end up being like coaches. Massa came to rely on his engineer, Rob Smedley, to coach him over the radio during races; telling him when to push harder, how to find time in certain corners, even geeing him up at times. He once called him '*Felipe baby*' over the radio, to the delight of the millions who heard it on TV. Together with the drivers they will analyse the data, look where time is being lost and suggest some alternative ways of driving certain sections of the circuit. But to a large extent it is then left up to the driver to sort out his own problems, and because of the nature of F1 he has a limited amount of time in which to do so. He can't just go out and try things because track time is strictly limited. Simulators are available in the team's headquarters, which perfectly model the racetracks on the F1 calendar, and the driver trains there before he travels out to a race. In future, these perhaps, will become a useful resource for coaching.

But F1 drivers seem to be obliged to rely on their talent more than other sportsmen. It's up to them to fix any problems and one wonders how much they improve as a result. The really good drivers are consistently on it every week, but many F1 drivers seem to have erratic performances. It is strange that they are so out on a limb in this respect, compared to their counterparts in other sports.

Fear and Resentment

Fear and resentment are around all of us, whether in the people around us or as part of the way we think. How we identify and deal with those seemingly negative aspects can have a major influence on our lives. Resentment is that deep feeling of displeasure or anger that we have towards someone because of a past offence. It is our painful memory of past hurts. Resentment is the great enemy of good relationships; it destroys friendships and turns friends into enemies. But the most damaging effect of resentment is the destruction of the one who holds it. Resentment makes people incapable of moving forward and stuck in their thought process. However, people sometimes get it wrong and the resentment they feel is misplaced. Fear and a lack of confidence can encourage individuals to find a '*way out*' and focus on misplaced resentment. I have seen, first-hand, how resentment and fear can be all-consuming; how talented individuals cannot move forward because the most important thing in their lives is to talk about how they have been hard-done-by, or how they should be doing better than they are. The ironic thing about fear and resentment is that although they are strongly connected, fear is rarely admitted. The opposite is often portrayed by people, who are too scared to succeed, but instead, use resentment as an excuse for why they haven't achieved. Resentment can cause havoc in the workplace and in relationships; the constant negativity and blaming of everyone is harmful and frustrating. Someone who is full of resentment is often the centre of attention and it's all '*me, me, me*!' In the situation of friends or family, people around the resentful one will try and make them happy because they care. You have probably been in a situation yourself where you have been trying to make someone happy but no matter what you do, they just don't respond in the right way. Even worse, trying to help someone who is full of resentment and fear makes you an enabler. You see, they will find reasons to stay in the same mind-set no matter what you do. Fear can be used in a positive way; my old mate, Linford Christie, always ran scared; he had the fear of losing when stepping out onto the track, but it helped him run fast. He might have had the fear of losing, but he wasn't scared of winning and that is where the huge difference lies.

You can have a fear of losing but the desire to succeed must supersede everything. To compete at a decent level, at any sport, you have to be so disciplined and work extremely hard. Most sportspeople don't get the recognition they deserve. In fact, there are athletes training so hard day in and day out for very little financial reward and respect from the general public. That, in itself, can breed some resentment; some athletes are winning gold medals at major competitions and not receiving the recognition they deserve. We even heard that the GB men's handball team slept on floors and cleaned toilets in their build-up to the 2012 London Olympics. These guys are exceptional; coming from a minority sport myself, I know how difficult it is to focus on your craft whilst going through major difficulties just to train and survive financially. Of all the bad and destructive things that can happen to us, resentment is one of the worst. It is like a disease working constantly to gain power and control us. No right-thinking person would happily nurture and harbour a disease in their body, knowing that this disease would eventually tear them apart. My opinion on the whole resentment thing is that, some people just think that it *'feels right'* and or *'so that's why I haven't succeeded'* or *'that's why I don't have a family and a great job'* because *'it's all his or her fault'* and so the disease begins. *Resentment feels justified – It's natural to resent that person or persons.* Many of us have had people resentful towards us, and for no justifiable reason. I've thought about this a lot; mainly because, like many of you, I have tried and tried to help certain people but without success. The truth is that in order to justify resentment, an often false image is built of the person being resented. People who live for resentment, push aside any good and selfless things that colleagues, friends and families have done and focus on any perceived grievances. I've realised that when someone behaves like that it gives them a feeling of superiority; an *'I'm better than that and I would never do anything like that.'* So the person feeling resentful hangs on to it. The really dangerous thing about having resentful people around, is that resentment turns into bitterness and then they have something to offset any future offenses they may commit. They want to be able to say: *'I did it because of what they did to me.'*

There are people around who love the pleasure they get out of being resentful; they enjoy feeling sorry for themselves and revelling in why they have been stopped from becoming the best in their field.The best thing I can say is don't hold onto resentment; let it go and forgive people if they have offended you because it takes up so much time and energy. When you look back it will be time wasted; time you could have spent achieving things. It can affect your health, mind, personality and the relationships with your colleagues, friends and family. Most importantly, you do not want to pass all that negativity on to your children. Your offspring should be inspired by you and have the world of opportunity. Illness can be caused by resentment, bitterness and fear. High blood pressure and many other problems can result from the above. My own beautiful and wonderful mother suffered a lot in the '60s, '70s and early '80s and she now suffers with many different ailments, including high-blood pressure. She has found it very difficult to deal with what happened to her. Even though her life is so much better now, she is still taking numerous tablets a day. My mum is the most fair, understanding and selfless person, but she was wronged badly and she has found it very difficult to deal with. Her problems are undeniably from the way she feels about the past. The reason why I am such a believer in anything being possible, no matter who is *In Your World*, is that my mum was trapped and wronged on a daily basis; but she found a way to bring up four children with great principles. Even in times of no money for food, she kept her dignity. Having given her all the love I have and anything she wants, I can see that this incredibly strong woman I love more than anything in the world lives with her past, every day. In order to stay positive, we need to think about things differently. If there are ten people in a room and one person doesn't like us, then we might focus on that person. Instead, we all need to focus on the nine people that we can have a reasonable relationship with and not spend years trying to help people who can't be helped. Once a colleague, friend or family member wants to be helped then we should all be there 100%.

Time is the most valuable commodity in existence, use it wisely.

Andy Murray

Behind every great man there is very often a woman doing all the hard work, so, it's widely stated. There has always been a great woman, Judy Murray.
But in tennis star Andy Murray's case, behind his success is not just a great woman but a massive team effort. A collection of trusted individuals who share Murray's life, are involved in the pain of defeat; the ecstasy of victory and the closeness of true friendship. Murray is the first to concede that without them, he might not have become a Grand Slam champion and a player who has become the world number one. They not only train together, they share their working day in close proximity to the British star. They take meals together, play practical jokes on each other, share the personal moments and yet, know when to allow the Scot the time he needs to be alone. Where the public might misunderstand Murray, is that he actually has a great sense of humour and loves watching comedy; Will Ferrell being one of his favourite comedians. But to be fair to the public they haven't seen very much of him displaying that side of his character. He is a complex character, who on the one hand loves a laugh and a joke, but on the other can live on a tightrope of pressure and expectation. At the top of the team is his coach; he has had many coaches but his greatest successes to date have been with Ivan Lendl, the former winner of eight Grand Slam titles. Then, his next coach was Amelie Mauresmo, a choice made jointly with his mother. But that relationship didn't go the distance and Murray again teamed up with Lendl in June 2016. It is to Lendl that Murray previously turned to for practical advice; for instance: When to stop hurting and confront the future and when emotion should be carefully folded away and put aside for another day. Lendl did that beautifully hence his nickname of *'Old Stoneface'*. Lendl as a top player, suffered so much from nerves that he would frequently be physically sick before a major match. He knew he had to get to grips with himself, so he reinvented a new Lendl; one who became cold, inscrutable and distant. He asked Murray to do the same. And that's when he became a winner. Murray himself admits: *'I still get nervous before a match, and of course during it.'* That is why he demands that his team be part of his matches; they fist-pump, are vocal and give him the fantastic support from the sidelines.

He thrives off that.
'I sometimes wish I had never allowed myself to become so emotionally involved after losing the 2012 Wimbledon final to Roger Federer. On reflection I should not have cried. It was a sign of weakness, and allows your opponent too much information.'

Lendl had spoken to Murray about showing too much of himself. When the Scot broke down on court at the presentation ceremony, following Federer's Wimbledon win, not a flicker of emotion crossed Lendl's face, while all around him in Murray's box his friends and family were weeping. Lesson learned. Lendl is good at breaking something down to the basics. He says simply: *'Crying is for babies.'* And he was able to soothe Murray's broken heart by getting him back playing, and, so successfully he won the U.S. Open title two months later. The two are both different and yet the same. Both are imbued with the same will to win, yet look at it differently. Murray is open with his friends, while Lendl has few close companions. Lendl wanted Murray to be hard mentally; the rest of his team work on him being hard physically. Matt Little is his fitness trainer, along with Jez Green. They prepare him; set out his training blocks and are behind the idea of Murray training for a week over Christmas in the Miami sunshine, when most take time off for the holidays. Instead they build Murray's constitution; put the strength into his legs, enlarge his lung capacity and work him to his physical limits. That's when physio Andy Ireland takes over. He will organise the stretching exercises, the recovery times and rehabilitation. Yoga sessions, and cold bathes, plus 400 metres sprints with just sixty seconds of recovery time. He will organise the massages, taking care to spend time on Murray's back problem and the worries about his right knee. Between them, it was the team who persuaded Murray it would be a good idea to withdraw from the French Open in June 2013 to make certain he was fully fit for Wimbledon. Murray said:

'You need good people around you; in a way they babysit you. I am very grateful for all they do for me; their help, patience and general imput.'

Team five became team six, when Murray's friend Danny Vallverdu came into the equation. He is around Murray's age and has been a friend for nearly ten years. Danny is a hitting partner; spending long hours on the court feeling Murray's back hand and forehands; working him to the right pitch of fitness, and then stopping the clock when any signs of fatigue set in. This was previsouly under the eagle eye of Lendl. They are all people Murray is comfortable with, can refer to and ask advice and opinions from. He values them so much that they have the official title of *'Team Murray'.* There can be as many as ten of them; all with a crucial role. The paradox with Murray, is that although he wants to be comfortable with the people around him, he almost wants the opposite when it comes to training and competing. He wants to win and be pushed to the absolute limit and that's a really difficult balancing act and one that Judy Murray helps with. Then there is his wife Kim Sears, and because her father Nigel was once head coach of women's tennis at the LTA, she understands its problems. Kim is there as a shoulder to cry on. She understands when to leave him alone, like when he becomes embroiled in his Play Station. She takes their dogs Maggie and Rusty for walks on the local common, and more importantly is a great partner who most of the backroom boys expected him to marry and he did. Being the wife of a tennis player is mainly a selfless task; the career of the player comes first. Andy Murray struck gold with Kim Sears because apart from being a genuinely lovely girl, she understands tennis and gives him the support he needs. Murray's mother Judy is the matriarch of the party. Fiercely competitive, she cooks for Andy, dispels Scottish common sense and oversees many of the financial deals that have so far earned the Scot a multi-million fortune. She was also partly responsible for putting the team together, picking people her son could interact with, have fun with when the hard work stops and enjoy the nonstop banter that draws the group together like an invisible cord. Judy travels with him, is a buffer to those who want to get to close. She is fiercely protective. Murray admitted that after winning the US Open title, he took special time to privately thank her for keeping the team ticking. Without them all, Murray would not be able to cope the way he does.

The calls on his time are becoming more and more demanding. Matt Gentry another back room boy who works for Murray's agents *XIX*, does much to field the demands on his time; for Andy isn't a natural communicator with the public and finds the media part of being a star the only tiresome aspect of fame. Murray would not know how to deal with the media and the pressure of fame without Matt and the rest of them. He admits, the workaholics who make his life style possible, are vital to him being a success. A team in every sense of the word. Also there in an understated role are Louise Irving, who specialises in management, and Rob Stewart who runs Murray's web site. He has learned the hard way. Talking to himself during a toilet break in the US Open final after winning the first two sets, Murray said: *'I told myself I was not going to lose. I had become fed up with walking around with my shoulders sloping and my head down. I needed to win for all the others with me who had such belief in what I could achieve. I couldn't let them down. As far as I'm concerned we are all in this together. My win was not just for me, but for the team too.'* That's why at his celebration party that night, Murray got more pleasure out of seeing his boys enjoy themselves. Not a drop of drink passed his own lips. He said:
'The most important thing is that they understand the person they are working with. If I am going through a tough time I will phone my Mum because she knows what I like to hear and don't like to hear. It is that kind of understanding that matters as much as forehands and backhands. There are of course still things I need to learn.'. 'I travel with a fitness trainer to keep me in shape - that for me is a wise investment. I have a physio because everyone complains I am injury-prone, so this is a great way of ironing out the niggles before they have a chance to develop into anything more serious.' And he believes it was the team who helped him recover from a fairly serious back injury a while ago that kept him out of the game for three weeks. Murray said: *'They helped a lot. They were so understanding, and it was because of them I was able to come through some tough matches.'* It is why when he wins, Murray always turns to the courtside box to salute the team who are so special to him. They are the mainstay of his career. But it took some time for Murray to get the right blend in his team.

He had gone through five coaches before he hooked up with Lendl. All offered experience and sound advice, but lacked that vital ingredient: the ability to get Andy's trust and belief to get him winning Grand Slams. Mauresmo became his seventh full-time coach and brought a more sensitive approach than Lendl. Murray's world now had his coach pushing a pram around Melbourne Park, but that is no problem to him. In fact he embraced that because his wife Kim would be doing the same with their their daughter.

Murray is a great team builder, one of the best in world sport.

He is the only top male player to have had a female coach. People may say that it's the influence of Judy, well maybe yes but it works. In his pursuit of building a great team, Murray leaves no stone unturned. He now has the experience of working with a female coach; something, his mother, Judy suggested. She also suggested he take on Lendl, even if the age difference was over twenty-five years. It was a gamble. Previously, Murray had worked with opinionated American, Brad Gilbert and the two grated on each other. Judy soon sensed Andy was uncomfortable with somebody with which he had nothing in common. Eating and drinking together put an intolerable strain on their relationship and Gilbert was sacked. After Mauresmo, Murray turned to Jamie Delgado for a short period then convinced Lendl to rejoin the team alongside Delgado. Now it is fair to say that when Lendl was back in the camp, he has the perfect team and success will come again. When more Grand Slam success arrives it will be with the additions to Murray's world – children. July 10th 2016, Andy Murray won his 2nd Wimbledon and this time Lendl looked emotional and with almost a tear in his eye. Murray punched the air with delight and his team celebrated another moment of history. Murray's example is, to some extent, replicated by Rafa Nadal, who travels everywhere with his uncle Toni as his chief companion, his doctor who supervises the injuries and his accommodating, loyal girlfriend who keeps a low profile.

Nadal once complained that when he was in his mid-twenties, he was becoming tired of the ranting and raving from Toni; a perfectionist who drilled Nadal to the point of exhaustion. But still he stayed with him; a loyal back up there at the court side for every match. And there again in practice: supervising, talking and consulting with the medical experts; worrying and fretting about the health of the young superstar. Nadal admitted he couldn't do what he does without support. He said:

'Those who are with me are very important to what I achieve. They can make things so much easier for me, take away the every day worries of life on the tournament circuit.'

Roger Federer goes everywhere with his wife Mirka. She has become his agent, travel adviser, companion and someone to return to every night where normality can be quaranteed. In the days when Bjorn Borg ruled tennis, he and his wife Marianne had set rules. Once again, she kept in the background as an organiser of his private life and at night would surrender the double bed to Borg, while she slept on the sofa so he would get a good night's rest. Tennis players are highly strung creatures, and in most cases lack selfconfidence, despite their fame and fortune and that is because they have never known a normal life. It is said that diva, Maria Sharapova, cannot go to the ladies' room unless someone goes with her. Yet on court she comes across as a powerful glamorous superstar; a diva in the game with a tremendous presence. So teams are important, especially if they can also be friends. They feed off of each other, offer comfort and solace and encouragement and praise. And that's all the majority of players ever want to hear. Novak Djokovic admits he is emotionally attached to his support team. It includes a coach, an assistant coach, a fitness trainer, a physiotherapist, an agent and his dog Pierre the poodle. He said:

'We enjoy a good life as tennis stars, but what is that without the people around you that love and respect you. They are the most valuable assets in my life.'

Djokovic is a great team builder; he keeps trusted people around him and adds to the team when necessary. In 2013 he added Boris Becker to longtime coaches Marian Vajda, Miljan Amanovic and Gebhard Phil-Gritsch. As I write this book, Andy Murray has just made a change to his backroom team. South African, Johan de Beer, replaced Andy Ireland as his physio.
Wimbledon 2013 looms and one of our great sporting *World Builders* prepares for history by being the first Brit in over seventy years to win the *'All England Championships'*. The thing to be most admired about Murray, is the lengths he goes to in order to get the absolute best out of himself. When you do that there are no excuses; you put yourself in a position where you know that no stone has been unturned. Lots of people in sport and everyday life say that they want to be the best they can be, but they often don't do everything possible, because they want an excuse for failure or are subconciously scared to put themselves in the firingline like Murray does. Murray likes to have fun in his camp, but is not scared of confrontation and wants people to be brutally honest with him. Again, some people think they want that, but in reality they don't want uncomfortable conversations. Murray's philosophy is to be admired, because it is a winning mentality at all costs. This guy has come from a back-drop of average tennis tradition; we are light years behind many nations in how they develop tennis players. But, he created his world and developed his mentality. It is very difficult to develop a winning mentality around the wrong people. Murray has changed the psyche of our sports people; history will show that his *'never die attitude'*, work ethic and character will transcend through generations.

He is a winner and an incredible World Builder.

Murray has always been aware of the necessity of a backroom team, competent enough to take care of business behind the scenes. Now that has culminated in him winning Wimbledon; a result he claims would not have happened if it was not for those who worked so hard to support him.That's why he held his celebrations in private; a table in a Sushi restaurant with just his pals around to share the moment, he accepts, will be difficult to ever emulate.

Murray eats up to thirty pieces of Sushi per-day, in a special diet, set for him by his nutritionist; another member of the team his mum, Judy, introduced.
She saw the improvement Novak Djokovic made when he went on a gluten free diet, and suggested Andy do the same. It enables him to work even harder because the Japanese food is easier to digest, and allows him to get back on the practice court or the gymnasium without wasting too much time. Everything is planned to the last degree; one of the attractions of inviting Ivan Lendl to the team was that Murray, who can be dour and serious, could rely on him to never speak of the training routines and coaching sessions they share together. Lendl has never been the most communicative of people and that has always appealed to the Murray camp.They are never afraid of any indescretions that could cause embarrassment to Andy, or that might divert him from being totally focused on his job. The team do the worrying for him; they look after his food, his fluid intake, his training schedules, his publicity work, shielding him from intrusion and fielding the many requests on his time that would be impossible to fulfil.

Worrying about things out of you control is such a waste of energy.

There's a famous saying that goes:

'Don't worry about anything, for worrying is the interest paid in advance on a debt you may never owe; you are a warrior, not a worrier' – Andy Murray is a warrior.

He doesn't have to worry, because he has someone who gives him unconditional support, Judy. And she makes sure her son uses all his energy in the right way. Judy is always hovering around talking to people, making the necessary phone calls and still finding time to see that his sponsorship deals are running smoothly. Winning Wimbledon will earn Murray enough money to probably become the wealthiest sportsman in the country; outstripping even David Beckham. And the team will ultimately benefit, because they will almost certainly receive bonus payment for whatever event he is successful in. Murray rewards loyalty, and looks after those who look after him.

In the background observing, watching and listening was Lendl; the man who helped Murray win his first Wimbledon and that's why he clambered into the players box after beating Djokovic to win the title. Lendl gave him a game plan and the mental advice which was so vital at emotional moments. The warm hug was one of grateful thanks. Lendl was responsible for getting things on track; never letting Murray get too far ahead of himself. His mantra has always been the same. *'We are here to win, not come second.'* So the team have flourished and bonded like a band of brothers and sisters. Between them they helped mould Britain's first Wimbledon champion for seventy-seven years. After two wonderful years, the partnership with Lendl ended; one of the reasons Ivan Lendl reneged on his original commitment to stay with Andy Murray, for the course of the Scot's career, was that he was wary of the travel and, particularly, he did not enjoy the aerial commuting in the US, nor the 10,000-mile slog from Miami to Melbourne for the first slam of the season. This was like a death in the family for Murray: *'It was tough; he was a big part of my life.' Great World Builders* evolve and Murray has done that by having a coach fundamentally different to Lendl. Firstly Amelie Mauresmo has made the sort of commitment that not only requires the usual sacrifices of time and hard yards, but comes with a unique rider: A five-month-old baby boy called Aaron. She took her first-born to Perth when Murray was warming up for the 2016 season, a gesture he appreciated for more than the obvious reasons. He and his wife, Kim, were expecting their own child, scheduled to arrive two weeks after the Australian Open 2016. Murray enjoyed the experience of having a baby's presence in a working environment. He said:

'Her boy has been great. He has come to a few dinners and stuff and been really well behaved. It looks easy, I guess, when you see a baby for an hour and a half per day. She seems to be handling everything very well and it hasn't affected her.'

Great team builders embrace different situations of their team and focus on the important common denominators. Murray didn't see Mauresmo's situation so much as a negative, but as a bonding situation. Mauresmo had the commitment, desire, personality and skillset to help Murray achieve his goals.

The challenge for Murray is to manage parallel emotions: His life with Kim, their child and family, whilst retaining the focus needed to be sharp and unforgiving at his workplace. *Murray's world* now has the forecast of children and the joys that brings. He is our first Wimbledon champion for almost eighty years and with the continued cleverness in team building he will enjoy success on and off the court. Way back in 1936, Fred Perry had only a locker room attendant to look after him; because Perry, a maverick, was not especially liked. When he won the last of his three consecutive titles in 1936, a Wimbledon official came up to the defeated Jack Crawford and said: *'Well old boy, the best man never won today.'* Perry overheard it and was furious. The same official was also there to present Perry with the purple and green club tie, but instead left it over the back of a chair and walked out. Perry was a loner; he aliented people because he came from *'the wrong side of the tracks'*, and would annoy opponents, by walking into the dressing room and saying: *'I'd hate to be playing Fred Perry today.'* He did things on his own and eventually left for the US, because he never fitted in. Murray would have been amused by Fred, but is wise enough to know great things cannot be achieved unless there are those around you similarly driven and similarly ambitious. It is a team sport in the truest sense of the word and Murray has proved it. From time to time, Murray will no doubt change the dynamics and personell in his world, but one thing will stay constant: His desire to build the world he lives in. November 2016, Murray beat Djokovic in the ATP World Tour Finals; he is the undisputed world no.1. The success he had with Ivan Lendl in past years had been rekindled. Even when he brought Lendl back, he kept Jamie Delgado in his team; a constant sat next to Lendl. Delgado had filled the gap as Murray's coach when Amélie Mauresmo left the team.There was a key moment on court just before Murray started his battle against Djokovic. When sat in the seat, he would have at change-overs he realised he couldn't see his team so he moved it. That is the importance of his team. He is not only the best on the planet at his craft, he gets the best out of himself because he is one of the best team builders ever seen in sport. December 2016, Djokovic announced he has split with coach Boris Becker. He is now behind Murray and looks to build a new team.

The Deal

Over the years so many people have been intrigued by the Sol Campbell deal, from Spurs to Arsenal and so on. Everyone seems to have an opinion on it. Some people think it was all planned.

Sol had a four year deal and planned to see it out. Even though a week is a long time in football, some think that with two years to go, Sol just decided to see out his contract. Here I will try and explain what was going on in Sol's world that culminated into the deal people will talk about for a long time to come. During the last two to three years of his contract at Spurs, he was also playing top class international football for England; he was probably the lowest paid player in the national team. For most footballers not being paid what they feel they should be on for any amount of time is not acceptable. In Sol's world, it was never about the money; he was desperate for Spurs to be a top team. He would go away with the England set-up and then come back excited about the experience. The only thing in his control was to be loyal to it and hope that a team could develop at Spurs to compete at the highest level. It was even put to him that for each month he was not signing a contract, he was losing money – even though for a long period a contract wasn't offered. How many of us would put principles aside because we thought we were losing money? Remember, Sol could have got injured at any time. I was obviously part of creating Sol's world and the focus was always on the football, no matter what was said, written or shouted from the terraces, the focus was on doing what was right for his career.

Earlier in this book I wrote about Beckham's strength of character; well, Sol is right up there in respect of that. Any person who is in a position of strength is a target for some, who will try to weaken or divide and conquer. It's fair to say that Sol and I were a very strong team. He wanted the most from his career and I made sure no one stole his dreams. We both came from one of the poorest parts of London – the *East End*. We both had to find our way in life and our families knew each other. We would exchange stories of life in the *East End* and felt a common bond in that. As Sol developed his career I think he was underestimated, because he was quiet and no one could see how strong and reolute he was.

With two years to go on his contract, all the fun and games started – but no contract offer.

When money doesn't control you and finance doesn't reflect your ego, then you are free to make choices.

People are expected to chase money and to throw numbers around sacrificing their integrity and possibilities. But Sol's focus was now: '*Show me ambition,*' as he was so frustrated with the fact that other teams were competing for major honours. Alan Sugar was chairman for a large part of Sol's stay at Spurs and I felt for him a bit. Because he did spend money prior to Sol's last couple of years but he was reliant on other opinions and judgements. I had respect for Sugar; I could see that he was a guy, who came from humble beginnings, and was basically a street fighter – he also loved a battle and if you were in the wrong, he would make you pay. He was a contradiction in many ways. On the one hand, he fronted people up; he could have a row and hated yes-men. but on the other he had very calm people around him who weren't argumentative. Although he would give an image of being quite insensitive and cold, he was astute at working people out and knowing who was a '*straight flyer*' and who wasn't. Like most chairmen, he didn't like dealing with agents; especially the ones he knew weren't representing their clients properly. But if an agent worked for the club and did an honest and fair job, he would also be fair. He didn't like double dealers and smoozers. He was straight and hated some aspects of football.

I learnt a lot from him; particularly about how important it is to have good legals. He was never really a people's person; he was tough but fair. Underneath the tough business man is a person that respects and appreciates loyalty and good work. He had the same people around him for a very long time and they wouldn't have hung around if he was as bad as some people said. I was one of few people that understood his jokes. I found him quite funny at times, even when he would say something blunt. Some situations didn't work out for him and he found himself pillored by some of the fans.

He was always brutally honest with me. For some reason I was never phased by any situations and never counted chickens before they hatched Alan accepted that I grafted for my client and I appreciated that because it's all too easy to criticise people (agents) if the situation doesn't go your way. He had a sense of humour, that only I found funny. Alan was just so blunt and he never saw the grey areas; it was black or white and some of his comments cracked me up.

All through our talks and discussions, I stood firm but listened to him. I think he couldn't understand me or Sol; he probably thought we were strange. In fact I know he thought I was strange. I think he saw how agents played the game with clients and couldn't understand why I wasn't playing the same game. During the more testing period with him, we played tennis first thing in the mornings. He was a good player, but my table-tennis background meant that I would do all these funny spins. My first serve was a bullet and second was a slow spinny serve that he hated; he called it a '*Shirley Temple*' serve. Straight after one of our tennis sessions he sent me an email starting '*Dear Shirley Temple.*' He did try to break me down with the tennis matches, but alas it didn't work and Shirley Temple came through victorious. We had a few heated talks in the boardroom at Amstrad. I can honestly say that he wanted the best for Spurs, but was just a bit disillusioned by some aspects of football. The fact that you don't necessarilly get what you pay for drove him mad. Football has aspects of it that doesn't make good business sense and people sometimes make emotional decisions. The one thing Spurs fans can be sure about is that he ran the club with a strong hand and never did anything for his own personal gain. Alan passed the baton on to Enic around the turn of 2001 and the new owners brought in Glen Hoddle. By then Sol had six months left on his contract; he was even more eager to see what was going to happen now. He was courted by some of the biggest clubs in the world but we had made a decision not to speak with anyone until the Spurs situation was sorted. In every step of any decision making we did not change the goal posts or make hypercritical descisons. By not speaking to European clubs (even though we could) it meant that some of them pulled out of the race to sign Sol.

We were determined to give 100% focus to the Spurs situation. The change in ownership and manager was a difficult situation, but Glen Hoddle was someone Sol respected and Glen had a good influence on Sol. We even had a discussion where he talked about giving it another year but it didn't work out and in late April, Spurs announced that Sol would be leaving as discussions had broken down. Until that point we had resisted formal discussions with interested parties. Arsenal were amongst interested parties and I can categorically say that he wouldn't have joined if it wasn't for the combination of David Dein and Arsène Wenger. I couldn't see the move to Arsenal until David Dein said his piece. He creates a world where if you're on his team then you are part of the family. There are people in football claiming to be the movers and shakers, but trust me the big 'D' got things done – he was, and probably still is, very smart. He made Sol feel like he was joining a family and that he would be protected. David did little things that people acknowledged and appreciated. He was the total opposite to Alan Sugar, but I liked them and have respect for both. Once Sol and I agreed to talk with people, I was surprised at how David made the possible switch sound so natural. Then once you are sat in a room with David and Arsène, you realised that the whole set-up was more than football; it was a family and that was not an easy thing to achieve in a huge institution.

Life, football – it all comes back to family. We all relate to family.

Arsène spoke about not making a decision based on hate. It was a major statement, because if you think about it, if Sol had decided not to make the move, it would have been a decision based on hate; not about the fans who would love him, but the people who would hate the decision. The reason why Sol went to any club had to based on football first and the personalities around the place second. Sol is someone who likes to discuss stuff in depth. He enjoys interesting conversations and Arsène offered that and Dean the Big 'D' had plenty in his locker. Right up until the morning of the announcement, the situation was totally confidential; the fact that the 9am press conference was decided the night before told you everything about the nature of the deal. The conference was called straight after Sol had agreed to join. Confidentiality is the norm in my world and it certainly is in Sol's and Arsenal FC's.

Football is a big business, but a small world; normally everybody knows everyone's business. But if you have confidentiality you have strength and it goes a long way when showing your character. When Sol stepped out from behind the boards to the flashing of cameras, nobody knew it was going to be him and then all hell broke loose. One camera-man said: *'xxxx me! it's Sol Campbell.'* The press conference came and went, then I switched my phone back on and got the shock of my life. Terrible messages from begrudged fans. Sandwiched in between them was a message from a female journalist who had befriended me for the year, to year and a half preceeding the announcement. It went something like: *'How could you do that to me? How could you not tell me or give me a heads-up? I thought we were friends? How silly am I gonna look now? I told my boss that I would break the story.'* This girl was in my world, but because of confidentiality being very important to me she didn't get her story and showed her true colours. That episode was scary because we have all got people in our world befriending us for the wrong reasons. Lack of confidentiality will cost us in the long-run as:

Loose Lips Sink Ships.

When Things Just Don't Work Out

The fear of failure or the possibility that someone will betray us are an example of reasons why some of us are discouraged to just try and make something happen; to try and reach our full potential or try to see where we can get to in life. The truth is that we have little control over people who choose to betray and decieve. The only thing we can do, is know that many people have become very successful with the back-drop of painful experiences. Sometimes there are people in our lives who stop us from our destiny and who become a crutch and we get stuck. We need mentors, but a good one will step back at the right moment and not stunt our growth. Good parents, mentors and teachers will show us the way and then let us fly. That is not an easy thing to do and it's not a nice feeling to know that someone doesn't need you anymore. When an important person leaves your world, it's not a time to feel sorry for yourself or to get depressed. If someone leaves your world their time was obviously up and it's your time to step up. A door will close and you will be disappointed but another will open and a challenge will be right in front of you. As an agent I have always given 100% and never compromised my commitment to my clients. When you use everything you have to protect, promote and guide a client in the right way with great results. You don't expect to be let down or indeed for the client to let themselves down. But sadly this can happen, because for all the long-term planning to make the correct decision, dark forces lurk in the background trying to get a short-term gain and turning the heads of young people with terrible advice. In any relationship, whether friendship, marriage or agent to client even, we can all be left flabbergasted by the decision of someone you thought was trustworthy and part of your team. We can be left feeling: '*wow! I put all that time and effort in you and this is how you repay me. I put my neck on the line for you; I gave you the best advice and support for you and can you not see where the dark forces are taking you?*' But, the truth is, we must all quit being down about people who walk away; we must quit being bitter about what didn't work out. If they were supposed to be in our lives, they would still be there. If we stop focusing on the people who let us down or left, we can use that energy to find the right people.

When you accept personal disappointment and move forward you will not only think on another level, the right people will come to you like a beam of light. All of us have either experienced or seen betrayal by someone close.

Sometimes we can all get lazy with what's going on around us and then the 'hornet's nest' is stirred to test our character.

In the representation business, it is common place to hear stories of clients or agents going behind each other's backs. If the agent has done a great job and the client has had their head turned by dark forces, then that person will struggle to reach their potential. If on the other hand the agent has not given due care and attention to their client because of money for instance, then the agent does not believe in the importance of a relationship and the client will find someone else and appreciate the right kind of relationship. But, that is nothing compared to your best friend sleeping with your spouse and so on. A girlfriend of a footballer once said to me: '*Having a one-night stand is one thing, but holding hands in the street is a real betrayal.*' This is because there is no chance of the betrayal being deemed a mistake or any other excuse someone could come out with. Unfortunately, when we trust someone and believe in them, we want to accept an excuse to not have to go through the pain of seperation. For some reason we have to be pushed out of our comfort zone by adversity. Betrayal can push us into better relationships and make us more determined to take notice of who is in our world. It can make us stronger, more resilient and even more determined to be successful. The pain we feel after a major betrayal, is the point at which we are about to reinvent ourselves. Steve Jobs is one of the brilliant minds of our generation. At twenty-one, he founded Apple and by twenty-three he was incredibly successful. Seven years later, he clashed with the board of directors and was fired from the company he founded. He told his friends how betrayed he felt and how wrong it was. But instead of sitting around in selfpity he went out and started another company and learned new skills. This company developed something that Apple needed and they were so successful that Apple purchased his company and brought him back as CEO. Jobs said if he hadn't been fired he would never have learned those new skills; the skills that made him into who he was.

The betrayal to Steve Jobs didn't stop him; it pushed him. Don't complain about who hurt you or who did you wrong. If that is going to keep you from where you need to go, then you have failed the test. Shake-off the selfpity and get prepared for all the opportunities and new skills you are about to develop. When things are stirring in your life, for example: a friend lets you down, someone's betrayed you, doors seem to be closing and you are uncomfortable with life in general, that is the moment to turn things around. That is the time for a turning point.

When the wrong people leave your life, the right things start to happen.

The Formula For Success

So we have looked at the importance of the people *In Your World* and the different mind-sets individuals have. We have analysed how successful people think and the environment needed to help individuals reach their goals.
In this last chapter, I am going to try and simplify the ingredients needed to help people fulfill their potential. When you decide that you want to be successful, the world becomes a different place; the world metamorphises into a completely different planet. Once you decide to build your world, people become interesting; fascinating in fact. Your world becomes 3D, because like a taxi looking for customers – your light is on. Success is all about having your '*light on*' and constantly being aware of people and opportunities. The important thing is to start because as the great Elton John said:

'If you don't start you've already finished.'

I believe there are a few fundamental things that should be assessed as a basic starting point. Apart from the fundamental:

1. Ability
2. Desire

The crucial things are

3. The view on situations
4. How you get in the zone

We've all heard the saying: half full or half empty?
That is a simple was of saying are you a positive or negative person?
If someone is taught how to look at every situation in the right way then success will come. This sounds simple: *'Just look at things in the right way and you will be succesful'* but it's a mental art to be able to get the good out of all situations. The way you look at each situation affects the way you go forward.

Similarly, in order to perform at your best, you need to learn how to get in the zone. Getting in the zone makes us perform infinitely better. All our senses are heightened and we almost become different people. *Lucy* is a film that maximised it's potential. It grossed $458 million against a budget of $40 million. It is about a girl that takes a drug called CP14 and it helps her untilise all her senses; obviously to the extreme as it's a movie after all. The question is how successful can someone be with:

1. The right people around them
2. Great advice
3. Getting in the zone

There are certain times when we all have to perform to the best of our ability and that just can't happen in a 'normal state of mind'. Also, people will get into the zone in different ways and that means understanding oneself and having people around us who understand what is needed. We are judged on certain moments; important moments. For instance, to be judged as the greatest football player of all time, there are certain moments and competitions where a player must perform, such as in a World Cup. Someone can do great business for years, then there comes a moment; a negotiation, where if they perform then it brings unrivalled success. At that moment, who advises, who's around them and how they perform is crucial. Remember the Swedish table-tennis players? When they are losing they are focusing on getting into their game and also looking forward because they know weaker players will be looking behind them. Even when they are losing 2-0 in a best of five, they still believe that when they get their game going they will be unstoppable. Remember Linford Christie telling me, '*Why not? Why can't it be me?*' There's the story about the guy who goes to a statue in his town every Saturday, closes his eyes and prays: '*Please let me win the lottery.*' Then one day the statue says to him: '*Why haven't you bought a ticket?*' When a risk is being weighed up, some people will see it as exciting and some traumatising. Same with chasing dreams; some will be excitied by the chance to achieve them and some scared by the possibility of not. Little quotes, messages and anecdotes from people in our world will build the blocks to help us have the right mind-set.

This is particularly important in formative years when we are all impressionable. When building one's world it is crucial not to be scared to bring people in and let people go. Your world is *Your World* and you have to be empowered to learn and build. The great thing with identifying the wrong people is, you should learn to see the common denominators and then identify the right people. There are billions of people in the world but not billions of completely different people; there are common denominators. You need people on the outside of your own thoughts to recognise and help you assess *Your World* at a given time. You should have situations that enable you to enjoy the moment and not drag in the past or worry yourself stupid about the future. In order to enjoy the moment and live in the present you have to learn from the past and let go and have people who can structure the future and take care of what's needed.

The past is gone, today is the moment, tomorrow is a new day.

A major key to clearing the path for talent is understanding the character and the motivation of individuals. Equally, a coach/mentor who understands an individual will help nurture the talent. Some coaches want to make their own life easier by disregarding talent with different characters. They take a view that if someone has certain traits then they won't make it; nothing is further from the truth. Too many talented people are judged in a negative way because they have character and are deemed not to be focusing on their craft. It's easy to see the obvious traits in people and those with common characters. It's much harder to have a group of people and take time to understand that they will have different characters and slightly different motivations. So, let's go back to an individual's motivation. A conversation about what motivates an indivudual is crucial to understanding where the desire and passion will come from. There has to be a core reason why someone would work hard and lead their lives in the right way. Lots of people don't know why they want something or why they are doing it. People's motivations are not to be sneered at but to be understood. American singer Demi Levato was bullied at school, and she developed a deep rooted desire to prove her bullies wrong; she is now a world star. Many will not be honest about their motivations.

When I first started as an agent/manager I would tell youngsters to forget about the money and to focus on the craft and the money would come. I painted a picture that if they did think about the money then it would not help them achieve what they wanted. The problem with that is that some would still focus on the money and even more significantly, those around them would sometimes soley think about the money. Friends and family who do not necessarily understand the importance of the craft can be sometimes more impressed with material things, like: Watches, cars and champagne nights out. So the pressure comes to show success by obvious things like these material possessions. Over the years, I started to realise that if someone (and their family) are motivated by money, then it needs to be addressed, harnessed and structured. It is crucial that a work contract is structured in a way that targets have to be reached before financial renumeration. Long-term goals have to be set like a house for mum and dad, financial security and business interests. For those who want the lifestyle, it's quite simple: Do the business and you can walk tall, go out on your nights out and have adulation. Another unsaid thing is that some sportsmen crave the attention from the opposite sex; it can't be underestimated how important that is to some at a young age. Again, this is something that wouldn't be admitted or discussed with their coaches, but those conversations will go on with the player's friends. The friends will reiterate the importance of being to attracted girls. Friends should, instead suggest the individual should stay away from girls and other materialistic distractions, and help focus the player on achieving performances they will be proud of. Because, with success comes the attention. The truth is that there are sports people who love their craft so much that they choose a partner and stick with that person. We see that a lot in tennis. It's not a coincedence that the top tennis players have long term relationships and have consistency in their private lives. Every individual is slightly different and in an ideal world a sportsperson would get married, have a family and focus on their career. But, that is unrealistic for some people, so should their talent be discarded? Is it more important to get the best out of people or to get everyone to tow the standard party line? There are many talented people who don't conform to the stereotype that is wanted by managers and coaches. People come from different backgrounds and some just do not have stereotypical characters.

I totally agree with the school of thought that it should always be about the team and that no one should be more important than the team. This is something Sir Clive Woodward used to the maximum with the England Rugby Team; enabling them to win the World Cup. But again, individuals who seem to be selfish and only care about themselves can be motivated to work for the team. They can be told: '*If you perform for the team imagine how much praise you will get?*' Everyone is basically selfish and inevitably do what is best for themselves. We all do what makes us feel good; even the amazing philanthropists and unselfish givers do what they do because it makes them feel good. The lucky ones are the people who put their necks on the line for others; none of us like the people who are purely selfish and have no care for others. Success isn't just about performance at work; it is also about happiness in your personal life. If you can take responsibility of who is *In Your World* , then your life can become forever fulfilling. The most difficult time for sportspeople is when their career is over. Many suffer depression and a complete loss of confidence and direction. When those in the sport and entertainment industry are working and things are going well, they often can't see the wood from the trees. People around them can get away with being lazy and the sportspeople themselves can adopt an attitude that the gravy train is never going to end. If you don't have loyal, smart, creative people around you during competing/performing years, it can be a very long fall. Sportspeople can literally go from adulation, respect and esteem, to being a complete nobody in society. For some it's not about not having adulation anymore; it's more – '*Who Am I?*' So, by having smart and loyal people around you, they will make sure you are aware of the long-term future and help you develop interests and skills. David Beckham developed himself and his brand because his eye was always on the future. Now, he is an ambassador/politician for life; just look at how he has developed the way he speaks and conducts himself. People would laugh at the way he spoke, but no one's laughing now. You can only start to improve yourself, if firstly you want to and secondly, someone *In Your World* is telling you that it's needed. So what is the measure of success? Well ultimately it is the people in our lives. So in our world, or more specifically, *In Your World*. So family, friends and work colleagues.

When we are young we have the future, as we get older, history with people becomes more and more important. So, try to keep people in your life who you can trust and know you. Then add people to your world who can help you achieve your goals and dreams. Old school talent managers like Billy Marsh (London Management) looked after two of our biggest talents in recent history - Eric Morcambe and Ernie Wise. Marsh brought the mercurial comedians into his office and agreed to look after them. Marsh explained to them: *'If you were ever unhappy, lawyers would get involved, and I would rather us just have a chat.'* He looked after Morcambe and Wise for their whole careers.

Turning Points

The penultimate chapter in this book is '*Turning Points*'. The search for them, belief in them and the mere fact of what they do. '*Turning Points*' play such a huge part in our lives, if we buy into the whole concept. We have to believe in a turning point, otherwise we might as well give up when things are going badly. The more we believe in turning points, the less time we spend in a negative frame of mind when things are not going right. The edge of disaster is also the brink of success. I was once having a massage at my gym and the masseur told me that she had split up from the man of her dreams because he had messed up and she was going to take a whole new direction in life. I sensed a real deep unhappiness in the way she spoke. A few months later I was back at the gym having another massage with the same masseur and we started discussing relationships again and I asked how she was and her reply surprised me: '*I'm so happy,*' she said. '*My boyfriend and I got back together and we're getting married.*' I was intrigued to hear what happened: '*He came to my house one day and knocked on the door; I just looked at him and asked what he was doing there. He said he wanted to talk. I still had feelings for him but had accepted that it was over. We sat down and he started talking. He apologised and talked about the mistakes; why they happened and how things would be different in the future. He said all the right things and as he was talking I fell in love with him all over again. We hugged, kissed then spoke for hours after about our future together.*' Now that is scary. What a fine line there is between happiness and sadness.
Every situation is recoverable but sometimes pride, confidence and stubborness gets in the way. In relationships we can all put things right and even when we think a situation is irreversible – it's not. When things are not going right for sportspeople during a competiton, a turning point can dramatically change the mental side and approach to the remaining part of the competition. In tennis, a player winning a five-set match, two sets to love up, is very close to victory and even closer to losing the whole match.This is because if they get close to winning and then don't, the whole psychology of the match changes and some players cannot get out of the change in their mental approach. The person two sets down can be down in the dumps or look for the turning point.

The turning point becomes greater, the closer someone gets to winning.Two sets to love up and having a match-point then losing it, can make someone unable to perform positively for the remainder of the match. When you hear players saying that they were *'hanging in there'* when being beaten, it's a positive way of looking for a turning Point. As I've mentioned before in this book – you can't be in control or winning all the time – so the best thing to do is to work or look towards a turning Point. The same theory above applies to football teams. Pundits often say that 2-0 up for a team is a dangerous scoreline; this is because of the mental change that happens when the losing team scores a goal to make it 2-1. The winning team are looking back and hanging on but the losing team are attacking and looking forward. When things are not going well for us, it can be easy to sink into a dark hole, then it becomes harder and harder to get out. Our thought process gives us no light at the end of the tunnel. But there is always a light, there is always a turning point and when it comes, we can go on a roll of positivity. Most of us have gone through difficult situations and have even been on the brink of despair. In order to feel the joy at the top of the mountain, we have to experience the pain of the bottom of the pit. When things are going bad and reach almost rock bottom, we are ironically on the brink of strength and achievement. We are also on the brink of defeat and the destroying of our belief. We just cannot buy the feeling of fighting our way back from the brink of defeat. In individual competitions, someone being match point down and winning in earlier rounds can make them feel fearless and indestructible. My sport was table-tennis, which has been dominated by the Chinese for many years. The Chinese are renowned for being mentally tough and invariably winning in tight situations. It is unacceptable for the world No. 1 or No. 2 Chinese player to lose in a major tournament after having match-points. At the 2003 World Championships in Paris, Austrian Werner Schlager made history and broke down major mental barriers. As the underdog, he played world No. 1 Wang Liqin in the Quarter-finals; it was best of seven, up to eleven. Schlager trailed three games to two and vitally 10-6 in the sixth game. 999 times out of a 1,000, the world No. 1 Chinese player wins the match 4-2 or 4-3 at worst. Werner Schlager played each point and won each point. When he got to 10-9, you could sense that Schlager was displaying an incredible strength of belief and character.

Could the mental strong-hold that the Chinese players had over the Europeans be broken? Schlager won the next point – incredible. The World Championships Quarter Finals of the Chinese national sport and the unthinkable was happening. Belief is an amazing thing to have; it can take you to places most people think are not possible. The crowd still saw only one winner and the Chinese coach had a few drops of sweat lingering around the top of his head. The Austrian, 100-1 outsider, against the world No. 1 in a sport where the Chinese always won and were always mentally stronger. So, 10-10 in the sixth game with Wang Liqin leading 3-2 in games in a best of seven; he had four match points and lost them all. Then it was one serve each and Liqin won the point; he had another match point. Surely it was all over? Schlager came back again. He looked into the eyes of the edgy Liqin; he won the next point. Game point for Schlager. The camera panned across to the Chinese national coach. He was worried. This would be devastating for him and his player. Schlager took the next point to square match 3-3 and then went on to win the match 4-3. This caused absolute jubilation for the Austrian team. Schlager then went on to win the semi-final beating Kong Linghui 13-11 in the deciding game. Yet another brutal seven game master-class in mental strength. Schlager overcame all the odds against him to beat, not one, but two of the great Chinese players. He had the opportunity to become the most unlikely winner ever of a World Championship. In the final he played Joo Se Hyuk of South Korea; Joo Se Hyuk was the world's finest defensive player and Schlager wasn't particularly good against defence. In the final Schlager found a way to win; another marathon match, 4-3 and another incredible mental performance. Everything is possible in life and when things are not going well look for turning points. Now, some of you may have never watched a table-tennis match and some of you may be questionning why I have gone into so much detail. Well, that was a sporting moment, where someone's belief against all the odds got him through. He searched for that crucial turning point and got it. Although the final was a gruelling match as well, there was only ever going to be one winner – Werner Schlager. The point being made here is, no matter how deep the hole you find yourself in, there is a turning point that changes everything. Imagine this:

A boxer is being whacked around the ring for eleven round;, he's losing on points and his face is all swollen up and his opponent is on the brink of winning. Then, Ding Ding, round twelve; the beaten-up and swollen-headed boxer is just about to give up, when he decides to swing one last punch … And it connects; his opponent goes down and is counted out. Now that is a turning point.

Don't Take Things Personally – Chris Moon

I am going to finish this book with a chapter about '*not taking things personally*' and an extraordinary man called Chris Moon. You may not know who Chris Moon is and if I told you he was an ultra-distance runner and had ran the marathon, you may lift an eyelid. Add to the above that he completed the gruelling Marathon De Sables and inspired many to follow in his footsteps, then this should be sparking your interest. If that hasn't impressed you then how about the fact he did the Badwater Death Valley 135 mile ultra and the 95 mile West Highland Way Race? Impressed yet? Well in 1995 he was blown up in a supposedly safe area of a minefield in remote East Africa and lost an arm and a leg. He survived initially because he treated himself. About fourteen hours after injury he arrived in South Africa where doctors said they'd never seen anyone live with such a small amount of blood. He recovered three or four times faster than was expected and was out of hospital in less than two months and within a year of leaving hospital, he ran the London Marathon. He raised significant sums to help disabled people in the developing world, worked to ban landmines and successfully completed a full time Master's Degree. Now I should have your attention. When someone, who has been through what he has, says: *'Get the absolute most you can get out of life!'* Then you should be ashamed if you are not trying to do so. He says that everybody has the ability to go one step beyond the point at which they feel they can go no further. Furthermore, that we must make the best of life and not waste the opportunities. Moon admits that when he was blown up by that landmine, he should have died. But, he fought for his life with every tiny bit of energy he had left; living and staying alive was the hardest thing he had ever done. When he was dying on the ground after being blown up, what he remembered was not the things he had done in his life – it was the things he hadn't done; the times he could have done better and the times when he didn't live life to the fullest with passion and enthusiasm, squeezing the last bit of juice out of life. When he was in hospital after the terrible incident, he laid there with one arm and one leg and felt sorry for himself. Moon decided to take ownership, believe in himself and to not take it personally.

He decided to get himself out and about; including asking girls out on dates. Although he would get a bit embarrassed at times, he found that humour and not taking things personally got him through. He said that if we take things personally, it stops us from seeing the big picture and makes us view situations in a blinkered way and purely about how we feel. If a man can lose 50% of his limbs and doesn't things personally, then who can have an excuse? If a man can suffer such a devastating event and still have a positive outlook, have a passion for life and live to inspire others, then how can others not be inspired by him? It is difficult not to take things personally, but if we do that too often then we spend a lot of time thinking about how we feel and the personal hurt, rather than learning or seeing the bigger picture of what is going on. We can end up being emotionally reactive and not intelligently proactive. What we can learn from Chris Moon is that our time spent alive has to be used in the most positive and fulfilling way and that sitting in a corner feeling sorry for ourselves is literally wasting precious time. Taking things personally takes a stranglehold over our thought process and stops us from taking a wider view.

Once we take something personally, all the creative, deep thinking and rational side of our brain stops working. Negative reactions like sulking, moods and tempertantrums all derive from being reactive to something taken personally. Once we learn not to take things personally and to see the wider reasons why situations happen, then we are set free from those shackles. One of the toughest situations to deal with as an advisor is when a client wants to react to a situation because it has been taken personally. An example of this is when a journalist writes something negative about a client and the reaction is: '*I'm never speaking to that journalist or newspaper again.*' That reaction would actually make the client feel better, because they have vented their frustration as a result of taking the article personally. But, if they stopped and thought about the situation rationally, newspapers have lots of journalists and 1) it is always better not to become alienated from a newspaper 2) the journalist probably wasn't being personal and just writing an opinion 3) think about how to manipulate the situation in a positive way, by getting the journalist to write a positive article in the future. By taking the article personally, it can actually harm a client's brand and future relationships.

Once the immediate period has passed; maybe a few days later then, the client themselves may have realised that the best thing was not to have had a knee-jerk reaction. However, many advisors, agents and manangers feel under pressure to react and create '*trench warfare*' because they may get pats on the back from the client; that is a short-term view. Long-term, it is always best to work with the media and have influence in those corridors of power. A scary aspect of taking things personally, is that it starts as a little seed, then flourishes into a weed-filled garden. It may start with a journalist writing an unfavourable article and then within a few months the client has all the negative energy of a battle with a media platform and the media platfrom is inspired to find reasons to write even more negative stories about the client. Not for one minute am I saying that it is easy not to take things personally, because it isn't. My point here is that if you have the right people around you then they will make you see the bigger picture for long-term benefits. When you learn to let go and not take things personally, a whole new world opens up; instead of wasting time and energy having grudges and limiting your thought process, you start to work out how to deal with situations for the best in the long-term. Taking things personally is a form of giving up; it's like something happens or somebody says something then there is an immediate reaction and no thought is given to the consequences. There's a saying: It's just business and Most successful business people don't take things personally when it comes to making business decisions, because they know the consequences. My mother has a saying and it goes: *wrong and strong*. What that means is there are people who make wrong decisions and say the wrong things but will never back down or admit they have made a mistake. There are some of us who actually know that taking something personally and saying the wrong things isn't the right way to go, but do it anyway. Because saying what they want to say and behaving how they want to behave is more important than what is actually best for them. In those situations we all need a strong voice to tell us not to do it and reasons why. So, by not taking things personally it opens up a whole new world; it gives us perspective, an understanding of people's intentions and the context, and also greater business insight and the ability to create positive environments.

No time is wasted having to mop up bad reactions, instead, your thought process becomes focused and positive. People around you will have to follow suit and feed off your positivity. But this doesn't happen over night; you have to try and keep trying and bit by bit you will see the benefits of not taking things personally. So, not taking things personally, is a vital part of us all being the absolute best we can possibly be. We should never accept defeat and chase our dreams; we have to live the fullest life possible. Chris Moon believes that many of us reach a level in life and then just accept that things won't get better. The truth is that we don't know what our full potential is until we try and keep trying. Chris Moon lay dying on the ground and had flashbacks of the things he never did; the times he didn't squeeze the last drop of juice out of life by living with the passion he should have. He laid there regretting the moments he had not made the best of his life.

The message to you is to live your life with passion and enthusiasm.
Find those people who will be part of your journey and belong *In Your World.*

Acknowledgements

Along with my views and opinions on the importance of having the right people around us, I wanted to give the reader an insight into the psyche of some of the elite sport achievers. Having that in mind, I consulted and received contributions from the following who have exceptional knowledge in their fields.

I would like to acknowledge:

James Allen
Pat Sheehan
John Cross
Guillem Balague
Peter Lockyer
Patrick Barclay
Nigel Clarke
Antonio Infantino

I would also like to give recognition to the following philosophers for usage of their quotes:

Eugene Luther Gore Vidal
Henry Brook Adams
Dr Brad Blanton
John Locke
Rudolph Steiner
David Hume

Bibliography

Dr Brad Blanton: Radical Honesty: How to Transform Your Life by Telling the Truth

BBC Sport (British Broadcasting Corporation) Secrets of Samba Football. 1999

Coyle, D. The Talent Code: Greatness Isn't Born, It's Grown. 2009.

Coyle, D. The Little Book of Talent: 52 Tips for Improving Skills. 2012

Douglas Fields, R. Myelination: An Overlooked Mechanism of Synaptic Plasticity. 2005

Dweck, C, S. Mindset: The New Psychology of Success. 2006

Dweck, C, S. Mindset: How You Can Fulfil your Potential. 2012

Epstein, D. The Sports Gene: Talent, Practice and the Truth about Success. 2013

Forbes, C. The Polgar Sisters: Training or Genius? 1992

Peters, S. The Chimp Paradox. 2012

Pfaff, D Barriers to Championship Performances, 2016

Syed, M. Bounce: The Myth of Talent and The Power of Practice. 2011

Syed, M. Black Box Thinking: The Surprising Truth about Success. 2015

David Whyte: Sweet Darkness, The House of Belonging, 1996

Patrick Barclay: Football - Bloody Hell!: The Biography of Alex Ferguson, 2011

Buzzfeed.com: 2014